Courtesy of the author

THOMAS FRANK is the author of *Pity the Billionaire*, *The Wrecking Crew*, and *What's the Matter with Kansas?* A former columnist for *The Wall Street Journal* and *Harper's*, Frank is the founding editor of *The Baffler*. He lives outside Washington, D.C.

ALSO BY THOMAS FRANK

Pity the Billionaire

The Wrecking Crew

What's the Matter with Kansas?

One Market Under God

The Conquest of Cool

Praise for *Listen, Liberal*

"A classic disaffected liberal's case—and a persuasive one—against what the Democratic Party has become."

—*The Philadelphia Inquirer*

"A simple and damning assessment." —*The Washington Post*

"No one has written more consistently and stylishly about the conservative onslaught in America and the betrayal of liberal democratic values than Thomas Frank, arguably the Left's leading essayist. . . . This is Mr. Frank's best book since *What's the Matter with Kansas?*" —*Pittsburgh Post-Gazette*

"*Listen, Liberal* documents a half-century of work by the Democratic elite to belittle working people and exile their concerns to the fringes of the party's platform. If the prevailing ideology of the Republican establishment is that of a sneering aristocracy, Democratic elites are all too often the purveyors of a smirking meritocracy that offers working people very little."

—*The Huffington Post*

"What makes Frank's book new, different, and important is its offer of a compelling theory as to how and why the party of Jefferson, Jackson, and Roosevelt is now so unlikely to champion the economic needs of everyday people. . . . In such a looking-glass world, *Listen, Liberal* is a desperately needed corrective." —History News Network

"Frank says Democrats need to take a good long look in the mirror if they want answers to why blue-collar workers are

feeling abandoned and even infuriated by what used to be their party."
—*New York Post*

"An astute dissection of contemporary Democratic politics that demonstrates, cogently and at times acidly, how the party lost the allegiance of blue-collar Americans."
—*Publishers Weekly*

"A tough and thought-provoking look at what's wrong with America . . . Frank puts forth an impressive catalog of Democratic disappointments, more than enough to make liberals uncomfortable."
—*Booklist*

"Important . . . Engaging . . . An edgy—even disturbing—analysis of the Democratic Party's jilting of its traditional base."
—*The National Book Review*

"Long overdue . . . *Listen, Liberal* is a powerful addition to America's political discourse. It is full of truths and, sadly, the truth hurts."
—*Washington City Paper*

"Democrats often use the fact that Republicans have gone off the deep end to ignore their left flank, on the grounds that those liberals have nowhere else to go politically. *Listen, Liberal* contributes to the literature that expresses deep frustration with that decision, the fuel for a revolt."
—*The Fiscal Times*

"As with Frank's other books, *Listen, Liberal* is a piece of contemporary history that tells us not only what the powerful are up to, but how the trick is being pulled, with an admirable deployment of irony. . . . While Frank's previous books are essentially about devils being devils, this one shows how the angels have fallen further than they realize." —*Prospect* (London)

"An indispensable read . . . Provocative and stimulating."
—*National Newswatch*

LISTEN, LIBERAL

LISTEN, LIBERAL

OR, WHAT EVER HAPPENED TO THE PARTY OF THE PEOPLE?

THOMAS FRANK

PICADOR

A METROPOLITAN BOOK

HENRY HOLT AND COMPANY NEW YORK

For information, address Picador, 175 Fifth Avenue, New York, N.Y. 10010.

picadorusa.com • picadorbookroom.tumblr.com
twitter.com/picadorusa • facebook.com/picadorusa

For book club information, please visit facebook.com/picadorbookclub or e-mail marketing@picadorusa.com.

The Introduction to *Listen, Liberal* incorporates several passages about income inequality that were published over the course of 2014 in *Salon*, the online magazine, as well as passages that appeared in columns for *Harper's* magazine, one from September 2012 and one from September 2013. Chapter Seven includes bits of an essay that appeared in *Bookforum* in the fall of 2013 and also expands on *Salon* essays that appeared in March 2014, August 2014, and January 2015. Chapter Eight incorporates part of a *Harper's* magazine column for September 2012. The Afterword includes passages from articles published in 2016 in *The Guardian*, *Le Monde diplomatique*, and *Harper's* magazine.

Designed by Kelly S. Too

The Library of Congress has cataloged the Metropolitan Books edition as follows:

Names: Frank, Thomas, 1965– author.
Title: Listen, liberal, or, what ever happened to the party of the people? / Thomas Frank.
Other titles: Listen, Liberal | What ever happened to the party of the people?
Description: First edition. | New York : Metropolitan Books, 2016. | Includes index.
Identifiers: LCCN 2015049351 | ISBN 9781627795395 (hardcover) | ISBN 9781627795401 (e-book)
Subjects: LCSH: Democratic Party (U.S.) | Liberalism—United States. | Politics, Practical—United States. | Elite (Social sciences)—Political activity—United States. | Political culture—United States. | BISAC: POLITICAL SCIENCE / Political Process / Political Parties. | POLITICAL SCIENCE / Political Ideologies / Conservatism & Liberalism.
Classification: LCC JK2316 .F73 2016 | DDC 324.2736—dc23
LC record available at https://lccn.loc.gov/2015049351

Picador Paperback ISBN 978-1-250-11813-4

Our books may be purchased in bulk for promotional, educational, or business use. Please contact your local bookseller or the Macmillan Corporate and Premium Sales Department at 1-800-221-7945, extension 5442, or by e-mail at MacmillanSpecialMarkets@macmillan.com.

First published by Metropolitan Books, an imprint of Henry Holt and Company, LLC

First Picador Paperback Edition: March 2017

10 9 8 7 6 5 4 3 2 1

It is doubtless important to the good of nations that those who govern have virtues or talents; but what is perhaps still more important to them is that those who govern do not have interests contrary to the mass of the governed; for in that case the virtues could become almost useless and the talents fatal.

—Alexis de Tocqueville, *Democracy in America*
(translated by Harvey C. Mansfield and Delba Winthrop)

McGeorge Bundy, then, was the finest example of a special elite, a certain breed of men whose continuity is among themselves. They are linked to one another rather than to the country; in their minds they become responsible for the country but not responsive to it.

—David Halberstam, *The Best and the Brightest*, 1972

CONTENTS

LISTEN, LIBERAL

INTRODUCTION

Listen, Liberal

There are consequences to excessive hope, just as there are to other forms of intemperance. One of these is disillusionment, another is anger, and a third is this book.

For a generation, Democratic politicians have talked of "hope" as though it were their unique selling proposition, a secret ingredient they had that no other major-party brand could offer. Today those same Democrats express annoyance at the suggestion that anyone could really have taken them seriously on this hope business. It is hard to govern, they say; you can't get everything you want from politics. Ordinary citizens are beyond disillusioned, though. It has been nine years since the last recession began, and whether the country is in a recovery or a slump or even a galloping bull market makes no difference to them anymore.

According to official measurements, the last few years have been a time of brisk prosperity, with unemployment down and the stock market up. Productivity advances all the time. For those who work for a living, however, nothing seems to improve. Wages do not grow. Median income is still well below where it was in 2007. Workers' share of the gross national product (as opposed to the share taken by investors) hit a record low in 2011—and then it stayed there right through the recovery. It is there to this day; economists now regard its collapse as a quasi-permanent development.[1]

In the summer of 2014, with the Dow Jones Industrial Average hitting all-time highs, a poll showed that nearly three-quarters of the American public thought the economy was still in recession—because for them, it was.[2]

There was a time when average Americans knew whether we were going up or going down—because when the country prospered, its people prospered, too. But these days, things are different. From the middle of the Great Depression up to 1980, the lower 90 percent of the population, a group we might call "the American people," took home some 70 percent of the growth in the country's income. Look at the same numbers beginning in 1997—from the beginning of the New Economy boom to the present—and you find that this same group, the American people, pocketed *none* of America's income growth at all. Their share of the good times was zero. The gains they harvested after all their hard work were nil. The upper 10 percent of the population—the country's financiers, managers, and professionals—ate the whole thing. The privileged are doing better than at any time since economic records began.[3]

To be a young person in this economy, just out of school and starting to feel the burden of now-inescapable student loans, is to sense instinctively the downward slope that most of us are on these days. People who are twenty-five today are doing worse than people of that age ten years ago, and much worse than people who were twenty-five back in 1996.[4] The same is true, incidentally, of people who are thirty-five, forty-five, and probably fifty-five, but for the young this reversal of the traditional American trajectory is acutely painful: they know that no amount of labor will ever catapult them into the ranks of the winners.

At the other end of the social ladder, meanwhile, it is all upside all the time. In 2012, corporate profits (measured as a share of gross domestic product) hit their highest level on record. In 2014, according to a much-discussed think tank report, the total of all the bonuses handed out on Wall Street was more than twice as much as the total earned by every person in the country who worked full-time for the minimum wage.[5] Measured in terms of wealth—of property and investments, stocks and bonds—matters are even more perverse. One particularly lucky American family, in fact, has as much wealth as does 40 percent of the American population. The main accomplishment of the six individuals who make up this fortunate bunch was to inherit shares in Wal-Mart, the retailer that has sucked the life out of thousands of middle-American towns. Sucked the wealth out of those towns and spent it on the six Wal-Mart heirs' tasteless mega-mansions, their degrees from prestigious colleges, their fancy racecars, and their sports teams. They own a bank, a ballet company, an art gallery (where you can see Norman Rockwell's painting of Rosie the Riveter), and of late the Wal-Mart bunch have begun "reforming" the public schools your kids go to.

Should all this go on—and it will—those kids of ours are going to be educated on certain matters far better than we ever were. They will know to laugh at the old middle-class promise—retirement, pension, a better life than the previous generation had—because it is propaganda so transparent it sounds like something the Soviet Union used to put out. They will understand that this isn't a commonwealth; it's a workhouse.

And that's where we are, eight years post-hope. Growth that doesn't grow; prosperity that doesn't prosper. The country, we now understand, is simply no longer arranged in such a way as to make its citizens economically secure.

A while ago I spoke at a firefighters convention in the Pacific Northwest, talking as I always do about the ways we have rationalized these changes to ourselves. Firefighters are the sort of people we honor for their bravery, but they also happen to be blue-collar workers, and they have watched with increasing alarm what has been happening to folks like them for the last few decades . . . watched as the people formerly known as the heart and soul of this country had their lives taken apart bone by bone. They themselves still make a decent living, I was told—they are some of the last unionized blue-collar workers who do—but they can see the inferno coming their way now, as their colleagues in other parts of the country get their contracts voided and their pensions reduced.

After I spoke, a firefighter from the Seattle area picked up the microphone. Workers had been watching their standard of living get whittled away for decades, he said, and up till now they had always been able to come up with ways to get by. The first adjustment they made, he recalled, was when women entered the workforce. Families "added that income, you got to keep your boat, or your second car, or your vacation, and everything was OK." Next, people ran up debt on their credit cards. Then, in the last decade, people began "pulling home equity out," borrowing against their houses. "All three of those things have kept the middle class from having to sink down into abject poverty," he said. But now all three coping mechanisms were at an end. There were no more family members to send to work, the expiration date had passed for the home-equity MasterCard, and still wages sank. His question was this: "Is there a fourth economic savior out there, or do you think that maybe we have reached the end?"

I had no good answer for him. Nobody does.

WHAT HAPPENED AT THE TURNING POINT

That these things are happening under the watch of the Democrats, the political party that was once such a militant defender of workers and the middle class, makes the triumph of inequality that much more startling.

This latest Democratic administration started so auspiciously, too, with a hero who was going to put things right. Do you remember what that felt like? The hundreds of thousands who would congregate to hear Barack Obama speak back in the dark days of 2008; the throng of revelers in Grant Park on the night he won; the million spectators who stood on the Mall in Washington to witness his inauguration.

The cool and eloquent champion arrived in a capital gripped by panic. Poisoned financial instruments had by that time killed several banks, countless hedge funds, and the savings of the nation. The investment banks that had survived had run to the government for help. A vast bailout was under way. Portents of fresh disaster were in every headline. The economic course on which we had traveled since the early 1980s was obviously finished. Deregulation had opened the floodgates; instant-millionaire paydays had removed every incentive to behave ethically; and an epidemic of fraudulent finance had duly swamped the system. All this was as plain as the line of desperate depositors out in front of IndyMac Bank. Now something was going to be done about it.

Our new president stepped up to fulfill his promise. He was living, breathing evidence that our sclerotic system could still function, that we could rise to the challenge, that we could change course.

It was the perfect opportunity for transformation. All the stars were in alignment. The president had carefully surrounded himself with some of the brightest minds of our time. Congress was controlled overwhelmingly by members of his own party. The public was prepared to back him in the most far-reaching reforms. History had dealt Barack Obama four aces. He could not lose.

Yet that is pretty much what happened. The crisis went to waste. The hero we put behind the wheel didn't heed the GPS device telling him to turn. He saw the warning lights flashing, and he heard that disturbing pounding under the hood, but he kept right on going.

To say "the center held," as one of his biographers does, is an optimistic way to describe Barack Obama's accomplishment.[6] Another would be to say he saved a bankrupt system that by all rights should have met its end. America came through an economic debacle, an earthquake that shook people's faith to the ground. Yet out of it, the system emerged largely unchanged. The predators resumed operations. Everything pretty much stayed the same.

OPPORTUNITY COST

This is a book about the failure of the Democratic Party—about how they failed when the conditions for success were perfect.

It is not another collection of familiar Beltway gripes—complaints about gridlock in Washington, or how appalling it is that Americans are so polarized. The failure I'm referring to is bigger than that. With the exceptions of global warming and the Soviet threat, it is the greatest public problem we have faced in our lifetimes.

President Obama himself has said that inequality is the "defining challenge of our time." That is a sweeping statement, but think about it for a moment and you realize it isn't anywhere near sweeping enough. "Inequality" is shorthand for all the things that have gone to make the lives of the rich so measurably more delicious, year on year for three decades—and also for the things that have made the lives of working people so wretched and so precarious.

It is visible in the ever-rising cost of health care and college; in the coronation of Wall Street and the slow blighting of wherever it is you live; in the dot-com bubble, in the housing bubble, in whatever bubble is jazzing the business pages as you read this. You catch a glimpse of it when you hear about the bankruptcy your neighbor had to declare when his child got sick. Or when you read about the lobbying industry that drives D.C., or the election fund-raising system, which allows a single Vegas billionaire to personally choose the acceptable candidates for a major political party. "Inequality" is a euphemism for the Appalachification of our world.

"Inequality" is what we say when we describe how the relationship of the very wealthy to the rest of us has come to approximate the relationship of Louis XVI with the peasantry of eighteenth-century France. Inequality is about you working harder than ever before while others work barely at all and yet are prospered by the market god with every imaginable blessing. Inequality is about the way speculators and even criminals get a helping hand from Uncle Sam while the Vietnam vet down the street from you loses his house. Inequality is the reason some people find such significance in the ceiling height of an entrance foyer or the hop content of a beer while others will never believe in anything again.

Inequality is not an "issue," as that term is generally used; it is the eternal conflict of management and labor, owner and worker, rich and poor—only with one side pinned to the ground and the other leisurely pounding away at its adversary's face.

"Inequality" is not even the right word for the situation, really, since it implies a technical problem we can solve with a twist of the knobs back in D.C. The nineteenth century understood it better: they called it "the social question," and for once their polite Victorian euphemism beats ours. This is nothing less than the whole vast mystery of how we are going to live together.

WHY SHOULD THE LIBERAL LISTEN?

It is the Republicans, certainly, who bear primary responsibility for our modern plutocracy. They are the party that launched us on our modern era of tax-cutting and wage-suppressing. They are the ones who made a religion of the market and who fought so ferociously to open our politics to the influence of money at every level. These days Republicans are rolling in deep fantasies of persecution and capitalist authenticity; not only will they not reverse course, but they often seem lost to reason itself. What afflicts them would take an expert in mass psychology to cure.

But it is time we understood that our current situation represents a failure of the Democratic Party as well. Protecting the middle-class society was the Democrats' assigned historical task, and once upon a time they would have taken to the job with relish. Shared prosperity was once the party's highest aim; defending the middle-class world was a kind of sacred mission for them, as they never used to tire of reminding us. And to this day, Democrats are still the ones who pledge to raise the minimum wage and the taxes of the rich.

When it comes to tackling the "defining challenge of our time," however, many of our modern Democratic leaders falter. They acknowledge that inequality is rampant and awful, but they cannot find the conviction or imagination to do what is necessary to reverse it. Instead they offer the same high-minded demurrals and policy platitudes they've been offering since the 1980s. They remind us that there's nothing anyone can do about globalization or technology. They promise charter schools, and job training, and student loans, but other than that—well, they've got nothing.

My fifty-year-old thesaurus offers "politician" as a synonym for "opportunist." But when Mr. Roget first put those two words together way back when, he wasn't reckoning with today's high-minded Democrats. Since 1992, Democrats have won the plurality of votes in every presidential election except one. For six of those years, they controlled Congress outright. But on matters of inequality they have done vanishingly little. They have stubbornly refused to change course when every sign said turn: when it would have been good policy to turn, when it would have been overwhelmingly popular to turn, when the country expected them to turn, when it was fully within their power to steer in a different direction.

Yes, I know, Democrats are the good guys, or rather the less bad guys. Many individual Democrats get enthusiastic, five-star approval ratings from me; many more are completely without blame in the narrative that follows. And it is largely thanks to the Democrats that mainstream pundits now feel it's OK to talk about inequality at all.

But as things have grown worse, income inequality has become an increasingly awkward issue for them. It just doesn't come naturally in the way that, say, talking about marriage equality now does. Looking back over their actual record, one starts to suspect that there's a better chance the party will resolve to kick Wyoming out of the union than to do something meaningful to halt the country's economic breakdown.

This is not because they are incompetent or because sinister Republicans keep thwarting the righteous liberal will. It is

Democratic failure, straight up and nothing else. The agent of change isn't interested in the job at hand. Inequality just doesn't spark their imagination. It is the point at which their famous compassion peters out.

What I am suggesting is that their inability to address the social question is not accidental. The current leaders of the Democratic Party know their form of liberalism is somehow related to the good fortune of the top 10 percent. Inequality, in other words, is a reflection of who they are. It goes to the very heart of their self-understanding.

SNOOZING THROUGH THE LIBERAL HOUR

This is an age of Democratic failure, but what gives the failure its bitter tang is that it is also an age of Democratic triumph—a "Liberal Spring," as a jubilant *New York Times* story put it in the summer of 2015. Yes, economic inequality is soaring, nothing can be done on that front, but in other realms these are times of extraordinary Democratic achievement. Gay marriage is legal now, the Confederate flag is coming down all across the Deep South, and America is led today by a black president, a formerly hypothetical scenario that pollsters long ago used to determine someone's relative liberalism. In 2008, that black candidate's campaign raised more money from the financial services industry—which is to say, from Wall Street—than did his Republican opponent.

And just cast your eyes over the long list of billionaires and venture capitalists who supported the campaign to legalize gay marriage, say the liberal optimists. Or consider the way the Silicon Valley brass swung into action when the state of Indiana passed a law permitting discrimination against homosexuals.

Or how the CEO of the country's largest chain of coffee shops urged his employees to instruct customers about the evils of racism. In terms of public righteousness, liberals are as conspicuous today as at any time in our history.

What's more, Democrats in Washington now believe they possess a permanent hold on the presidency, thanks to the country's demographic shifts. "The coalition of the ascendant" is the phrase journalists began to use in 2008 to describe the Democrats' victorious and inexorably growing army—"young people, minorities, [and] upper middle class white professionals," to quote the pundit who coined the locution[7]—and what it means is that every augury now points the Democrats' way. Yes, they might lose a Congressional election here and there, but they are the natural majority party now, they think; when they encounter an obstacle, all they have to do is stand by and let the natural process of demographic "ascendancy" work.

Talk about the coalition of the ascendant causes Democratic hearts to race joyfully. For so many years they were the loser party, the wimp faction, the party of McGovern and Carter and Mondale and Dukakis. Now, suddenly, they have been transformed into the dominant party, the rightful occupants of the White House. The righteous will be rewarded, goes the proverb, and to Washington Democrats their advancing ascendancy feels a lot like cosmic justice.

For them it is an awesome vindication. So what if Republicans trounced them in 2010 and 2014? So what if the GOP dominates the state legislatures and both houses of Congress? Democrats now know with the certainty of political science itself that those Republican advances will slowly but surely be reversed. Democrats no longer need to plead, explain, or persuade; henceforth they need merely to wait.

"NOTHING MUCH CHANGED"

Trying to pinpoint where and when the hope drained out of the Obama movement is something of a parlor game for my disgruntled friends. Some say they lost their faith in Obama even before he took office, when he named the bailout architect Tim Geithner as his choice for Treasury secretary and the deregulation architect Larry Summers as his main economic adviser. A big chunk of the public came to believe the fix was in two months into his first term, when a round of bonuses—not reprimands or indictments, mind you, but bonuses—went out to executives of the financial sinkhole known as AIG.

But all that is mere speculation. Thanks to journalistic science, we can now pinpoint the exact moment when the Obama administration formally renounced any intention of making the big historical turn it had been elected to make: it was the meeting between the new president and a roomful of nervous Wall Street CEOs on March 27, 2009. After warning them about the "pitchforks" of an angry public, Obama reassured the frightened bankers that they could count on him to protect them; that he had no intention of restructuring their industry or changing the economic direction of the nation. "Lots of drama," is how one mogul described the meeting to the journalist Ron Suskind, "but at day's end, nothing much changed."[8]

I clung to the "hope" for a little while longer than that. I can remember the exact moment when I finally gave it up—it was the first time I heard the phrase "grand bargain," Barack Obama's pet term for his proposed deficit and tax deal with the Republicans. In a split second I understood the whole thing: that big compromises like this were real to the president, but "change" was not. I had known that Obama had a passion for centrist talk; everyone did. Bipartisan conciliation was the theme of Obama's famous keynote speech at the 2004 Democratic convention. It was one of the themes of his 2008 stump speech, when he talked so inspiringly about "the politics of addition, not the politics of division."

What was shocking about all this was to realize that *Obama believed these clichés.* Consensus, bipartisanship, the "center": *those* were the things this admirable and intelligent man was *serious* about—the kind of stale, empty verbiage favored by Beltway charlatans on the Sunday talk shows. The other things Obama used to say—like when he connected deregulation, corruption, and income inequality in his Cooper Union speech in 2008—those things were just to reel in the suckers. The suckers being the people who could hear the pillars of their middle-class world snapping. The suckers being the people who could see that the system was crumbling and thought maybe we ought to do something about it.

What I realized in the instant when I heard that phrase was that this man, in whom I and so many others had placed such faith, was in fact another ordinary consensus Democrat with ordinary consensus ideas. He believed the same tired partisanship-deploring platitudes as everyone else. Nothing could budge our leadership class from this illusion. Unemployment could hit 50 percent, foreclosures could sweep through entire states, there could be riots in every city in the land, and the TV hosts would *still* be moaning about how dreadful it is that Democrats and Republicans don't agree on things.

Which brings us face-to-face with our mystery: how is it that, in our moment of utmost need, a fake crisis like the problem of "extreme partisanship" was able to trump the real deal?

These are not Obama's shortcomings alone. They are failings of the party he leads. They are, in a word, ours. It's time to own up.

1

Theory of the Liberal Class

Let us put the question bluntly. What ails the Democrats? So bravely forthright on cultural issues, their leaders fold when confronted with matters of basic economic democracy. Why? What is it about this set of issues that transforms Democrats into vacillating softies, convinced that the big social question is beyond their control?

The standard explanation is money and the way it runs through politics, adjusting incentives and distorting priorities wherever it flows. The country's leaders, this theory goes, are the products of a corrupt campaign finance system, their values whacked by the revolving door between Congress and K Street, between the Treasury Department and the banks. While parts of the oligarchy that rules this land and funds our politicians might not really object to something like gay marriage, when it comes to putting big banks into receivership—oh, no. In the land of money, that kind of thing is *verboten*.

There is plenty of evidence for this theory, and I will present quite a bit of it in the pages that follow.* But the Democrats'

---

* For a more comprehensive examination of this evidence, especially as it pertains to the Republicans, see my 2008 book, *The Wrecking Crew.*

problems go deeper than this. To diagnose their particular malady we must understand that there are different hierarchies of power in America, and while oligarchy theory exposes one of them—the hierarchy of money—many of the Democrats' failings arise from another hierarchy: one of merit, learning, and status.

Money and merit: sometimes these two systems of power overlap and sometimes they are separate. Occasionally they are in conflict, but more frequently they are allies—contented partners in power.

We lampoon the Republican hierarchy of money with the phrase "the One Percent"; if we want to understand what has wrecked the Democratic Party as a populist alternative, however, what we need to scrutinize is more like the Ten Percent, the people at the apex of the country's hierarchy of professional status.

PARTY OF THE PEOPLE

Let us start with the institution of the political party itself. There are countless reasons why voters come together in factions and why they register for this party instead of that one: race, ethnicity, region, religion, generation, and gender, to name a few of the categories we like to talk about nowadays. There is another criterion, however, that we sometimes have trouble acknowledging: social class.

Once you start thinking about it, though, the role of class in political parties is obvious, and it goes back to America's very beginning. In *Federalist Paper* No. 10, published in 1787, James Madison famously identified "unequal distribution of property" as the main cause of political "faction." Madison deplored these factions, but he also made them seem, well, natural:

> Those who hold and those who are without property have ever formed distinct interests in society. Those who are creditors, and those who are debtors, fall under a like discrimination. A landed interest, a manufacturing interest, a mercantile interest, a moneyed interest, with many lesser interests, grow up of necessity in civilized nations, and divide them into different classes, actuated by different sentiments and views.

"Classes" were thus observed to be the very stuff of faction and parties, and it is a surprisingly short walk from the antipartisanship of the *Federalist Papers* to the fulminating, class-based factionalism of U.S. Senator Thomas Hart Benton, a fiery Democrat in the Jacksonian tradition. "There are but two parties, there never has been but two parties," Benton thundered in 1835, "founded in the radical question, whether PEOPLE, or PROPERTY, shall govern? Democracy implies a government by the people. . . . Aristocracy implies a government of the rich . . . and in these words are contained the sum of party distinction."[1]

Benton's exact phrases may not be familiar these days, but his sentiment certainly is. Democrats have fancied themselves as the "Party of the People" since the beginning, squaring off against what they love to caricature as the party of the highborn. This populist brand-positioning has served them well on many occasions, as Mitt Romney can no doubt attest. On other occasions it has had about as much to do with reality as the theory that the moon is made of green Play-Doh. After all, the Party of the People was also, once, the Party of Slavery and the Party of the Klan.

But the idea of two great parties corresponding to two great economic groups has been accurate enough often enough for the idea to stick. Whatever the class conflict happens to be at a given time—creditors versus debtors, bankers versus farmers, owners versus workers—the Democrats have usually sided with the weak and the downtrodden. For a few reminders of what this sounds like, here is William Jennings Bryan, in his "Cross of Gold" speech in 1896:

> There are two ideas of government. There are those who believe that, if you will only legislate to make the well-to-do prosperous, their prosperity will leak through on those below. The Democratic idea, however, has been that if you legislate to make the masses prosperous, their prosperity will find its way up through every class which rests upon them.

And here is Franklin Roosevelt, deploring the rise of "economic royalists" in 1936:

> The hours men and women worked, the wages they received, the conditions of their labor—these had passed beyond the control of the people, and were imposed by this new industrial dictatorship. . . . Those who tilled the soil no longer reaped the rewards which were their right. The small measure of their gains was decreed by men in distant cities. Throughout the Nation, opportunity was limited by monopoly.

Lastly, here is Harry Truman, speaking to farmers at a plowing competition in Iowa in 1948:

> The Democratic Party represents the people. It is pledged to work for agriculture. It is pledged to work for labor. It is pledged to work for the small businessman and the white-collar worker. The Democratic Party puts human rights and human welfare first. But the attitude of the Republican gluttons of privilege is very different. The bigmoney Republican looks on agriculture

> and labor merely as expense items in a business venture. He tries to push their share of the national income down as low as possible and increase his own profits. And he looks upon the Government as a tool to accomplish this purpose.

This was rhetoric, of course, but there was also something real behind it. Working people, or rather, their organizations, once carried enormous clout within the Democratic Party. Thanks to its solid identification with the common folk, Democrats held a majority in the House of Representatives from the early 1930s all the way to the mid-1990s, with two short GOP interludes. "It was a proletarian House of Lords," is how one political journalist has described that body in the late 1960s.[2]

Today, the American class divide is starker than at any time in my memory, and yet Congress doesn't seem to know it. Today, the House of Representatives is dedicated obsessively to the concerns of the rich—to cutting their taxes, to chastising their foes, to holding the tissue box as they cry about the mean names people call them.

How is this possible? Just about everyone not among the top tier of the income distribution these days expresses a kind of bitter cynicism about our financial overlords. Regardless of party, everyone is furious about the Wall Street bailouts. Books about the disappearing middle class have gone from the fringe to the mainstream. Our economy has been reliving the 1930s; why hasn't our politics?

The answer is staring us in the face, if we care to see it. Yes, social class is still all-important in politics, just like Madison, Benton, Bryan, and Truman thought it was. And yes, the Democrats are still a class party. In fact, they show admirable concern for the interests of the social class they represent.

It's just that the class they care about the most doesn't

happen to be the same one Truman, Roosevelt, and Bryan cared about.

THE HIGH-BORN AND THE WELL-GRADUATED

In his syndicated *New York Times* column for November 21, 2008, David Brooks saluted president-elect Obama for the savvy personnel choices he was then announcing. This was before Brooks had become one of the president's favorite columnists; before the fabled "bromance" between the two men burst into the raging blaze of mutual admiration it would one day become. But the spark was there already.

It was the educational pedigree of the then-forming Team Obama that won the columnist's esteem. Nearly every person Brooks mentioned—the new president's economic advisers, his foreign policy advisers, even the first lady—had collected a degree from an Ivy League institution, more than one in most cases. The new administration would be a "valedictocracy," Brooks joked: "rule by those who graduate first in their high school classes."

Brooks has been obsessed with the tastes and habits of the East Coast meritocracy for as long as I've been reading him, and though he sometimes mocks, he always comes back to his essential conviction, the article of faith that makes a writer like him fit so comfortably at the *Times:* the well-graduated are truly great people. And on that day in 2008 when Brooks beheld the incoming Obama crew, with their Harvard-certified talent—Lord!—he just about swooned. "I find myself tremendously impressed by the Obama transition," he wrote. Why? Because "they are picking the best of the Washington insiders": "open-minded individuals" who are "not ideological" and who exhibit lots of "practical creativity." They were "admired professionals," the very best their respective disciplines had to offer.

Brooks did not point out that choosing so many people from the same class background—every single one of them, as he said, was a professional—might by itself guarantee closed minds and ideological uniformity. Nobody else pointed this out, either. We always overlook the class interests of professionals because we have trouble thinking of professionals as a "class" in the first place; like David Brooks, we think of them merely as "the best." They are where they are because they are so smart, not because they've been born to an earldom or something.

Truth be told, lots of Americans were relieved to see people of talent replace George W. Bush's administration of hacks and cronies back in 2008. Those were frightening times. Still, if we want to understand what's wrong with liberalism, what keeps this movement from doing something about inequality or about our reversion to a nineteenth-century social pattern, this is where we're going to have to look: at the assumptions and collective interests of professionals, the Democratic Party's favorite constituency.

The historian Christopher Lasch—a kind of cosmic opposite of David Brooks—wrote in 1965 that "modern radicalism or liberalism can best be understood as a phase of the social history of the intellectuals."[3] My goal in this book is to bring Lasch's dictum up to date: the deeds and positions of the modern Democratic Party, I will argue, can best be understood as a phase in the social history of the professionals.

Who are professionals? To begin with, they are not the same thing as Lasch's "intellectuals." His category is made up mainly of writers and academics; it is defined by the critical stance they take toward the workings of society. There aren't really enough intellectuals to make up a distinct social class, in the way that term is traditionally used.

"Professionals," on the other hand, are an enormous and

prosperous group, the people with the jobs that every parent wants their child to grow up and get. In addition to doctors, lawyers, the clergy, architects, and engineers—the core professional groups—the category includes economists, experts in international development, political scientists, managers, financial planners, computer programmers, aerospace designers, and even people who write books like this one.

Professionals are a high-status group, but what gives them their lofty position is learning, not income. They rule because they are talented, because they are smart. A good sociological definition of professionalism is "a second hierarchy"—second to the main hierarchy of money, that is—"based on credentialed expertise."[4] Which is to say, a social order supported by test scores and advanced degrees and defended by the many professional associations that have been set up over the years to define correct practice, enforce professional ethics, and wage war on the unlicensed.

Another distinguishing mark of the professions is their social authority. Ivan Illich, a critic prominent in the 1970s, once defined professionals by noting their "power to prescribe."[5] Professionals are the people who know what ails us and who dispense valuable diagnoses. Professionals predict the weather. They organize our financial deals and determine the rules of engagement. They design our cities and draw the traffic patterns through which the rest of us travel. Professionals know when someone is guilty of a moral or criminal misdeed and they also know precisely what form of retribution that culpability should take.

Teachers know what we must learn; architects know what our buildings must look like; economists know what the Federal Reserve's discount rate should be; art critics know what is in good taste and what is in bad. Although we are the subjects of all these diagnoses and prescriptions, the group to which professionals ultimately answer is not the public but their peers (and, of course, their clients). They listen mainly to one another. The professions are autonomous; they are not required to heed voices from below their circle of expertise.

In this way the professions build and maintain monopolies over their designated fields. Now, "monopoly" is admittedly a tough word, but it is not really a controversial one among sociologists who write about the professions. "Monopolizing knowledge," according to one group of sociologists, is a baseline description of what professions do; this is why they restrict entry to their fields.[6] Professions certify the expertise of insiders while negating and dismissing the knowledge-claims of outsiders.

Specialized knowledge is, of course, a necessity in this complicated world of ours. From ship captains to neurosurgeons, modern society depends heavily on people with technical expertise. And so nations grant professionals their elevated status, the sociological theory continues, in exchange for a promise of public service. The professions are supposed to be disinterested occupations or even "social trustees"; unlike other elements of society, they are not supposed to be motivated by profit or greed. This is why we still find advertising by lawyers and doctors somewhat off-putting, and why Americans were once shocked to learn that radio personalities took money to play records they didn't genuinely like: because professionals are supposed to answer to a spirit more noble than personal gain.[7]

With the rise of the postindustrial economy in the last few decades, the range of professionals has exploded. To use the voguish term, these are "knowledge workers," and many of them don't fit easily into the old framework. They are often employees rather than independent practitioners, taking orders from some corporate manager instead of spending their lives in private practice. These modern professionals aren't workers per se, and they aren't capitalists either, strictly speaking. Some professions share certain features with these other groups, however. The accountants at your neighborhood tax preparation chain, for example, are sometimes just scraping by. And teachers are often union members, just like blue-collar workers. At the other end of the scale, certain lucky professionals in Silicon Valley happen to be our leading capitalists. And the gulf between professional hedge fund managers and the rich folks whose money they invest is small indeed.

As these last two examples suggest, the top ranks of the professions are made up of highly affluent people. They are not the billionaire Wal-Mart clan, but they have a claim to leadership nevertheless. These two power structures, one of ownership and the other of knowledge, live side by side, sometimes in conflict with one another but usually in comity.

The concern of this book is not investigating the particular expertise of any given profession, but rather the politics of professionalism in a larger sense. As the political scientist Frank Fischer writes in *Technocracy and the Politics of Expertise*, professionalism is more than an occupational category; it is "a postindustrial ideology."[8] For many, it provides an entire framework for understanding our modern world.

As a political ideology, professionalism carries enormous potential for mischief. For starters, it is obviously and inherently undemocratic, prioritizing the views of experts over those of the public.[9] That is tolerable to a certain degree—no one really objects to rules mandating that only trained pilots fly jetliners, for example. But what happens when an entire category of experts stops thinking of itself as "social trustees"? What happens when they abuse their monopoly power? What happens when they start looking mainly after their own interests, which is to say, start acting as a class?

"RULING IN THE NAME OF KNOWLEDGE"[10]

Americans have pondered these questions before. The professions' claims of superior authority and of a monopoly on the power to prescribe rubbed early Americans the wrong way, and in the first decades of the Republic the country reacted harshly against them. In the Jacksonian period, a time of profound anti-aristocratic feeling, "the ideology of merit clashed in America with the ideological egalitarianism of the political system," as the sociologist Magali Larson writes. It was impossible to reconcile equality, Americans believed, with the professional ideal of a legally sanctioned clique of experts. Cartels and monopolies were in bad odor back then, and the public rebelled against the professions as attempts to maintain aristocratic entitlement through "mystification and concealment," as an 1835 newspaper put it. Many states in those days took the revolt against professionalism so far as to repeal medical licensing requirements.[11]

The anti-professional spirit persisted for decades. The Farmers' Alliance and the Knights of Labor, two nineteenth-century workers' organizations, specifically excluded lawyers from membership. I myself have seen a Populist-inspired sculpture garden in western Kansas in which a figure labeled "Labor" is crucified by statues representing the professions: "Doctor," "Preacher," "Lawyer," "Banker."[12]

Amid the enormous strikes and the sudden, catastrophic recessions of the Gilded Age, however, a group of reformers who came to be known as "progressives" came to see professionalization as a positive thing—indeed, as the only hope for a society being torn apart in the war between capital and labor. Professionals, recast now as an enlightened managerial class, were supposed to bring about an industrial peace that would be impossible under the profit motive alone. The progressives of this period could be frankly and openly elitist on the subject: Herbert Croly, the author of the seminal work *The Promise of American Life* and later a founder of the *New Republic*, openly advocated for a sort of neo-aristocratic order led by "exceptional" citizens, and left-wing critics ranging from Thorstein Veblen to R. H. Tawney imagined capitalism tamed by professional expertise.

The progressives had a point. Many of the industrial world's problems were—and are—highly technical ones that require the attention of well-trained experts. Markets could obviously not be counted on to bring about democratic solutions to the scourge of exploitation, layoffs, and workplace injuries. There were no easy, Jeffersonian ways around these problems.

For many years the progressive ideal seemed like a brilliant success. Franklin Roosevelt's "brain trust," for example, still stands today as a symbol of the liberal possibilities of professionalism, as do the New Deal's many interventions in the workings of the market. Economies could be managed, at least in part; world wars could be planned and won; an assortment of consumer goods could be essentially guaranteed to each and every member of the broad middle class. The administration of FDR was something of a golden age for government-by-professionals, although (as we shall see) one that was different in important ways from our current regime of rule-by-expert.

Let me confess here a nostalgia for the managerial professionalism that I have just described. It was, after all, the system that administered the country's great corporations, its news media, its regulatory agencies, and its welfare state in the more benevolent years of the American Century. Here and there, in certain corners of our national life, this older organizational form still survives, keeping our passenger jets from exploding and our highway bridges from collapsing.

But generally speaking, that system of professionalism was long ago subverted and transformed into something different and more rapacious. Today we live in a world of predatory bankers, predatory educators, even predatory health care providers, all of them out for themselves. The corruption of the professions is a grand story in its own right, and one that parallels the story told in this book: it starts at roughly the same time, it features a number of the same characters, and so on. With a few exceptions, however, it is not my subject here.

What concerns us instead are popular attitudes toward the professions, and by the 1970s they were definitely starting to sour. "Technocracy" was the new term for describing the reign of professionalism, and its connotations were almost entirely negative. Rule-by-expert, it began to seem, excluded rule-by-the-people. It was dehumanizing and mechanical. In a technocracy, the important policy decisions were made in faraway offices that were insulated from the larger whirl of society. The people making the decisions identified far more with society's rulers than they did with the ruled, and their decisions often completely ignored public concerns. Busing was one of the era's classic examples of failed technocratic overreach; another was the Vietnam War, a catastrophic intervention in which tens of thousands of working-class Americans were sent to their deaths—not to mention the vast death toll among the Vietnamese themselves—largely because foreign-policy professionals in Washington were unwilling to listen to voices from outside their discipline, bearing uncomfortable news.[13]

The problems of technocracy were never solved. Instead technocracy became a way of life, with its own mass constituency. Today, as we are so often reminded, we live in a "postindustrial" age, and in this advanced state of civilization, the demand for expertise has become enormous. Knowledge industries such as software, finance, communication, surveillance, and military contracting are the vital economic sectors of our time, and the corporate world has proceeded to bulk up with armies of middle managers, efficiency experts, laboratory scientists, and public-relations specialists.

As the professional-managerial class grew, its political alignment also changed. Between the Eisenhower era and today, professionals undertook a mass migration from the Republican to the Democratic Party, for reasons that will become apparent as we proceed. In fact, according to the sociologists Jeff Manza and Clem Brooks, professionals went from being the *most Republican* social formation in the country in the 1950s to being the *most Democratic* by the mid-Nineties.[14]

Professionalism is "postindustrial ideology," and today the Democrats are the party of the professional class. The party has other constituencies, to be sure—minorities, women, and the young, for example, the other pieces of the "coalition of the ascendant"—but professionals are the ones whose technocratic outlook tends to prevail. It is their tastes that are celebrated by liberal newspapers and it is their particular way of regarding the world that is taken for granted by liberals as being objectively true. Professionals dominate liberalism and the Democratic Party in the same way that Ivy Leaguers dominate the Obama cabinet. In fact, it is not going too far to say that the views of the modern-day Democratic Party reflect, in virtually every detail, the ideological idiosyncrasies of the professional-managerial class.

Liberalism itself has changed to accommodate its new constituents' technocratic views. Today, liberalism is the philosophy not of the sons of toil but of the "knowledge economy" and, specifically, of the knowledge economy's winners: the Silicon Valley chieftains, the big university systems, and the Wall Street titans who gave so much to Barack Obama's 2008 campaign. Liberal thinkers dutifully return the love, fussing over their affluent, highly educated sweethearts with all manner of flattering phrases: these high-achieving professionals are said to be the "wired workers" who will inherit the future, for example. They are a "learning class" that truly gets the power of education. They are a "creative class" that naturally rebels against fakeness and conformity. They are an "innovation class" that just can't stop coming up with awesome new stuff.

The phrase I will apply to them in the pages that follow is the "liberal class," a designation I borrow from the radical writer Chris Hedges, although with a pretty big caveat.[15] The premise of Hedges' book on the subject, *Death of the Liberal Class*, is that the cohort behind liberal politics is disappearing or has lost its nerve. He writes to mourn their passing; I write to protest their triumph.

POP TECHNOCRACY

To protest their triumph? Why would a person of vivid pink sentiments like me object to the ascendancy of any liberal group? What difference does it make if the driving force behind Democratic victory comes from below or from on high?

Put it a different way: what does it mean when the dominant constituency of the left party in a two-party system is a high-status group rather than the traditional working class?

One thing we know for sure that it means is soaring inequality.

When the left party in a system severs its bonds to working people—when it dedicates itself to the concerns of a particular slice of high-achieving affluent people—issues of work and income inequality will inevitably fade from its list of concerns.

We know this, for starters, because this is exactly what has happened. Issues of income inequality have been recontextualized so thoroughly in our time that certain Democrats even have trouble understanding what their forebears of the 1930s and '40s meant when they talked about the subject. For our modern liberals, it is obvious that careers should be open to talent and it is an outrage when barriers of any kind prevent the able from rising to the top.

Another term for this understanding of equality is meritocracy, which is one of the great, defining faiths of the professional class. Meritocracy is about winners, and ensuring that everyone has a chance to become one. "The areas in which the left has made the most significant progress," writes the journalist Chris Hayes, "—gay rights, inclusion of women in higher education, the end of de jure racial discrimination—are the battles it has fought or is fighting in favor of making the meritocracy more meritocratic. The areas in which it has suffered its worst defeats—collective action to provide universal public goods, mitigating rising income inequality—are those that fall outside the meritocracy's purview."[16]

Another reason we know that a party of professionals will care little about inequality is because professionals themselves care little about it. While this segment of the population tends to be very liberal on questions of civil liberties and sexual mores, the sociologist Steven Brint tells us that professionals are "not at all liberal on economic and equality-related issues." On anything having to do with organized labor, as we shall see, they are downright conservative.[17]

The problem with such broad-brush generalizations about any social stratum, of course, is that there are lots of exceptions, and a group of educated and often sophisticated individuals naturally contains lots of honorable folks who care sincerely about society's well-being. Many of them understand the madness of a deregulated market system as it spins out of control. But in a sweeping sociological sense, professionals as a class do not get it. This is because inequality does not contradict, defy, or even inconvenience the logic of professionalism. On the contrary, inequality is essential to it.

Professionals, after all, are life's officer corps. They give the orders; they write the prescriptions. Status is essential to professionalism; according to sociologist Larson, achieving a more exalted level in life's hierarchy is "the most central dimension of the professionalization project." What she means is that inequality is what it's all about. Sometimes the privileges accorded to the professions are enshrined in law—not just anyone is allowed to step into a courtroom and start pleading before a judge, for example—and even when they aren't, they are maintained by artificial scarcity, by what Larson called, in her classic 1977 book on the subject, a "monopoly of expertise."[18]

Meritocracy is what makes these ideas fit together; it is "the official professional credo," according to one group of sociologists—the conviction that the successful deserve their rewards, that the people on top are there because they are the best.[19] This is the First Commandment of the professional-managerial class.

These days meritocracy has come to seem so reasonable that many of us take it for granted as the true and correct measure of human value. Do well in school, and you earn your credential. Earn your credential, and you are admitted into the ranks of the professions. Become a professional, and you receive the respect of the public plus the nice house in the suburbs and the fancy car and all the rest. Meritocracy makes so *much* sense to us that barely anyone thinks of challenging it, except on its own terms.

For President Barack Obama, for example, belief in meritocracy is a conviction of the most basic sort. "Obama's faith lay in cream rising to the top," writes Jonathan Alter in his account of the early days of the Obama presidency. The president believed this, Alter continues, for the most personal of reasons: because this was the system that had propelled him to the top. "Because he himself was a product of the great American postwar meritocracy," Alter continues, "he could never fully escape seeing the world from the status ladder he had ascended."

Obama proceeded to fill his administration with the graduates of the most prestigious universities and professional schools, in turn causing David Brooks to feel such optimism for the country. "At some level," Alter writes, "Obama bought into the idea that top-drawer professionals had gone through a fair sorting process, the same process that had propelled him and Michelle to the Ivy League, and were therefore in some way deserving of their elevated status."[20]

What this doctrine means for the politics of income inequality should be clear: a profound complacency. For successful professionals, meritocracy is a beautifully self-serving doctrine, entitling them to all manner of rewards and status, because they are smarter than other people. For people on the receiving end of inequality—for those who have just lost their home, for example, or who are having trouble surviving on the minimum wage, the implications of meritocracy are equally unambiguous. To them this ideology says: forget it. You have no one to blame for your problems but yourself.

There is no solidarity in a meritocracy. The very idea contradicts the ideology of the well-graduated technocrats who rule us.

As we shall see, leading members of the professional class show enormous respect for one another—what I will call "professional courtesy"—but they feel precious little sympathy for the less fortunate members of their own cohort—for the adjuncts frozen out of the academic market for tenure, for colleagues who get fired, or even for the kids who don't get into "good" colleges. That life doesn't shower its blessings on people who can't make the grade isn't a shock or an injustice; it's the way things ought to be.[21]

This has all sorts of important consequences for liberalism, but let us here take note of just one before proceeding: professionals do not hold that other Democratic constituency, organized labor, in particularly high regard. This attitude is documented in study after study of professional-class life. One reason for this is because unions signify lowliness, not status. But another is because solidarity, the core value of unions, stands in stark contradiction to the doctrine of individual excellence that every profession embodies.[22] The idea that someone should command good pay for doing a job that doesn't require specialized training seems to professionals to be an obvious fallacy.

THE PANACEA OF EDUCATION

It is not a coincidence that the two most successful Democratic leaders of recent years—Bill Clinton and Barack Obama—were both plucked from obscurity by prestigious universities. Nor is it surprising that both of them eventually signed on to a social theory in which higher education is the route to individual success and to national salvation as well.

Educational achievement is, after all, the foundation of the professions' claim to higher status. It should not surprise us that the liberal class regards the university as the greatest and most necessary social institution of all, or that members of this cohort reflexively propose more education as the answer to just about anything you care to bring up. College can conquer unemployment as well as racism, they say; urban decay as well as inequality. Education will make us more tolerant, it will dissolve our doubts about globalization and climate change, it will give us the STEM skills we need as a society to compete. The liberal class knows, as a matter of deepest conviction, that there is no social or political problem that cannot be solved with more education and job training. Indeed, the only critique they will acknowledge of this beloved institution is that it, too, is not meritocratic enough. If we just launch more charter schools, give everyone a fair shot at the SAT, and crank out the student loans, then we will have done all it is humanly possible to do.

To the liberal class, every big economic problem is really an education problem, a failure by the losers to learn the right skills and get the credentials everyone knows you'll need in the society of the future. Take inequality. The real problem, many liberals believe, is that not enough poor people get a chance to go to college and join the professional-managerial elite. Driving this point home is the object of report after report from the Hamilton Project, a Democratic think tank that is named, tellingly, for the original advocate of an American ruling elite.[23] Other leading members of the liberal class have flogged the point relentlessly over the years. A sampling:

- "If there is an income divide in America it is over education," wrote Democratic media strategist Bill Knapp in the *Washington Post* in 2012, "and this makes sense: People who are better educated should make more money."[24]
- "What I fundamentally believe—and what the president believes," Arne Duncan, Obama's secretary of education,

told a reporter in 2012, "is that the only way to end poverty is through education."[25]

- "The best way by far to improve economic opportunity and to reduce inequality is to increase the educational attainment and skills of American workers," declared Federal Reserve Chairman Ben Bernanke to the graduating class at Harvard in 2008, a group much perturbed by inequality.[26]
- Thomas Friedman, Obama's other favorite newspaper columnist, comes back to the subject again and again. "The biggest issue in the world today is growth, and, in this information age, improving educational outcomes for more young people is now the most important lever for increasing economic growth and narrowing income inequality," he wrote in 2012. "In other words, education is now the key to sustainable power."[27]

To the liberal class this is a fixed idea, as open to evidence-based refutation as creationism is to fundamentalists: if poor people want to stop being poor, poor people must go to college.

But of course this isn't really an answer at all; it's a moral judgment, handed down by the successful from the vantage of their own success. The professional class is defined by its educational attainment, and every time they tell the country that what it needs is more schooling, they are saying: Inequality is not a failure of the system; it is a failure of you.

This way of thinking about inequality offers little to the many millions of Americans—the majority of Americans, in fact—who did not or will not graduate from college. It dismisses as though a moral impossibility the well-known fact that there have been and are places in the modern world where people with high school diplomas can earn a good living—like, say, the northern states of the USA between 1945 and 1980 or the Germany of today.

Then there are disturbing reports like the recent study showing that, in terms of wealth, black and Hispanic college graduates actually "fared significantly worse" in the late recession than did members of those groups who hadn't gone to college. The people in question were the ones who did everything right, who went through life the way our society instructs us to, and they were punished for it.[28]

And that's only the beginning of the problems. Who is to say that a college degree by itself is the silver bullet? In the arms race of merit, perhaps it's getting straight As that makes you worthy, or going to a "good school," or studying the STEM subjects, or not wasting time on the STEM subjects. Even then, the education panacea offers nothing to the ones who check every box and who still find, after they graduate, that there are simply no jobs out there, or that the jobs that exist pay poorly.

But nothing can dissuade the leaders of the liberal class from this faith—not the many scandals reverberating through the universities, not the much-discussed misery that has engulfed high-achieving humanities PhDs, not the crushing weight of the student loans, not the perverse fact that the quality of American higher ed has declined while its price tag has grown so massively.

Nor can the leaders of the professional class see the absurdity of urging everyone else to do exactly as they themselves did to make their way to the top. It is as if some oil baron were to proclaim that the unemployed could solve their problems if they just found good places to drill for oil. Or if some mutual-fund manager were to suggest that the solution to inequality was for everyone to put their savings in the stock market.

THE PATHOLOGIES OF PROFESSIONALISM

Having people of talent run the vast federal apparatus is clearly a desirable thing. The EPA and the Nuclear Regulatory Commission ought to be under the direction of people who know what they're doing, as surely as qualified engineers should design our bridges and historians should be the ones who teach history.

But what are we to make of our modern-day technocracy, a meritocracy of failure in which ineffectual people rise to the top and entire professions (accountants, real-estate appraisers, etc.) are roiled by corruption scandals?

The answer is that the professional ideology brings with it certain predictable, recurring weaknesses. The first of these pitfalls of professionalism is that the people with the highest status aren't necessarily creative or original thinkers. Although the professions are thought to represent the pinnacle of human brilliance, what they are actually brilliant at is defending and applying a given philosophy. In *Disciplined Minds*, an important description of the work-life of professionals, the physicist Jeff Schmidt tells us that "ideological discipline is the master key to the professions." Despite the favorite Sixties slogan, professionals do not question authority; their job is to apply it. This is the very nature of their work and the object of their training, according to Schmidt; by his definition, professionals are "obedient thinkers" who "implement their employers' attitudes" and carefully internalize the reigning doctrine of their discipline, whatever it happens to be.[29]

In addition, the professions are structured to shield insiders from accountability. This is what defines the category: professionals do not have to listen. They are the only occupational group, as the sociologist Eliot Freidson put it many years ago, with "the recognized right to declare . . . 'outside' evaluation illegitimate and intolerable."[30]

Exhibit A of these interlocking pathologies is economics, a discipline that often acts like an ideological cartel set up to silence the heterodox. James K. Galbraith has written a classic description of how it works:

> Leading active members of today's economics profession . . . have joined together into a kind of politburo for correct economic thinking. As a general rule—as one might expect from a gentleman's club—this has placed them on the wrong side of every important policy issue, and not just recently but for decades. They predict disaster where none occurs. They deny the possibility of events that then happen. . . . No one loses face, in this club, for having been wrong. No one is disinvited from presenting papers at later annual meetings. And still less is anyone from the outside invited in.[31]

Professional economists screw up again and again, and no one cares. The only real accountability they face is from their endlessly forgiving peers in economics departments across the country. Granted, economics is an extreme case, but its thoroughgoing application of the right to disregard criticism has made it a kind of fascinating anti-profession, a brotherhood of folly rather than of expertise.

The peril of orthodoxy is the second great pitfall of professionalism, and it's not limited to economics. Every academic discipline with which I have some experience is similar: international relations, political science, cultural studies, even American history. None of them are as outrageous as economics, it is true, but each of them is dominated by some convention or ideology.

Those who succeed in a professional discipline are those who best absorb and apply its master narrative.[32]

Our modern technocracy can never see the glaring flaw in such a system. For them, merit is always synonymous with orthodoxy: the best and the brightest are, in their minds, always those who went to Harvard, who got the big foundation grant, whose books are featured on NPR. When the merit-minded President Obama wanted economic expertise, to choose one sad example, he sought out the best the economics discipline had to offer: former treasury secretary and Harvard president Larry Summers, a man who had screwed up time and again yet was shielded from the consequences by his stature within the economics profession.

Look back to the days when government-by-expert actually worked and you will notice an astonishing thing. Unlike the Obama administration's roster of well-graduated mugwumps, the talented people surrounding Franklin Roosevelt stood very definitely outside the era's main academic currents. Harry Hopkins, Roosevelt's closest confidant, was a social worker from Iowa. Robert Jackson, the U.S. Attorney General whom Roosevelt appointed to the Supreme Court, was a lawyer who had no law degree. Jesse Jones, who ran Roosevelt's bailout program, was a businessman from Texas with no qualms about putting the nation's most prominent financial institutions into receivership. Marriner Eccles, the visionary whom Roosevelt appointed to run the Federal Reserve, was a small-town banker from Utah with no advanced degrees. Henry Wallace, who was probably the nation's greatest agriculture secretary, studied at Iowa State and came to government after running a magazine for farmers. Harry Truman, FDR's last vice president, had been a successful U.S. senator but had no college degree at all.

Even Roosevelt's Ivy Leaguers were often dissenters from professional convention. John Kenneth Galbraith, who helped to run the Office of Price Administration during World War II, spent his entire career calling classical economics into question. Thurman Arnold, the Wyoming-born leader of FDR's Antitrust Division, wrote a scoffing and derisive book called *The Folklore of Capitalism*. Just try getting a job in Washington after pulling something like that today.

A third consequence of modern-day liberals' unquestioning, reflexive respect for expertise is their blindness to predatory behavior if it comes cloaked in the signifiers of professionalism. Take the sort of complexity we saw in the financial instruments that drove the last financial crisis. For old-school regulators, I am told, undue financial complexity was an indicator of likely fraud. But for the liberal class, it is the opposite: an indicator of sophistication. Complexity is admirable in its own right. The difference in interpretation carries enormous consequences: Did Wall Street commit epic fraud, or are they highly advanced professionals who fell victim to epic misfortune? As we shall see again and again, modern-day liberals pretty much insist on the latter view, treating Wall Street with extraordinary deference despite all that went on during the last decade. This is no doubt due, in part, to Wall Street's enormous political contributions. But anyone seeking to understand this baffling story must also take note of the widely shared view among Democrats that Wall Street is a place of enormous meritocratic prestige, on a level equivalent to a high-end graduate school. Wall Street's veneer of professionalism is further buttressed by its complicated technical jargon, which (like other disciplines) the financial industry uses to protect itself from the scrutiny of the public.[33]

One final consequence of the ideology of professionalism is

the liberal class's obsessive pining for consensus. I have already mentioned President Obama's remarkable zeal for bipartisan agreement; as we shall see, this is not his passion alone. Most of the Democratic leadership has shared these views for decades; for them, a great coming-together of the nation's educated is the obvious objective of political work.

This obsession, so peculiar and yet so typical of our times, arises from professionals' well-known disgust with partisanship and their faith in what they take to be apolitical solutions.[34] If only they could bring Washington's best people together, they believe, they could enact their common-knowledge program. That the Obama administration chose to fritter away months and even years pursuing this fantasy—with its health care proposal, with its deficit-reduction commission—could probably have been predicted based strictly on the educational pedigree of the president's cabinet choices. Not to be too reductionist here, but it was all a class performance. It was the essence of professionalism.

ON THE LIBERALISM OF THE RICH

I am pressing on a sensitive point here. Democrats cherish their identification as the Party of the People, and they find it unpleasant to be reminded that affluent professionals are today among their most dedicated supporters. Democrats' close relationship with the successful is not something they advertise or even discuss openly.

Exceptions to this rule are rare. One of the few works I know of that seems to approve, albeit with reservations, of liberalism's alliance with a segment of the upper crust is the 2010 book *Fortunes of Change*, written by the philanthropy journalist David Callahan.[35] The premise of his argument is that our new, liberal plutocracy is different from plutocracies of the past because rich people today are sometimes very capable. "Those who get rich in a knowledge economy," the journalist tells us, are well-schooled; they often come from the ranks of "highly educated professionals" and consequently they support Democrats, the party that cares about schools, science, the environment, and federal spending for research. It is not a coincidence, Callahan continues, that "some of the biggest zones of wealth creation are near major universities." The smart get richer and the dumb get . . . Republicans, I guess.

If we accept this equation between wealth and educational accomplishment, it begins to seem unremarkable that, in 2008, hedge funds and investment banks made Barack Obama the first Democrat to outraise his Republican opponent on Wall Street.[36] There's a simple reason that financial firms rallied to the Democrat on that occasion, Callahan suggests: because people on Wall Street, being very smart and very well-educated, are natural liberals. As the journalist reminds us, financial companies these days are populated not by "jocks" but by "quants," by people who are familiar with "new financial products for managing risk or structuring debt, such as derivatives."

As an example, Callahan points us to the D. E. Shaw Group hedge fund, which was founded by a man with a PhD from Stanford who gives enormous sums to Democratic candidates and who also employed former Treasury Secretary Larry Summers for a few years between Summers's gig as president of Harvard and his next gig running President Obama's National Economic Council. Callahan quotes at length from D. E. Shaw's recruiting materials:

> Our staff includes a number of Rhodes, Fulbright, and Marshall Scholars, Putnam Fellows, and the winners of more than 20

> medals in the International Math Olympiad. Current employees include the 2003 U.S. Women's Chess Champion, a Life Master bridge player, and a *Jeopardy* winner, along with a number of writers, athletes, musicians, and former professors. Over 100 of our employees hold PhDs, almost 40 are entrepreneurs who previously founded their own companies, and approximately 20 percent are published authors whose work ranges from highly technical papers in specialized academic journals to award-winning mystery novels.

To this honor roll of intellectual and financial achievement, Callahan appends the following observation: "This is definitely not the Sarah Palin demographic."[37]

No. But neither is it a demographic with any particular concern for the fate of working people.

2

How Capitalism Got Its Groove Back

Democrats have been wondering who they are and squabbling over what they believe for virtually my entire life. It has taken them years to get to wherever it is they are today; years filled with quarrels and vituperation and occasional bouts of manic self-love. It has required long periods of slow evolution, usually in the wrong direction; runs of rapid but lousy choices; epochs of soft-headed enthusiasm for fad ideas, each of which was then followed by a savage Thermidor in which hard-headed party toughguys promoted different fad ideas that turned out to be even worse.

Throughout it all burned the basic questions: Who are the Democrats? What is their purpose, and whom do they serve?

What remained constant throughout these decades of wandering was a certain knowledge of what Democrats were *not*. On this, everyone agreed: Democrats could no longer be the party of Franklin Roosevelt's New Deal coalition, with its heavy reliance upon organized labor and its tendency to see issues through the lens of social class. Through the Seventies, the Eighties, the Nineties, and into the Aughts, as different Democratic reform movements came and went, this was the universal thesis: The New Deal coalition was done for. The reasons for its demise changed as the years passed, however. Some said it was because manufacturing had been overtaken by white-collar work. Others said it was because people were moving to the suburbs . . . or because people were moving to the Sun Belt . . . or because unions were dying . . . or because unions deserved to die . . . or because white Southerners represented the only hope . . . or because white Southerners were a lost cause . . . or because universal, effortless prosperity . . . or because globalization, or because entrepreneurs, or because computers . . . or merely because certain groups who made up the old Democratic electorate were now considered a liability.

Though these many diverse theories, offered up by many different Democratic reform movements, were complicated if not outright contradictory, they all pointed toward the same North Star, toward the same constantly growing awareness of what Democrats had to become in the future: the party of well-educated professionals.

THE POWELL MEMO OF THE DEMOCRATS

Our story begins in the smoking aftermath of the 1968 election, with its sharp disagreements over the Vietnam War, its riots during the Democratic convention in Chicago, and with a result that Democrats at the time took to be a disastrous omen: their candidate for the presidency, Vice President Hubert Humphrey, lost to Richard Nixon. Soul-searching commenced immediately.

There was one bright spot in the Democrats' 1968 effort, however. Organized labor, which was the party's biggest constituency back then, had mobilized millions of working-class voters with an enormous campaign of voter registration, pamphlet-printing, and phone-banking. So vast were their efforts that some observers at the time credited labor with almost winning for Humphrey an election that everyone believed to be lost.[1]

Labor's reward was as follows: by the time of the 1972 presidential contest, the Democratic Party had effectively kicked the unions out of their organization. Democratic candidates still wanted the votes of working people, of course, as well as their donations and their get-out-the-vote efforts. But between '68 and '72, unions lost their position as the premier interest group in the Democratic coalition. This was the result of a series of reforms authored by the so-called McGovern Commission, which changed the Democratic party's presidential nominating system and, along the way, changed the party itself.

Most of the reforms the McGovern Commission called for were clearly healthful. For example, it dethroned state and local machines and replaced them with open primaries, a big step in the right direction. The Commission also mandated that delegations to its 1972 convention conform to certain demographic parameters—that they contain predetermined percentages of women, minorities, and young people. As it went about reforming the party, however, the Commission overlooked one important group: it did nothing to ensure representation for working-class people.[2]

The labor leaders who, up till then, had held such enormous sway over the Democratic Party could see what was happening. After decades of toil on behalf of liberalism, "they were being taken for granted," is how the journalist Theodore White summarized their attitude. "Said Al Barkan, director of the AFL/CIO's political arm, COPE, early in 1972 as he examined the scenario about to unfold: 'We aren't going to let these Harvard-Berkeley Camelots take over our party.' "[3]

But take it over they did. The McGovern Commission reforms seemed to be populist, but their effect was to replace one group of party insiders with another—in this case, to replace leaders of workers' organizations with affluent professionals. Byron Shafer, a political scientist who has studied the 1972 reforms in great detail, leaves no doubt about the class component of the change:

> Before reform, there was an American party system in which one party, the Republicans, was primarily responsive to white-collar constituencies and in which another, the Democrats, was primarily responsive to blue-collar constituencies. After reform, there were two parties each responsive to quite different white-collar coalitions, while the old blue-collar majority within the Democratic party was forced to try to squeeze back into the party once identified predominantly with its needs.[4]

Years ago, when I first became interested in politics, I assumed that this well-known and much-discussed result must have been an unintended effect of an otherwise noble reform effort. It just had to have been an accident. I remember reading about the McGovern Commission in my dilapidated digs on the South Side of Chicago and thinking that no left party in the world would deliberately close the door on the working class. Especially not after workers' organizations had done so much for the party's flat-footed nominee. Besides, it all worked out so very, very badly for the Democrats. Neglecting workers was the opening that allowed Republicans to reach out to blue-collar voters with their arsenal of culture-war fantasies. No serious left politician would make a blunder like that on purpose.

But they did, reader. Leading Democrats actually *chose* to reach out to the affluent and to turn their backs on workers.[5] We know this because they wrote about it, not secretly—as in the infamous "Powell Memo" of 1971, in which the future Supreme Court justice Lewis Powell plotted a conservative political awakening—but openly, in tones of proud idealism, calling forthrightly for reorienting the Democratic Party around the desires of the professional class.

I am referring to a book called *Changing Sources of Power*, a 1971 manifesto by lobbyist and Democratic strategist Frederick Dutton, who was one of the guiding forces on the McGovern Commission. Taken along with the Republican Powell Memo, it gives us the plans of the two big party organizations as the country entered upon the disastrous period that would give us Reagan, Bush, Clinton, Gingrich, and the rest. Where Powell was an arch-conservative, however, Dutton was a forthright liberal. Where Powell showed a certain cunning in his expressed desire to reverse the flow of history, Dutton's tone is one of credulity toward the inflated sense of world-historical importance that surrounded the youth culture of those days. In the book's preface, for example, he actually writes this: "Never has the future been so fundamentally affected by so many current developments."

Dutton's argument was simple: America having become a land of universal and soaring affluence, all that traditional Democratic stuff about forgotten men and workers' rights was now as relevant as a stack of Victrola discs. And young people, meaning white, upper-middle-class college kids—oh, these young people were so wise and so virtuous and even so holy that when contemplating them Dutton could scarcely restrain himself. They were "aristocrats—en masse," the Democratic grandee wrote (quoting Paul Goodman); they meant to "rescue the individual from a mass society," to "recover the human condition from technological domination," to "refurbish and reinvigorate individuality." Better: the young were so noble and so enlightened that they had basically transcended the realm of the physical. "They define the good life not in terms of material thresholds or 'index economics,' as the New Deal, Great Society, and most economic conservatives have done," Dutton marveled, "but as 'the fulfilled life' in a more intangible and personal sense."

Yes, the young were beyond the reach of economics, and seen from the vantage point of 1971, the Great Depression—the period that formed the identity of the Democratic Party—was a far-off country suffering from incomprehensible troubles. The New Deal was quickly becoming irrelevant. Dutton acknowledged that the Democratic coalition that came together during the dark years of the 1930s—he mentioned city dwellers, farmers, and blue-collar workers—still had some life in it, but it either couldn't or *shouldn't* survive much longer. These were two very different kinds of judgments, but for Dutton they seemed to overlap. The main thrust of *Changing Sources of Power* was that Democrats needed to reach out to the young, educated professionals-to-be because they were better, more liberal people; but Dutton also suggested from time to time that Democrats needed to do this because that was the direction the world was going. "Contending economic classes" no longer defined the political drama, Dutton wrote; instead, the great players on the national stage were the Now Generation and "an affluent and liberating upper-middle-class element."

In those days, when American prosperity looked like it would never end, the old economic issues felt to many like they had lost their vitality. Enlightened people didn't really care anymore about the minimum wage or workers' rights. But the stuff about authenticity and personal fulfillment—the stuff that appealed to "the young existentialists"—that stuff would win elections. The "balance of political power," Dutton wrote, had gone "from the economic to the psychological to a certain extent—from the stomach and pocketbook to the psyche, and perhaps sooner or later even to the soul."

Then Frederick Dutton, Democratic Party power broker, went farther: he identified workers, the core of the New Deal coalition, as "the principal group arrayed against the forces of change." They were actually, to a certain degree, the enemy. Dutton acknowledged that it was strange to contemplate such a reversal of the moral alignment that had put his own party into power, but you couldn't argue with history. "In the 1930s, the blue-collar group was in the forefront," Dutton recalled. "Now it is the white-collar sector." Specifically: "the college-educated group." That was who mattered in the future-altering present of 1971.

Put yourself in Dutton's place, and you can perhaps understand where he was coming from. In the Sixties, labor unions seemed like big, unresponsive, white-dominated organizations that were far closer to the comfortable and the powerful than they were to the discontented. *Changing Sources of Power* appeared shortly after a disturbing presidential run by Alabama governor George Wallace, an arch-segregationist whose appeal was then thought to be greatest among working-class whites. The culture in those years was saturated with depictions of blue-collar bigots doing scary things like shooting the main characters in *Easy Rider* and rioting in *support* of the Vietnam War.[6] Everyone back then knew what reactionary clods FDR's old constituents had become; just look at *All in the Family*.

Still, a man like Dutton should have known better. A glance at the union placards carried by marchers at Martin Luther King's 1963 March on Washington—or at the way the United Auto Workers lobbied for the Civil Rights Act of 1964—or at the 1968 strike of black sanitation workers in Memphis—should have been enough to suggest that the Archie Bunker stereotype was not the whole story. Besides, what kind of Democrat gives up on basic economic issues in order to focus on matters of "the psyche" and "the soul"? This was not politics; it was psychotherapy. Worse: it was aristocratic hauteur disguised as enlightenment.

Worse still: regardless of how sclerotic and self-interested unions were in 1971, closing the door on working people's organizations also meant closing the door on working people's issues. That, in turn, consigned future generations of Americans—young or old, enlightened or obtuse, it mattered not—to spend their lives in a society more similar to the Gilded Age than to the affluent 1960s. Although Dutton surely didn't intend for matters to unfold this way, his reverence for the professional class and his contempt for the "legatees of the New Deal" opened the way for something truly unfortunate: the erasure of economic egalitarianism from American politics.

A REALIGNMENT OF CHOICE

What distinguished Dutton's call for realignment from so many of the others that have appeared over the years was that, thanks to his position on the McGovern Commission, he had a certain amount of power to put his theories into effect. "Every major realignment in U.S. political history," he declared in *Changing Sources of Power*, "has been accompanied by the coming of a large new group into the electorate." There's something to that, but what Dutton proposed, and what the Democratic Party in fact undertook, was something very different: a realignment of choice. Democratic leaders decided to reorient the party after 1968 not because this was necessary for survival but because they distrusted their main constituency and had started to lust after a new and more sophisticated one.

The crucial moment in that realignment, as I have mentioned, came in 1972, after the Democrats had reformed their presidential nominating process and chosen George McGovern himself as their candidate. The result was not a good one for Democrats, but they stayed the course. As a senator from South Dakota, McGovern had a decent record on working-class issues, but the public identified him with the Democratic Party's new favorite group: affluent suburban liberals. In fact, according to one account, McGovern did better among these "highly skilled professionals" than he did with the Democrats' traditional blue-collar constituency, many of whom were lured away by the Richard Nixon reelection campaign. What this meant was that McGovern romped in prestigious college towns and also came out ahead in the college-heavy and distinctly professional state of Massachusetts. Nearly everywhere else, however, his particular demographic appeal was a recipe for disaster. He went down in one of the greatest electoral wipeouts in American history.[7]

Not everything was doom and debacle. Among other things, the McGovern campaign launched the political careers of several new-generation Democrats, including the future senator Gary Hart and the future president Bill Clinton, who worked on the 1972 campaign in Texas. And if you looked beneath the surface of McGovern's results, according to a 1974 book by the future Clinton associate Lanny Davis, you discovered that taking the professional vote away from Republicans wasn't necessarily a bad idea. The title of Davis's account was *The Emerging Democratic Majority*—a title that would reappear later in the long, dark decades of Democratic infighting and exile—and his argument was as follows: if Democrats could win back white, working-class voters while hanging on to their new, affluent-suburban electorate, their triumph would be assured.

But that never really happened. Instead, the party intensified its courtship of the comely professional-managerial class. In 1974, in reaction to the Watergate scandal, a huge group of Democrats was elected to Congress—new-school Democrats, that is, who seemed to be largely uninterested in traditional Democratic issues of economic equality. "The new Democrats came out of the anti-war protests and the McGovern campaign, the Peace Corps and the women's movement, the professions and the suburbs," writes historian Jefferson Cowie, "but not the union halls and the wards."[8]

Their de facto leader was the newly elected senator Gary Hart, McGovern's former campaign manager, a man who made his name denouncing old-fashioned, working-class politics in favor of a more tech-friendly vision. Hart became a symbol of the Sixties generation's revolt against the workerist politics of their parents. "The End of the New Deal" was the title of Hart's standard 1974 campaign speech; he liked to mock old-school libs as "Eleanor Roosevelt Democrats." Later on, Hart would lead the technology-minded politicians the media nicknamed the "Atari Democrats"; his 1984 run for the Democratic presidential nomination was celebrated as a blow against the New Deal past. It was also the occasion for the media's discovery of the affluent and tasteful "yuppie"—the "Young Urban Professional" whose rise was supposed to signal yet another break from the Democrats' traditional blue-collar demographic.[9]

The Jimmy Carter presidency was an earlier milestone. At

first Carter had seemed like a man who could recover the party's historic constituencies. But once in office, he broke with the New Deal tradition in all sorts of highly visible ways, cancelling public works projects and conspicuously snubbing organized labor. With the help of a Democratic Congress, he enacted the first of the era's really big tax cuts for the rich and also the first of the really big deregulations. As though to prove how tough and post-partisan he could be, in 1980 he and Paul Volcker, his hand-picked Fed chairman, put the country on an austerity diet that was spectacularly punishing to the ordinary working people who had once made up the Democratic base.

Carter turned out to be a sort of archetype, the first in a series of passionless Democratic technocrats. That working people felt the brunt of Carter's policies was no coincidence; this was not a group for whom his administration felt a great deal of sympathy. In a 1981 interview looking back at the administration's deeds, Carter adviser Alfred Kahn, an economist, had this to say about the fights over deregulation and inflation:

> I'd love the Teamsters to be worse off. I'd love the automobile workers to be worse off. You may say that's inhumane; I'm putting it rather baldly but I want to eliminate a situation in which certain protected workers in industries insulated from competition can increase their wages much more rapidly than the average without regard to their merit or to what a free market would do, and in so doing exploit other workers.[10]

This is a Democrat, remember, and what he was objecting to was the way unions supposedly allowed workers to prosper "without regard to their merit." It is a view we shall hear again as we proceed.

All these Democrats worked to sever their ties with the past, but for the nation's mainstream political commentators the Democrats' reorientation was always and forever insufficient. Regardless of what they did, they still hadn't distanced themselves from the New Deal finally enough; they were still too beholden to manufacturing and blue-collar workers. Democrats would run for the presidency on a professional-friendly platform of high-minded post-partisanship and be rejected by the electorate—and then, in the aftermath, those same Democrats would be ritually denounced by Washington's TV thinkers as examples of the New Deal's exhaustion and irrelevance. It happened to the post-ideological Jimmy Carter in his bid for reelection; it happened to the budget-balancing Walter Mondale; it happened to the technocratic centrist Michael Dukakis—each one of them magically transformed on the day of their defeat into an instructional film on why Democrats needed to embrace post-ideological, budget-balancing, technocratic centrism.[11]

"The collapse and end of the New Deal is one of the most frequently announced events in American media," wrote a political scientist in 1985. It was announced so often and so predictably in those days that cataloguing it became an academic exercise in itself. The historian William Leuchtenburg filled several chapters of his 1989 book, *In the Shadow of FDR*, with New Deal death notices of this kind. For example, after Carter's electoral disaster in 1980, Senator Paul Tsongas said, "Basically, the New Deal died yesterday." After the electoral disaster of 1984, syndicated columnist Joseph Kraft announced that "the repudiation of Mondale was a repudiation of the Democratic Party that had emerged from the old Roosevelt coalition." After the electoral disaster of 1988, it was the same, even though candidate Michael Dukakis had worked hard to distance himself from the New Deal and even from the word "liberal." On the eternal return of the death-of-the-New-Deal, Leuchtenburg himself wondered, "It was far from clear why if, as Gary Hart claimed, the New Deal was dead in 1974, it was necessary for him to kill it off in 1980 and again in 1984."[12]

Can we really blame the media for telling the story this way, time after time? All the bright young Democrats with the post-partisan ideas were saying the same thing. All through the Seventies and Eighties, in fact, new waves of liberal thinkers kept washing up, divining from the political stars the same ideas: that labor unions were an economic drag and/or dying fast; that industrial society itself had gone into eclipse; and that the future belonged to people like them, meaning—always—affluent professionals or some other highly educated and market-savvy cohort.

The most exciting of these bright young thinkers were the tech-minded Washingtonians who called themselves the "Neo-Liberals"; in the early 1980s their bold thinkings were the subject of a manifesto, an anthology, a collective biography, and countless news stories. To the reader of today, however, what stands out in their work is the distaste they expressed for organized labor and their enthusiasm for high-tech enterprises. The 1983 Neo-Liberal manifesto, for example, blamed unions for the country's industrial problems, mourned all the waste involved in the Social Security program, and called for a war on public school teachers so that we might get a better education system and thereby "more Route 128s and Silicon Valleys." It was all so modern, so very up-to-date. "*The solutions of the thirties will not solve the problems of the eighties*," proclaimed a book-length account of this band of cutting-edge thinkers. "Our hero," announced one of the leaders of the bunch, "is the risk-taking entrepreneur who creates new jobs and better products."[13]

THE COMING OF THE NEW DEMOCRATS

Success came eventually to these different Democratic prophets of postindustrialism, but it was brought, ironically, by a group that initially distanced itself from the McGovern turn. I refer to the Democratic Leadership Council (DLC), established by a group of white Southern politicians in 1985 and supposedly committed to the working-class voters the Democratic Party had left behind. As the DLC saw it, whenever Democrats lost an election, it was because their leaders were too weak on crime, too soft on communism, and too sympathetic to minorities.

The DLC had a single-factor theory of politics: that voters had grown disgusted with the cultural liberalism of the post-McGovern era. Why did Carter lose in 1980? Too damn liberal. Why did Mondale lose in 1984? Still too liberal. Why did Dukakis lose in 1988? Liberal again. The DLC also had but a single prescription for this malady: the Democratic Party could only win if it moved to "the center," severing ties with its constituent groups and embracing certain free-market policies of the right. The essential flaw in this neat little syllogism flashed on and off like a neon sign—that all three of the Democratic candidates in the 1980s had followed this exact strategy of shifting rightward and had lost anyway.

What made the DLC succeed where others had failed were the contradictions it managed to juggle. It was a bluntly pro-business force—friendly with lobbyists and funded by corporate backers—that nevertheless proclaimed itself as a warrior for the working class. It was a strictly inside-the-Beltway operation that presented itself as the champion of "forgotten Democrats." One of its early manifestos, for example, berated "higher socioeconomic status Democrats" for antagonizing working-class voters both culturally and economically, by embracing (among other things) "no-growth policies in the mid-seventies just as the economy was beginning to grind to a halt."[14]

Why working-class voters were supposed to pine for balanced budgets, free-trade treaties, and the rest of the items on the DLC wish-list was a mystery. The answer, it would soon become clear, was that the DLC didn't really care all that much about working people in the first place. The aim of the group was to capture the Democratic Party for its lobbyist supporters by whatever means were at hand, and in the 1980s, claiming to represent the overlooked middle American probably seemed like a good gambit.

By the early 1990s, however, the DLC's proletarian period was over. Instead, the group used different rhetoric to persuade Democrats to let them drive. Now its leaders talked about getting "beyond left and right," about occupying the "vital center," about themselves as visionary "New Democrats," empty phrases that nevertheless carried—that carry still—a kind of hypnotic power over the technocratic Washington mind. Before long, the DLC had discovered the great Cause on whose behalf it would henceforth make its demands: not the forgotten worker but the future—the "postindustrial, global economy." It was in order to "do business" in this new realm, the group's many manifestoes declared, that we needed to reform "entitlements" (i.e., Social Security), privatize government operations, open charter schools, get tough on crime, and all the rest of it.[15]

This was the DLC's "futurist" period, with everything exactly the same as in its earlier phase except that the New Economy had taken the place of the "forgotten Democrat" as the factor everyone needed to consider. Indeed, the group now seemed to revel in the imminent downfall of the working class. A remarkable artifact of this period was a 1995 cover story in the

DLC magazine entitled "Beyond Repair: The Politics of the Machine Age Are Hopelessly Obsolete," in which the reader learns that, "Thanks to the near-miraculous capabilities of microelectronics, we are vanquishing scarcity." The reign of plenty that was to come meant that "the venerable politics of class warfare . . . is dying," but also that lots of people in society's lower ranks were going to get nowhere in the future. The insufficiently educated, it was said, would eat the dust "like illiterate peasants in the Age of Steam."[16]

By then, one of the DLC's leaders had seated himself in the Oval Office, a story I will tell in the next three chapters. But allow me to step away from that chronological sequence for a moment to relate how the saga of the DLC ended. At first, remember, the group was critical of "higher socioeconomic status Democrats" for being too liberal; by 1998, however, they had completely reversed themselves. In that year, the Democratic Leadership Council published a manifesto announcing who history's lucky winners were going to be—and it was the same group of people the DLC had once reviled for dragging the Democrats to the left. To find this out, readers had to make their way through a preface declaring yet again that "the New Deal era has ended," but then political scientists William Galston and Elaine Kamarck were ready to divulge their finding: "The New Economy Favors a Rising Learning Class Over a Declining Working Class."

Yes, a "learning class." This cohort, which the authors also called "Wired Workers," was made up of individuals who were "better educated, more affluent, more mobile, and more self-reliant" than others. These fine people were scheduled to "dominate at least the first half of the 21st century," and both of the country's political parties would be required—on pain of utter destruction—to compete single-mindedly for their votes.

Amazingly, the things that Wired Workers wanted were exactly the things that the Democratic Leadership Council had been pushing since its inception—entitlement reform, free markets, charter schools, and the rest of it.[17]

ENTER THE BUBBA

The different schools of Democratic Party reform that I have briefly described here are usually regarded as separate if not mutually despising tendencies. Frederick Dutton and his fellow worshippers at the shrine of enlightened youth were part of what is called the "New Politics" persuasion; among other things, they were open to cultural radicalism and strongly opposed the Vietnam War. The Democratic Leadership Council, on the other hand, were a faction of hippie-punching white Southerners who loved free markets and who ultimately discredited themselves many years later by whooping it up for the Iraq War.[18]

These factions appeared to be opponents, and yet there was a persistent habit of thought that united them: regardless of what it was they were demanding, they all agreed that what stood in their way was the legacy of the New Deal—the Democratic Party's commitment to equality for working people. That was what had to end.

Here is where our story takes its remarkable turn: slowly but relentlessly, these different loser reform traditions came together, and as they did, the Democratic Party became a success. Bad ideas plus bad ideas turned out, in this case, to yield electoral victory.

The exact point where these trajectories intersected was occupied by one Bill Clinton, governor of Arkansas, a Rhodes Scholar and a McGovern campaign worker who had grown up to become the chairman of the DLC. He led the idealistic Sixties generation *and* he warred with the teachers' union; he smoked dope *and* he never got high; he savored Fleetwood Mac *and* he got tough with welfare mothers. Here was the one-man synthesis of the grubby dialectic I have been describing, and he arrived in Washington to fulfill the sordid destiny of his class like Lenin arriving at the Finland Station.

3

The Economy, Stupid

As the Nineties began, public fury over inequality was beginning one of its great cyclical eruptions. For the twenty preceding years, pundits and politicians had hoped, predicted, and declared that the egalitarian impulses of the Depression years had been cured; instead, the economic effects of Reaganism made their revival inevitable. The rich were richer than at any time since World War II, while small farmers and manufacturing workers were seeing their livelihoods destroyed. The cult of the entrepreneur had produced a group of buyout artists and savings and loan owners who were little better than criminals. The stock market had been galloping along at a tremendous pace—until the crash of 1987 suggested the whole thing was built on sand.

The former Republican strategist Kevin Phillips kicked things off with his best-selling 1990 book, *The Politics of Rich and Poor*, asserting that upper-bracket excess could only go so far before it triggered a populist backlash—and that America had reached that point. The book was filled with the now-familiar sorts of charts showing how income inequality had accelerated over the years and how the top percentages were pulling away from everyone else. "Only for so long," Phillips wrote, "will strung-out $35,000-a-year families enjoy magazine articles about the hundred most successful businessmen in Dallas or television programs about the life-styles of the rich and famous."[1]

The following year, two reporters for the Philadelphia *Inquirer* published an even more bitter account of how the wealthy had plundered the country's productive enterprises during the 1980s, "pushing the nation toward a two-class society." In 1992, the series appeared in book form under the title *America: What Went Wrong?*, with a then-shocking inverted flag on the cover; it, too, spent many weeks on the best-seller lists. A typical passage fumed that in 1989

> the top 4 percent of all wage earners in the country collected as much in wages and salaries as the bottom 51 percent of the population. Mull over the numbers carefully: The top 4 percent of America's work force earned as much as the bottom 51 percent. That is in wages and salaries alone.[2]

Class outrage was in the air. The Eighties boom had soured into a sharp recession in 1990, but the president at the time, the patrician George H. W. Bush, seemed less than concerned. In December 1991, General Motors announced plans to close 21 plants and lay off an astonishing 70,000 workers. The month after that, TV news footage showed almost 10,000 people lined up in the bitter Chicago cold for 1,000 job openings at a new hotel.

In the presidential campaign then unfolding, economic populism was the flavor of the moment, the clear way to voice the spirit of the times and to challenge the uncaring, high-born incumbent. Four different candidates in 1992 struggled to make themselves the favorite of the discontented voter; the one who pulled it off most convincingly was the young governor of Arkansas, Bill Clinton, who preached the old-time religion with everything he had. Not only did Clinton wave a copy of *America: What Went Wrong?* during his speeches, but he talked like its authors, too. Middle-class Americans now "worked harder for less," he would say. "One percent of America's people at the top of the totem pole now have more wealth than the bottom 90 percent," he liked to add, calling it "the biggest imbalance in wealth in America since the 1920's right before the Great Depression." Indeed, Clinton said, we were now facing the danger of raising "the first generation of Americans to do worse than their parents."[3]

When he was finally offered the nomination of the Democratic Party, he accepted it "in the name of the hardworking Americans who make up our forgotten middle class." Then he added this: "When I am president, you will be forgotten no more."

It was the kind of campaign that old-style Democrats loved to run, a hard-times set piece in which a clever commoner squares off against a bored grandee who yawns at the suffering all around him—a man who actually checks his watch when asked a question about the woes of the "common people." It was the election of 1932 all over again, with Bush standing in for the hated Herbert Hoover. The fieriest rhetoric of all came from one of Clinton's chief surrogates, Democratic Georgia governor Zell Miller. Twelve years later, Miller would appear at the Republican convention, endorsing George W. Bush and winning renown as one of the greatest turncoats in Democratic Party history, but in 1992 he was still a flamboyant Southern populist, a purveyor of proletarian bombast so purple he actually began his keynote speech by boasting about the authenticity of his accent and the hardness of his upbringing. He laced into "aristocrats," "the rich," and the "billionaire" third-party candidate, Ross Perot. He recalled the days of Franklin Roosevelt. He blasted Republicans in classic style. "I know what Dan Quayle means when he says it's best for children to have two parents," Miller thundered at one point. "You bet it is! And it would good if they all had trust funds, too!" He continued:

> I'm for Bill Clinton because he is a Democrat who does not have to read a book or be briefed about the struggles of single-parent families, or what it means to work hard for everything he's ever received in life. There was no silver spoon in sight when he was born, three months after his father died. No one ever gave Bill Clinton a free ride as he worked his way through college and law school.

SPEAKING TRUTH TO WEAKNESS

Zell Miller's later career as a double-crosser gives some hint of how phony it all was. The Democratic rhetoric of 1992 may have made you feel like the heroes of the Thirties were still with us, standing ready to take up the old fight against arrogant wealth—in fact, their campaign talk was patently designed to create exactly that impression. In truth, however, erasing the memories and the accomplishments of Depression-era Democrats was what Bill Clinton and his clique of liberals were put on earth to achieve.

That is not the conclusion of some sour and cynical Clinton hater, of which there were once so many; that is the sober and considered judgment of a responsible journalist, Martin Walker of the British *Guardian* newspaper and author of the 1996 book, *The President We Deserve*. Walker was clearly an admirer of the forty-second president, and after acknowledging Clinton's failings, he urged his readers to think bigger: the president's shortcomings were "in the end balanced and even outweighed by his part in finally sinking the untenable old consensus of the New Deal, and the crafting of a new one." Only a Democrat was capable of such a deed, and Clinton did it. That was his great and undeniable achievement: He put the Thirties sensibility down so forcefully it would never again be revived.

Let us recall that Bill Clinton came to national prominence as the leader of the Democratic Leadership Council, whose object was to shift the party to the right using whatever ideological tools were at hand. It is ironic, given the damage they proceeded to do to working-class people, that the New Democrats finally got their chance to move into the executive branch as the result of a distinctly populist campaign pounding away at the oldest of left-wing themes.

The truth of the New Democrats' purpose was presented by the journalist Joe Klein in his famous 1996 roman à clef about Clinton's run for the presidency, *Primary Colors*. Although the novel contains more than a nod to Clinton's extramarital affairs, Klein seems broadly sympathetic to the man from Arkansas as well as to the DLC project more generally. Toward the equality-oriented politics of the Democratic past he is forthrightly contemptuous. Old people who recall fondly the battles of the Thirties, for example, are objects of a form of ridicule that Klein thinks he doesn't even need to explain; it is self-evident that people who care about workers are fools. And when an old-school "prairie populist" challenges the Clinton character for the nomination, Klein describes him as possessing "a voice made for crystal radio sets" and "offering Franklin Roosevelt's jobs program (forestry, road-building) to out-of-work computer jockeys." Get it? His views are obsolete! "It was like running against a museum."

That was the essential New Democrat idea: The world had changed, but certain Democratic voters expected their politicians to help them cling to a status that globalization had long since revoked. However, a true statesman—a real New Democrat—would challenge them to open their eyes. The climactic point in *Primary Colors* comes when the Clinton-figure visits a union hall in New Hampshire—"an obscure local of a dying craft . . . a fraternal organization for people left behind." To these working-class losers, the candidate decides to tell the hard, unpleasant truth:

> "So let me tell you this: No politician can bring these shipyard jobs back. Or make your union strong again. No politician can make it be the way it used to be. Because we're living in a new world now, a world without borders—economically, that is. Guy can push a button in New York and move a billion dollars to Tokyo before you blink an eye. We've got a world market now. That's good for some. . . . But muscle jobs are gonna go where muscle labor is cheap—and that's not here. So if you all want to compete and do better, you're gonna have to exercise a different set of muscles, the ones between your ears."
>
> "Uh-oh," said the woman.
>
> And Stanton [read: Clinton] did something really dangerous then: he didn't indulge her humor. "Uh-oh is right," he said. "And anyone who gets up here and says he can do it for you isn't leveling with you. So I'm not gonna insult you by doing that. I'm going to tell you this: This whole country is gonna have to go back to school. We're gonna have to get

smarter, learn new skills. And I will work overtime figuring out ways to help you get the skills you need."

That's the magic moment that turns the fictional presidential race around: when the Clinton character speaks truth to weakness. In Klein's cosmogony, this is something noble, something honest, something Democrats must do in order to win. Although this particular story was made up, as a description of a certain Democratic outlook it was exactly right. What workers need, this passage tells us, is to be informed that, in the face of global markets, there's nothing anyone can do to protect them. That resistance is futile. That only individual self-improvement is capable of lifting you up—not collective action, not politics, not changing how the economy is structured. Americans can only succeed by winning the market's favor, and we can only do that by proving ourselves worthy in school.

Klein was right to make this scene the fulcrum of his novel. It raises the basic question of what to do about inequality—collective action or individual effort—raises it and then dismisses it with a glib call to go out and get some "skills." It is the glibness of that dismissal, the professional-class certainty that has been repeated in a thousand presidential statements and Senate hearings and casual conversations on the Acela train, that explains the Democratic Party's flat inability to rise to the challenge of plutocracy.

EVERY MAN A YUPPIE

In reality, remember, Bill Clinton owed his election to hard times and his remarkable ability to make people think he cared about their suffering. With an assist from the plain-speaking billionaire Ross Perot, Clinton succeeded in winning back many of the working-class voters his centrist, technocratic predecessors had lost to the Republicans.

Once elected, Clinton expressed his thoughts in a December 1992 speech to his "economic summit." Here is how he proposed to deal with the various economic problems he had identified on the campaign trail:

> Our new direction must rest on an understanding of the new realities of global competition. The world we face today is the world where *what you earn depends on what you can learn.* There's a direct relationship between high skills and high wages, and therefore we have to educate our people better to compete. We will be as rich and strong and rife with opportunity as we are skilled and talented and trained.

I put Clinton's line about "what you earn" in italics because it may well be the most important passage of them all for understanding how his party—how our entire system—has failed so utterly to confront income inequality. It's a line Clinton repeated a number of times in the course of his years in government,* and here, in a single sentence, is the distilled essence of the theory that has governed the politics of work and compensation from that day to this: *You get what you deserve, and what you deserve is defined by how you did in school.* Furthermore, this is supposedly true both for individuals and for the nation. Everyone says this. Barack Obama says it, David Brooks says

* One of the more remarkable occasions on which Clinton uttered this favorite aphorism was while signing a 2000 law that vastly expanded the number of H-1B visas for foreign high-tech workers, thereby diluting the earning power of all those Americans who'd been dutifully learning all those New Economy skills.

it, George W. Bush says it, even Wisconsin governor Scott Walker says it, by implication, when he demands that the mission of the University of Wisconsin be changed from the "search for truth" to making people employable.

There is a sense in which this is obviously true; a platitude, even: None of us would get very far if we didn't know how to read or to do math. Research and development is indeed important. People have to have the right skills before they can run the big machinery.

But it doesn't take an advanced degree to figure out that this education talk is less a strategy for *mitigating* inequality than it is a way of *rationalizing* it. To attribute economic results to school years finished and SAT scores achieved is to remove matters from the realm of, well, economics and to relocate them to the provinces of personal striving and individual intelligence. From this perspective, wages aren't what they are because one party (management) has a certain amount of power over the other (workers); wages are like that because the god of the market, being surpassingly fair, rewards those who show talent and gumption. Good people are those who get a gold star from their teacher in elementary school, a fat acceptance letter from a good college, and a good life when they graduate. All because they are the best. Those who don't pay attention in high school get to spend their days picking up discarded cans by the side of the road. Both outcomes are our own doing.

One source of this idea, obviously, was the country's traditional Protestant work ethic. There was also an important contemporary source. A few pages ago, I described a handful of popular authors who wrote on inequality in the early Nineties, but I left out the one whose views turned out to be most consequential of them all: Harvard professor Robert Reich, a close Clinton friend who became secretary of labor in 1993. On the campaign trail, Clinton had carried with him an oft-consulted copy of Reich's 1991 magnum opus, *The Work of Nations*, and the plan for job training and infrastructure spending that Clinton announced as a candidate followed the strategy Reich outlined.[4] Like the other books I mentioned, *The Work of Nations* acknowledged that most of us were sinking while others were enjoying fabulous success. In his gently ironic style, Reich told the story of how the well-to-do—the "fortunate fifth," he called them—were engaged in a kind of "secession" from the larger American community, withdrawing into exclusive suburbs and private schools. Here they were "able to shop, work, and attend the theater without risking direct contact with the outside world."

Today Robert Reich is something of a populist prophet and a fighter for economic justice, but in those days he was a very different sort of thinker. Inverted-flag distress signals were not for him. Despite his acknowledgement of rising inequality, he seemed rather satisfied with the way things were unfolding. *The Work of Nations* appeared to be a critique, but it was in fact a long valentine to society's winners—the "symbolic analysts," as Reich famously dubbed them, the professionals and consultants whose work was creative and pleasant and intellectual and who rode effortlessly on the waves of the international market, electronically connected at all times even as they jetted around the world. While manufacturing workers drifted hopelessly toward history's dustbin, the symbolic analysts were the coming class, the only people who really mattered: "Never before in history," Reich wrote, "has opulence on such a scale been gained by people who have earned it, and done so legally."

That bit about the winners having "earned" their wealth is a critical moral point. For some, the social crevasse that began to open in the Eighties was an outrage; for Reich, the success of the symbolic analysts was entirely legitimate. These were creative people who were "adding substantial value." They were highly educated. Their innovations were in worldwide demand. They had *merit.*

In Reich's understanding of the world circa 1991, not a whole lot could be done for that part of the population who worked in traditional blue-collar jobs. In the future, people would either have to become servants of the symbolic analysts or become symbolic analysts themselves. Reich assured us that the latter was possible, if we dedicated ourselves to spending more on education, infrastructure, and job training. Unlike other dominant classes in history, there was technically no limit on the number of people who could join this favored cohort, who could grow up and "sell symbolic-analytic services worldwide." In theory, everyone could become a yuppie.

A more serious objection is that Reich's plan to put people on the path to symbolic analysis simply missed the point. The problem of inequality was more fundamental than upgrading the jobs people did. During the '92 campaign, one of Clinton's best lines had been that Americans were "working harder for less"; what he was acknowledging when he said this was one of the basic facts of the decades-long inequality debate: that worker productivity was going up but wages were not.

This was—and remains—essential to the inequality problem. Before the late 1970s, productivity and wage growth had always increased in unison—as workers made more stuff, they earned more money. But by the early 1990s, the two had clearly separated. Workers made more stuff than ever before, but they no longer prospered from what they made.[5] Put differently: Workers were working as hard and as well as ever; they simply weren't reaping the profits from it. Wall Street was. This was a massive and fundamental disorder, but one thing it was *not* was a failure of education. Had the problem been one of inadequate worker skills, productivity would not have been increasing so fast.

The real problem was one of inadequate worker power, not inadequate worker smarts.* The people who produced were losing their ability to demand a share in what they made. The people who owned were taking more and more.

Today the separation of productivity from reward is a feature of nearly every sort of work—white-collar, blue-collar; symbolic, literal; physical, mental; analytic, representational; all of us going nowhere while owners ascend the stratosphere. But because it happened to production workers first, it was possible for Democrats like Reich and Clinton to look at the situation and conclude that the real problem was those workers' lousy educations.

It was a costly mistake. While this interpretation might have made a kind of narcissistic sense to the well-graduated, it allowed Democrats to ignore what was happening in the real economy—from monopoly power to financialization to labor-management relations—in favor of a moral fantasy that required them to confront no one. In the Clinton view, which would become the standard Democratic view, the only ones who had to change their ways were the victims themselves.

INEQUALITY COMES TO TYPICALTOWN, USA

Clinton and company would have done well to pay attention to what was going on in Decatur, Illinois, a prairie town of home-

* To his credit, Robert Reich has since come around to a version of this viewpoint. For example, see his article, "The Political Roots of Widening Inequality," published in *The American Prospect* in Spring 2015.

grown hamburger stands, WPA murals, and numerous statues of Abraham Lincoln, a local boy who made good. During World War II, Decatur was so exactly the quintessence of who-we-are that it scored 99 out of 100 on an East Coast professor's "most typical" scale; that professor proceeded to send the then-unknown sociologist C. Wright Mills to Decatur to study its completely average population. What Mills found in Decatur later became the nucleus of *White Collar*, his famous study of the middle-class mind.[6]

Mills should have stuck around a little longer. Shortly after the Clinton administration took office, this most average of American cities descended into class war, with industrial actions at three different local factories. It all started in 1993 when the managers of a Decatur corn-processing plant, owned by the Tate & Lyle multinational sweetener concern, locked out their unionized employees. Contract negotiations had been going nowhere. The union was upset about what they saw as unsafe working conditions in the plant, and management was demanding concessions that were so extreme—for example, they wanted to put the workers on twelve-hour rotating shifts in place of the conventional eight-hour day—they seemed designed to provoke a strike. Instead, the union members had launched a campaign in which they worked exactly as they were instructed to work by managers and operating manuals; no more, no less. Production declined. Management responded by bringing in replacement workers to do their jobs.[7]

Shortly after the lockout began, the unions representing workers at Decatur's Firestone tire plant and its Caterpillar earth-mover factory also went on strike. Here, too, the twelve-hour shift was an issue, in addition to two-tier pay scales in which new employees would never be able to earn as much as those who had hired in previously. These were no ordinary concessions. As I learned when I went to Decatur in 1994, a worker's internal clock never adjusts to a rotational system, in which one's shift moves all the time. More ominously, the twelve-hour rotating shift system would make it impossible for workers to participate in the life of their family or town: no more league sports or church choirs for them.[8]

The three union locals in Decatur quickly made common cause with one another, and before long a big part of the working population in that most typical American town were out protesting. With billboards, placards, newsletters, and the other publicity tools of that pre-Internet era, these aggrieved Midwesterners reached out across the country to tell the story of how their town had become a "war zone," by which they meant to suggest that working-class Americans were in the crosshairs of a merciless new economic order.

The workers turned out to be right about the war zone. Before long the local police escalated the conflict with a spectacular bit of violence, using pepper spray on a crowd of peaceful protesters at the Tate & Lyle factory gate. I lived in Chicago at the time and I remember being shocked by the pictures of that incident, in particular by a poignant one of a middle-aged protester holding an American flag as the pepper spray hit his face.

That detail was fairly typical. The union members in Decatur grew increasingly radical as time went on, but they always took care to start their meetings with the Pledge of Allegiance. And those meetings themselves—it is painful to recall how earnestly those people believed in democracy, how deeply they seemed to feel that if average Americans could just get together and talk it over and settle on a plan, why, they could take on multinational corporations. Solidarity would prevail over everything. It was like something out of Lincoln's time. Or Roosevelt's, anyway.

What I remember above all—what I will never forget—is a march I observed in October 1994 that passed by Decatur's three affected factories. Seven thousand people from all over the region had come to the war zone to participate, and I climbed up onto an overpass at one point to look back at the parade. The street was filled from side to side and as far as the eye could see with an advancing multitude of workers and average citizens—even the police had given up trying to exert control by this point—and as I beheld all this I experienced a spontaneous apprehension of what liberalism was all about, of what it stood for and of where its power came from—or, rather, where its power *used* to come from.

According to company management, the real problem was that employees were in denial; the union "still thinks it is 1950," declared the CEO of Caterpillar.[9] Those aggrieved Midwesterners simply hadn't understood how the world had changed, how savage the competitive environment had become—and how ridiculous it was now for working-class people to expect to live middle-class lives. (It's something CEOs still say, incidentally, about anyone who expects to be paid decently.)

The Democratic administration in Washington, meanwhile, did virtually nothing to remedy the situation in the Midwestern war zone; Robert Reich had actually wondered in a 1993 interview with the *New York Times* "whether the traditional union is necessary for the new workplace."[10]

The union workers themselves had a grittier—and, as it turned out, far more accurate—impression of where events were taking us. At a contentious union meeting in 1994, I was talking with a bunch of people about the labor struggles of times past, and a locked-out worker at Tate & Lyle named Royal Plankenhorn told me this: "Now it's our turn. And if we don't do it, then the middle class as we know it in this country will die. There will be two classes, and it will be the very very poor and the very very rich."[11]

YUPPIE CRIMES

But Decatur was far away from Washington, and its problems made no impression that I could detect on Bill Clinton's wise brain trust. The New Economy was dawning, creativity was triumphing, old industry was evaporating, and those fortunate enough to be among the ascendant were absolutely certain about the direction history was taking.

How could they be so certain? How did the liberal class know so confidently that education and training were the solution for inequality as well as the explanations for individual and national success?

Their certainty came, for one thing, from the fact that just about *everyone* was repeating the same platitudes. Postindustrialism! Globalization! The information superhighway! These were gods before whom everyone bowed back then, deities who made their will known to the country's opinion columnists and management theorists.

Another reason so many were convinced so completely that education determined everything from personal prosperity to national competitiveness was, again, that it was true for them personally. Going to fancy colleges is what had allowed them to succeed, what had defined them as a generation, what had kept them out of trouble in Vietnam; it was natural for them to think that it could do the same for all people at all times in all situations.

Consider the new president's own story. Higher education had been what opened the doors for Bill Clinton, what had allowed a talented commoner from a backward place to travel the wide world and to enter the highest circles of the power elite. And so it was with nearly all Clinton's close confidants: they were successful professionals whose worth was established by their achievements in college or graduate school. Martin Walker, the journalist who wrote *The President We Deserve*, starts his biography by marveling at Clinton's different circles of well-graduated friends—the ones from his college days at Georgetown, the ones from his days as a Rhodes Scholar, the ones from Yale Law School—and then he speculates about the kind of high-powered synergies that could happen when Bill brought one group of smart friends into contact with another.

Clinton's cabinet was a kind of yuppie Woodstock, a gathering of the highly credentialed tribes. Critics at the time tallied up how many of them had attended this institution and how many that; how many were married to important journalists and how many were married to important college professors. It was such a tight little network of enlightened strivers, all these hard-working, well-graduated people who not only knew the answers but who knew one another, too. "The Clinton Administration was to fulfill Cecil Rhodes's dream," wrote the British journalist Walker. "Seldom has any foreign country been run so completely by such a narrowly defined elite."[12]

Clinton had famously promised to appoint a cabinet that would "look more like America than any previous administration." Look like us they did—black, white, brown, male, female. Examined from any perspective other than their external appearances, however, they were not representative at all. In

1992, the Democratic convention had laughed at George H. W. Bush's posh-boy entourage for being ignorant of life as it's lived in some Appalachian hollow, and now came the news that there were more millionaires among the populist Bill Clinton's cabinet than there had been in Bush's. In addition, more than three-quarters of them were lawyers. The country had merely exchanged one elite for another; a cadre of business types for a collection of high-achieving professionals.

One point where Clinton's obliviousness to the situation of ordinary people became conspicuous was in the brief tussle over his first choice for attorney general: one Zoë Baird, a typically well-connected corporate lawyer who was married to a famous law professor at Yale. Between the two of them, Baird and her husband made more than six hundred and fifty grand per year, but still they saw fit to pay their two undocumented domestic servants a little more than $250 per week, without having initially made the required Social Security payments. Had Baird been a Bush appointee, this would no doubt have constituted a living lesson in how class and inequality work—a teachable moment, as people like to say. But of course it wasn't that at all. It was scarcely anything. The Clinton vetting team wasn't put off by it in the least. They thought it was just a "yuppie crime," the columnist Clarence Page joked. Offensive to you, maybe, but in the circles in which these people traveled it was about as dreadful as the rule-breaking fun of Ferris Bueller and his pals.[13] Congress did not find it so petty, however, and the Baird nomination had to be withdrawn.

Bill Clinton was often described as the leader of his generation, but it's more accurate to say he was the leader of a particular privileged swath of his age group—the leader of a *class*. And this was the moment for his cohort to take their turn at the controls. As the sentimental music of Judy Collins played, one privileged group was taking over from another. A few journalists got it at the time: looking over the rosters of Clinton appointees, their spouses, and their interlocking circles of friends, Jacob Weisberg of the *New Republic* fretted about the "increasingly cozy relationships between press, law, academia and government" that he saw there. "There's rarely been a time," he concluded, "when the governing elites in so many fields were made up of such a tight, hermetic and incestuous clique."[14]

There was something else Weisberg understood in those early days of the administration. "The Clinton circle has a pronounced class consciousness that tells them they're not just lucky to be here," he wrote. "They're running things because they're the best."

4

Agents of Change

Everyone remembers the years of the Bill Clinton presidency as good times. The economy was booming, the stock market was ascending, and the mood was infectious. You felt good about it even if you didn't own a single share.

And yet: What did Clinton actually do in his eight years on Pennsylvania Avenue? While writing this book, I would periodically ask my liberal friends if they could recall the progressive laws he got passed, the high-minded policies he fought for—you know, the good things Bill Clinton got done while he was president. Why was it, I wondered, that we were supposed to think so highly of him—apart from his obvious personal affability, I mean?

It proved difficult for my libs. People mentioned the obvious things: Clinton raised the minimum wage and expanded the Earned Income Tax Credit. He secured a modest tax increase on the wealthy. There was his ban on assault weapons. And he did propose a national health program, although it was so poorly designed it could be a model of how not to do big policy initiatives.

Other than that, not much. No one mentioned any great but

hopeless Clintonian stands on principle; after all, this is the guy who once took a poll to decide where to go on vacation. His presidency was all about campaign donations, not personal bravery—he rented out the Lincoln Bedroom, for chrissake, and at the end of his time in office he even appeared to sell a presidential pardon.

It's easy to remember the official, consensus reasons why we're supposed to admire Bill Clinton—the achievements which the inevitable Spielberg bio-pic will no doubt illustrate with poignant and whimsical personal glimpses. First was the economy, which did really well while he was in office. So well, in fact, that we had something close to full employment for several years while the Dow hit 10,000 and the Nasdaq stock index went effing *vertical*—flush times that are almost inconceivable from our present-day vantage point. Surely that trumps everything.

The other great source of the Clinton myth is the insane vendetta against him launched by the Republicans—what his former aide Sidney Blumenthal has called the "Clinton Wars." The attacks began soon after Clinton took office—the Whitewater pseudoscandal actually made page one of the *New York Times* in 1992—and the Clinton Wars were so patently, so outrageously unfair that you couldn't help but stand behind their victim. Clinton's enemies spent millions trawling Arkansas for his old paramours. Congress actually *impeached* the guy for lying about a blowjob.

For many of the authors who have examined the Clinton presidency, the Clinton Wars eclipse everything else. For instance, take Carl Bernstein, the eminent journalist who wrote a meticulously researched biography of Hillary Clinton, Bill's wife and "co-president." So many of the pages Bernstein allots to the couple's White House years are filled with details about Vince Foster and the Travel Office and the Independent Counsels and the Grand Juries and the missing billing records that Bernstein ultimately relegates Bill Clinton's actual achievements as president to a few desultory paragraphs here and there.[1]

The Clinton Wars were what politics was all about, and Bill Clinton won those wars. The priggish, boorish, pharisaical right raged against him, and he soldiered on. He defied the Republicans and got himself reelected even as his party lost control of Congress. He outmaneuvered the GOP during the budget wars of 1995 and '96 and convinced the public to blame it for the government shutdown.

Flush economic times and victory in the Clinton Wars: These two are enough to secure the man a spot among the immortals.* In fact, before the Crash of 2008, my fellow Washingtonians tended to regard the Clinton administration as a transparent triumph. This was what a successful Democratic presidency looked like. This was the model. To do as Clinton did was to follow the clearly marked path of wisdom.

YESTERDAY'S GONE

Evaluating Clinton's presidency as heroic is no longer a given, however. After the bursting of the dot-com bubble in 2000, the corporate scandals of the Enron period, and the collapse of the real estate racket, our view of the prosperous Nineties has

---

* I'm not going to go into the third great source of the Clinton myth, which is the man's legendary personal charm. How can anyone dislike a guy from Hot Springs, Arkansas, whose great ambition as a youth was to be a second Elvis Presley?

changed quite a bit. Now we remember that it was Bill Clinton's administration that deregulated derivatives, deregulated telecom, and put our country's only strong banking laws in the grave. He's the one who rammed the North American Free Trade Agreement (NAFTA) through Congress and who taught the world that the way you respond to a recession is by paying off the federal deficit. Mass incarceration and the repeal of welfare, two of Clinton's other major achievements, are the pillars of the disciplinary state that has made life so miserable for Americans in the lower reaches of society. He would have put a huge dent in Social Security, too, had the Monica Lewinsky sex scandal not stopped him. If we take inequality as our measure, the Clinton administration looks not heroic but odious.

Some believe it is unfair to criticize President Clinton for these deeds. At the time of his actions, they recall, these initiatives were matters of almost universal assent. In the tight little group of credentialed professionals who dominated his administration as well as the city they worked in, *almost everyone agreed* on these things. Over each one of them there hovered a feeling of inevitability and even of obviousness, as though they were the uncontroversial policy demands of history itself. Globalization wanted these things to happen. Technology wanted them to happen. The Future wanted them to happen. Naturally the professional class wanted them to happen, too.

The term Clinton liked to use to summarize this sense of inevitability was "change." This word is, obviously, a longstanding favorite of politicians of the left; what it means is that We the People have the power to shape the world around us. It is a hopeful word. But when Clinton said in a speech about free trade in 1993 that

> Change is upon us. We can do nothing about that,

he was enshrining the opposite idea as the progressive creed. Change was an external force we could neither escape nor control; it was a reality that limited what we could do politically and that had in fact made most of our political choices for us already. The role of We the People was not to make change but to submit to its dominion. Naturally, Clinton thought to describe this majestic thing, this "change," by referencing a force of nature: "a new global economy of constant innovation and instant communication is cutting through our world like a new river, providing both power and disruption to the people and nations who live along its course."[2]

Clinton spoke of change the way other politicians would talk about God or Providence; we could succeed economically, he once announced, "if we make change our friend."[3] Change was fickle and inscrutable, an unmoved mover doing this or that as only it saw fit. Our task—or, more accurately, your task, middle-class citizen—was to conform to its wishes, to "adjust to change," as the president put it when talking about NAFTA.

Worship of "change" was standard stuff in the business literature of that period, but Clinton brought it into the public sphere. For him, this was how politics worked: Every deal was always a done deal. Every legislative program was a way of reckoning with some irresistible onrushing historical force that he and his advisers had divined. The role of Congress was to figure out how to bow to the new reality as Clinton's cohort perceived it.

BAD BRAINS

The first time I myself tuned in and noticed some version of this inevitability-speak was in 1993, during the fight over NAFTA. The deal had been negotiated by the departed president, George H. W. Bush, but the Democratic majority in Congress had balked at the original version of the treaty, forcing the parties back to the table. As with so many of the achievements of the Clinton era, it eventually took a Democratic president, working with Republican members of Congress, to pass this landmark of neoliberalism.

According to the president himself, what the agreement was about was simple: "NAFTA will tear down trade barriers," he said when signing it. "It will create the world's largest trade zone and create 200,000 jobs in this country by 1995 alone." The stationery of an outfit that lobbied for the treaty was emblazoned with an even briefer version of this reasoning: "North American Free Trade Agreement—Exports. Better Jobs. Better Wages."[4]

But it wasn't reason that sold NAFTA; it was a simulacrum of reason, by which I mean the great god inevitability, invoked in the language of professional-class self-assurance. "We cannot stop global change," Clinton said in his signing speech. The phrase that best expressed the feeling was this: "It's a no-brainer." Lee Iacocca uttered it in a pro-NAFTA TV commercial, and before long everyone was saying it.[5] The phrase struck exactly the right notes of simplicity combined with utter obviousness. Globalization was irresistible, the argument went, and free trade was always and in all situations a good thing. So good, it didn't even really need to be explained. Everyone knew this. Everyone agreed.

Yet there *were* people who opposed NAFTA, like labor unions, for example, and Ross Perot, and the majority of Democrats in the House of Representatives. The agreement was not a simple or straightforward thing: it was some 2,000 pages long, and according to reporters who actually read it, the aim was less to remove tariffs than to make it safe for American firms to invest in Mexico—meaning, to move factories and jobs there without fear of expropriation and then to import those factories' products back into the U.S.[6]

One reason the treaty required no brains at all from its supporters is because NAFTA was as close to a straight-up class issue as we will ever see in this country. It "boils down to the oldest division of all," Dirk Johnson wrote in the *New York Times* in 1993: "the haves versus the have-nots, or more precisely, those who have only a little." The lefty economist Jeff Faux has even told how a NAFTA lobbyist tried to bring him around by reminding him that Carlos Salinas, then the president of Mexico, had "been to Harvard. He's one of us."[7]

That appeal to technocratic unity gives a hint of what Clintonism was all about. To owners and shareholders, who would see labor costs go down as they took advantage of unorganized Mexican labor and lax Mexican environmental enforcement, NAFTA held fantastic promise. To American workers, it threatened to send their power, and hence their wages, right down the chute. To the mass of the professional-managerial class, people who weren't directly threatened by the treaty, holding an opinion on NAFTA was a matter of deferring to the correct experts—economists in this case, 283 of whom had signed a statement declaring the treaty "will be a net positive for the United States, both in terms of employment creation and overall economic growth."[8]

The predictions of people who opposed the agreement turned out to be far closer to what eventually came to pass than did the rosy scenarios of those 283 economists and the victorious President Clinton. NAFTA was supposed to encourage U.S. exports to Mexico; the opposite is what happened, and in a huge way. NAFTA was supposed to increase employment in the U.S.; a study from 2010 counts almost 700,000 jobs lost in America thanks to the treaty. And, as feared, the agreement gave one class in America enormous leverage over the other: employers now routinely threaten to move their operations to Mexico if their workers organize. A surprisingly large number of them—far more than in the pre-NAFTA days—have actually made good on the threat.[9]

Mexico has not fared much better. In the decades before NAFTA, its economy often grew rapidly; since NAFTA was enacted, Mexico has experienced some of the feeblest growth of any country in Latin America, despite all the stuff it now makes and exports to the U.S. The country's poverty rate has not changed much at all while every other country in the region has made considerable progress. One reason for all this is the predictably destructive effect that free trade with American agribusiness has had on the fortunes of millions of Mexican family farmers.[10]

These results have never really shaken the "no-brainer" consensus. Instead, that contemptuous phrase returns whenever new trade deals are on the table. During the 1997 debate over "fast track," restricting the input of Congress in trade negotiations, Al From, the founder of the Democratic Leadership Council, declared confidently that "supporting fast track is a no-brainer." The *New York Times* columnist Thomas Friedman, who is fond of the phrase, has gone so far as to claim that free-trade treaties are so good that supporting them doesn't require knowledge of their actual contents. "I wrote a column supporting the CAFTA, the Caribbean Free Trade Initiative," he told Tim Russert in 2006. "I didn't even know what was in it. I just knew two words: free trade."[11]

Twenty years later, the broader class divide over the subject persists as well. According to a 2014 survey of attitudes toward NAFTA after two decades, public opinion remains split. But among people with professional degrees—which is to say, the liberal class—the positive view remains the default. Knowing that free-trade treaties are always for the best—even when they empirically are not—seems to have become for the well-graduated a badge of belonging.[12]

THE JOURNEY

One of the strangest dramas of the Clinton literature, in retrospect, was the supposed mystery of Bill's developing political identity. Like a searching teenager in a coming-of-age movie, boy president Bill would roam hither and yon, trying out this policy and that, until he finally learned to be true to himself and to put Democratic tradition behind him. He campaigned as a populist, he tried to lift the ban on gays in the military, then all of a sudden he was pushing free trade and deregulating telecom. Who was this guy, really?

How the question seemed to vex the president's friends and advisers! There was "a struggle for the soul of Bill Clinton," said his aide David Gergen just after the Republicans took Congress in 1994. A month later, Clinton's press people (to quote the hilarious deadpan of the *Washington Post*) were actually forced to deny "that Clinton lacks a sense of who he is as president and where he wants to go."[13]

Clinton's wandering political identity fascinated both his admirers and biographers, many of whom chose to explain it as a quest: Bill Clinton had to prove, to himself and the nation, that he was a genuine New Democrat. He had to grow into presidential maturity. And the way he had to do it was by somehow damaging or insulting traditional Democratic groups that represented the party's tradition of egalitarianism. Then we would know that the New Deal was truly dead. Then we could be sure.

This became such a cherished idea among Clinton's campaign team that they had a catchphrase for it: "counter-scheduling." During the 1992 race, as though to compensate for his friend-of-the-little-guy economic theme, Clinton would confront and deliberately antagonize certain elements of the Democratic Party's traditional base in order to assure voters that "interest groups" would have no say in a New Democrat White House.[14] As for those interest groups themselves, Clinton knew he could insult them with impunity. They had nowhere else to go, in the cherished logic of Democratic centrism.

The most famous target of Clinton's counter-scheduling strategy was the civil rights leader Jesse Jackson, the bête noir of centrists and the living embodiment of the politics the Democratic Leadership Council had set out to extinguish. At a 1992 meeting of Jackson's Rainbow Coalition, with Jackson sitting to his left, Clinton went out of his way to criticize a controversial rapper called Sister Souljah who had addressed the conference on the previous day. The exact circumstances of Clinton's insult have long been forgotten, but the fact of it has gone down in the annals of politicking as a stroke of genius, an example of the sort of thing that New Democrats should always be doing in order to discipline their party's base.[15]

Once Clinton was in the White House, counter-scheduling mutated from a campaign tactic to a philosophy of governance. At a retreat in the administration's early days, Bill's chief political adviser, Hillary Clinton, instructed White House officials how it was going to be done. As Carl Bernstein describes the scene, Hillary announced that the public must be made to understand that Bill was taking them on a "journey" and that he had a "vision" for what the administration was doing, a "story" that distinguished good from evil. The way to dramatize this story, the first lady continued (in Bernstein's telling), was to pick a fight with supporters.

> You show people what you're willing to fight for, Hillary said, when you fight your friends—by which, in this context, she clearly meant, *When you make them your enemy.**

NAFTA would become the first great test of this theory of the presidency, with Clinton defying not only organized labor but much of his own party in Congress. In one sense, it achieved the desired results. For New Democrats and for much of the press, NAFTA was Clinton's "finest hour," his "boldest action," an act befitting a real he-man of a president who showed he could stand up to labor and thereby assure the world that he was not a captive of traditional Democratic interests.[16]

But there was also an important difference. NAFTA was not symbolism. With this deed, Clinton was not merely insulting an important constituency, as he had done with Jesse Jackson and Sister Souljah. With NAFTA he connived in that constituency's ruin. He assisted in the destruction of its economic power. He did his part to undermine his party's greatest ally, to ensure that labor would be too weak to organize workers from that point forward. Clinton made the problems of working people materially worse.

It is possible to regard this deed as fine or brave, as so many New Democrats did, if you understand the struggles of workers

---

* Hillary was not alone in pushing this strategy. One of the most prominent contributions to the battle for Bill Clinton's soul was a 1995 *Washington Post Magazine* article called "Can This President Be Saved?" Among other things, it was filled with exhortations to Clinton to "fight with your old liberal friends." The Bernstein passage about Hillary at the White House retreat is found on p. 269 of *A Woman in Charge*; italics are in the original.

as a cliché you've grown sick of hearing. However, if you understand those workers as humans—humans who contributed to Bill Clinton's election—NAFTA starts to appear like betrayal on a grand scale as well as a sizable political blunder. By making it clear to labor, his party's strongest combatant, that he did not care about them or their issues, Clinton essentially encouraged them to stay home on election days. To this day, for working people, the lesson of NAFTA glares like the headlight of an oncoming locomotive: These affluent Democrats do not give a damn about inequality except as an election-year slogan.

Workers were the first casualties of Bill Clinton's quest for his New Democratic self. But the journey went on. The next great milestones were his big, first-term legislative accomplishments: the great crime crackdown of 1994 and the welfare reform measure of 1996. Both were intended to swipe traditional Republican issues and to demonstrate Clinton's independence from the so-called special interests.

Back in 1992 Clinton had briefly departed the campaign trail to return to Arkansas and be visibly present while his state went about executing one Ricky Ray Rector, a convicted killer who was so mentally damaged he had no idea what was happening to him or why. Clinton's design was to signal his toughness and thus avoid the fate of Michael Dukakis, whose presidential run had been done in by TV commercials suggesting he was too much of a wuss to keep dangerous black men behind bars. In the precise words of Christopher Hitchens, Rector was a "human sacrifice" for Clinton's presidential ambition.[17]

The reasoning that led Clinton to turn the Rector execution into a ritual appeasement of the electoral gods brought him, in 1994, to call for and then sign his name to the most sweeping police-state bill that modern-day America has seen. Among other things, the measure provided for the construction of countless new prisons, it established over a hundred new mandatory minimum sentences, it allowed prosecutors to charge thirteen-year-olds as adults in some cases, and it coerced the states into minimizing parole. It also increased the number of federal death penalties from three to *sixty*, including some for nonlethal offenses—and this from a political party that in 1972 had called for the abolition of capital punishment in its national platform. Clinton's aides referred to this bid for mass imprisonment as "upping the ante," as though it were a poker game with the Republicans. Winning that game was the subject of boasting for Democrats. Said Joe Biden, then a Democratic senator from Delaware, during the debate on the bill:

> The liberal wing of the Democratic Party is now for 60 new death penalties. That is what is in this bill. The liberal wing of the Democratic Party has 70 enhanced penalties. . . . The liberal wing of the Democratic Party is for 100,000 cops. The liberal wing of the Democratic Party is for 125,000 new State prison cells.[18]

None of this happened because of an increase in crime, by the way—violent crime had actually crested several years before—but rather to demonstrate Clinton's hard-heartedness. "The one way Bill Clinton defined himself as a different Democrat was his tough position on crime," said Senator Joe Lieberman on the occasion of the bill's passage. "And he has redeemed that promise."[19]

In an ugly coda that was delayed by about a year, the '94 law also required President Clinton personally to sign off on the infamous 100-to-1 sentencing disparity between crack and powder cocaine. The former drug was thought to be the scourge of the planet—and 88 percent of the people arrested for it were black—while the latter, even though it was essentially the same thing, was regarded as just another harmless yuppie crime. Handing down prison sentences of many decades for one drug but not the other was both racist and insanely cruel. But Clinton went out of his way to ensure that this practice continued. The number of young black citizens who, in this manner, lost years of their lives to advance Bill Clinton's journey to political manhood will probably never be known. Let a thousand Ricky Ray Rectors burn, but please God, get this man reelected.[20]

Unfortunately, building the greatest gulag in the world was not enough to demonstrate Bill Clinton's disregard for the lives of the poor. The right wing actually mocked his crime bill as a kind of government handout to the poor.[21] He would have to do more.

Which brings us to the 1996 welfare reform act, one of the proudest deeds of the Clinton presidency. It is difficult to overstate the level of genius that punditry and political science used to attribute to this measure. An act of highest bipartisanship, it was said. Joe Klein wrote that Clinton "made work pay," a bewildering but nevertheless common description of the statute. To say that welfare reform succeeded, in the sense that there are now fewer people on welfare, is also a well-worn cliché; Clinton himself made this point on the op-ed pages of the *New York Times* in 2006.[22]

The story, in brief, was as follows. The country's welfare system was deeply unpopular in the 1990s. Its centerpiece was a 1935 program called Aid to Families with Dependent Children (AFDC) that dispensed cash assistance to impoverished single mothers. AFDC was one of the basic guarantees of the American welfare state, but it was also a program hated both by resentful taxpayers as well as by the poor themselves, because it made no provision for employment or training. The hate was also racialized. In a cover story calling for Clinton to do away with the program, the *New Republic* magazine, the voice of the professional class, illustrated its message with a crass "welfare queen" stereotype: a photo of a black mother, having an insouciant smoke, under the words "Day of Reckoning." Instead of fixing the system or defending it against conservative attacks, Clinton signed a 1996 Republican bill that deleted it once and for all. AFDC was replaced with a program called Temporary Assistance to Needy Families (TANF) that leaves welfare up to the states—and gives the states plenty of incentive to kick people off the rolls.

Whether that was the right thing to do with poor moms and impoverished children was of little interest in Washington. What thrilled the pundit class was the sheer counter-scheduling genius of it all. Welfare reform was the glorious moment when Bill Clinton arrived at the end of his long search for himself; when he and the world knew for sure that he was a New Democrat and he was announcing it, loud and proud. "When he signed the bill, the final cornerstone of our Clinton revolution was in place," rejoiced DLC chieftain Al From. "There would never again be a doubt that he was a different kind of Democrat." John Harris, the founder of *Politico*, interpreted it in the same way: "With his signature Clinton had proven that he was indeed an authentic New Democrat, ready to break with old liberalism, even at personal cost."[23]

It had all the elements of the magic formula. Welfare reform "triangulated" between the positions of the two parties, to use the term made famous by Clinton's advisers. It erased one of the fundamental achievements of the New Deal. It harmed an important constituency of Clinton's party, meaning the poor, and simultaneously it negated one of the GOP's most potent issues, thus allowing the president, as his aide Sidney Blumenthal put it, to "undercut the Republicans and begin transforming politics."[24]

Some would say he had transformed politics quite a bit already. As a result of the many flanking maneuvers Clinton had pulled on his own party, Americans now had *two* conservative presidential candidates to choose from. In the 1996 election, which happened just a few months later, Americans resoundingly chose the friendly young conservative Bill Clinton over the dour old conservative Bob Dole.

I jest, but I probably shouldn't. We are dealing here with the raw material of the Clinton myth: *The Democrat won a second term*, and that is all that matters. What he had to do to purchase that victory is irrelevant. Within the confines of the two-party system, Clinton was a veritable acrobat: He leaped and pirouetted and triangulated all around; he undermined his allies; he signed his enemies' legislation; he got himself elected twice, and he even avoided being kicked out of the White House after his impeachment. Clinton was "The Survivor," as per John Harris's book title; he was "The Natural," as per Joe Klein's. Some believe he was even greater than those honorifics imply. Presidential historian Steven Gillon, for example, writes of Clinton's royal progress to the 1996 Democratic Convention in Chicago as a kind of generational redemption:

> By crushing Gingrich [meaning, blaming him for the government shutdown], scaling back the Republican Revolution, and returning to his New Democrat roots, [Clinton] hoped to complete the unfulfilled mission of Robert F. Kennedy. He had devoted his public life to repairing the party's tattered political fabric. Now he was leading the party back to Chicago,

> to the place where it all came apart, to show that a new party could emerge from the ashes of the old.[25]

But celebrating this achievement feels a little like cheering for yesterday's bump in the share price of Novartis or the victory of the Valencia soccer team: Our stake in the win is far from obvious.

LUCKY MISTAKES

If Clinton's posture toward the Democratic Party's base was frosty, his attitude toward Wall Street, his party's onetime archenemy, was the opposite: a combination of enthusiastic support and practiced obsequiousness.

Clinton didn't learn this stance easily, but he certainly learned it well. According to the version of the story made famous by Bob Woodward in *The Agenda*, it wasn't until after the 1992 election was over that Clinton was advised that the deficit he would inherit from the Republicans was going to negate his planned program of stimulus spending. The bond market simply did not trust politicians, he was told, and therefore if Clinton wanted interest rates to come down—the only way to make the economy bounce back, everyone said—he would have to persuade investment bankers he was serious about taking on the federal deficit. There was to be no clever counter-scheduling of this group; no act of triangulation that could exile them to the outer political darkness. They had to be seduced, not tricked or disciplined; their confidence was critical.

They were, in short, too big to criticize. A famous passage in *The Agenda* has Clinton aide Robert Rubin, the former co-head of Goldman Sachs, facing off against the populist consultant Paul Begala over the subject of what to say about "the rich":

"'Look,' Rubin said impatiently, 'they're running the economy and they make the decisions about the economy. And so if you attack them, you wind up hurting the economy and wind up hurting the president.'"[26] History records that Rubin got his way, not merely on the immediate matter of presidential messaging, but on the direction of political history itself.

Realizing the predicament he was in is what set off Clinton's famous explosion in the Oval Office one day in early 1993, which we also know about from Woodward:

> "I hope you're all aware we're all Eisenhower Republicans," he said, his voice dripping with sarcasm. "We're Eisenhower Republicans here, and we are fighting the Reagan Republicans. We stand for lower deficits and free trade and the bond market. Isn't that great?"[27]

Here we get a rare glimpse of the Bill Clinton that might have been. But the president was a quick study. He abandoned stimulus and reconciled himself to austerity with remarkable speed. He then convinced himself that puffing up the confidence of financiers was just as good, just as populist, as pushing some old-fashioned Democratic spending program through Congress. According to Woodward, the rationalization came easily: When markets prospered, the president told himself, all Americans benefited. So when Clinton made deficit reduction the centerpiece of his economic program, Woodward recounted, "He was not trying just to help the bond market, he claimed. The bond market was just the vehicle for helping the middle class."*

---

* There was no criticism or mockery intended here, as far as I can tell. Woodward seems to have meant this as a straightforward description of the president's views.

This was in the aftermath of the sharp recession that got Clinton elected, remember. Bringing down the federal deficit, however, is not ordinarily the Keynesian strategy for encouraging economic recovery in hard times; in fact, it's the opposite of what most Keynesian economists would recommend. Thanks to the peculiar and complicated circumstances of 1993, however, it worked for Bill Clinton this one time. Joseph Stiglitz, the economist who chaired Clinton's Council of Economic Advisers, actually calls this sequence of deficit reduction and recovery an "inadvertent effect," a "lucky mistake."[28]

"Lucky" is a kind word for it, I suppose; a more accurate one would be "deceptive" or "treacherous." Assuming an attitude of meek deference toward Wall Street, Bill Clinton hacked away at the federal deficit; for unrelated reasons, the economy proceeded to boom. Everyone who was watching learned the obvious but wrong lesson from Clinton's apparent success: austerity is the right policy for hard times. Running for president in 2000, Clinton's vice president, Al Gore, actually promised he would reduce federal spending in the event of a recession.[29]

This is how the party of Jefferson, Bryan, and Roosevelt became its opposite—the party of the bankers.* Clinton had made an early offering to the gods of the market by choosing

---

* In the pro-Clinton book *Bull Run: Wall Street, the Democrats, and the New Politics of Personal Finance* (PublicAffairs, 2000), financial journalist Daniel Gross writes:

> The figures of William Jennings Bryan and William Jefferson Clinton, who rose to the national stage one hundred years apart at the head of the same party, make neat bookends—and not just because of the similarity of their names. Rather, Bryan's enduring legacy was as an antagonist of the "moneyed interests," a dogma to which the Democratic party held firm for nearly a hundred years. By contrast, one of Clinton's most enduring legacies may be his party's accommodation to those same interests. (p. 21)

Robert Rubin and Roger Altman, two prominent investment bankers, to fill high positions in his administration. Before long there were numerous others, many of them protégés of Rubin from his days at Goldman Sachs. Twice did Clinton go on to reappoint Wall Street's favorite libertarian, Alan Greenspan, to chair the Federal Reserve. By April 1994, according to the *New York Times*, the president was even taking the stability of financial markets into account in foreign policy decisions.[30]

Whatever was required to gratify the markets was done. Interstate banking was deregulated in 1994 in order to "let the strong take over the weak so that we can move forward," as one prominent banker put it. There was a memorable capital-gains tax cut in 1997, causing the One Percent to leap for joy. There was telecommunications deregulation in 1996 and a big if incomplete push for electricity dereg as well. There were high-profile decisions not to rein in corporate practices that were clearly out of control, like granting executives stock options in lieu of pay. Again, the brilliant political logic of counter-scheduling was at work. "The New Democrats wanted to differentiate themselves from the Old Democrats, who were seen as pro-regulation and anti-business," writes Stiglitz in *The Roaring Nineties*, his account of the Clinton years. "They wanted to earn their pro-business stripes by pushing deregulation still farther than it had gone before."[31]

Each of the bold endeavors I just mentioned eventually ended in disaster. The day the president signed the bill deregulating interstate banking, a memo went around the White House crowing that Clinton "has accomplished what had eluded the Carter, Reagan and Bush administrations." What a proud moment for a Democrat. Unfortunately, what the Clinton team had actually done was to doom local and regional banks and transform the financial system into an oligopoly dominated by a handful of enormous players—the familiar Citis, Chases, Wells Fargos and Bank of Americas—none of which were really accountable to state legal systems any longer. The smaller banks Clinton was pushing toward extinction (i.e., "the weak") tended to be much more prudent lenders than their giant cousins ("the strong"), which before long were issuing mortgages to anyone who wanted one. After the orgy of insane lending climaxed in catastrophe a decade later, of course, "the strong" had to be bailed out. They were "too big to fail" by then.[32]

Let us continue down the list of Democratic achievements of the 1990s. Telecom deregulation turned out to encourage monopoly building, not innovation; its main effects were the extinction of locally controlled radio stations and the bidding up of telecom shares in the great stock market bubble that burst during Clinton's last year in office. Electricity deregulation, as it was implemented by the states, allowed Enron to engineer the California power shortage. The rage for stock options fed the epidemic of corporate fraud that came to light soon after Clinton left office, while the capital-gains tax cut was rocket fuel for inequality—"one of the most regressive tax cuts in America's history," according to Stiglitz's recollections of his service in the Clinton administration.

Bailouts were another market-pleasing specialty of the era, with the Clinton team riding to the rescue after each of the era's great financial failures. Treasury Secretary Robert Rubin organized an executive-branch rescue of the Mexican government in 1995, after that country's leaders had spent the previous few years issuing highly questionable bonds that happened to be very popular with American financiers. The Mexican operation probably served as a back-door bailout for Rubin's old colleagues on Wall Street, but more important, it was what the admiring financial journalist Daniel Gross called "a turning point for Clinton" in his relationship with investment bankers: it "allowed Clinton to ingratiate himself with big investors at the institutional level."[33]

The final great accomplishment of Bill Clinton's presidency was another act of sweeping bank deregulation, the 1999 repeal of the Glass-Steagall Act, which had separated commercial from investment banking since 1933. Treasury Secretary Rubin had long argued that the old law had to go so that Wall Street could achieve "revenue diversification" and stay competitive with foreign banking establishments.[34] Banking lobbyists agreed with him, as did lobbyists for the insurance industry and—well, lobbyists for just about everyone with money.

In fact, among members of the professional class, the cancellation of Glass-Steagall was another no-brainer, what with globalization and the New Economy and all. The term of art this time around was "Depression-era" (as in "Depression-era barriers" or "Depression-era rules" or "Depression-era walls"), which cast the old law's repeal in the familiar terms of political rejuvenation, with the Democratic party symbolically casting off the conditions of its New Deal heyday.

As with NAFTA, every expert who mattered was on the same page. A retrospective on the banking law published by the Minneapolis Fed in 2000 casually referred to it as "the now infamous Glass-Steagall Act of 1933." "Almost everybody agreed that Glass-Steagall was an anachronism in a global economy," proclaimed a 1995 *New York Times* news story on the effort to repeal the law. "Enacted in 1933 to prevent a recurrence of financial skulduggery that many believed touched off the Great Depression, the act is widely viewed today as a drag on the economy."[35]

Not only did *everybody agree* on what was *widely viewed*, but repealing it was a bridge to the future itself. Quoth the new Treasury secretary, Larry Summers, on the occasion of the final termination of Glass-Steagall in 1999, "At the end of the 20th century, we will at last be replacing an archaic set of restrictions with a legislative foundation for a 21st-century financial system."[36]

Some foundation. Nine years later, after the greatest wave of insider looting ever seen, the deregulated 21st-century financial system had to be rescued almost in its entirety. To say this was a system built on sand would be charitable. Its foundations actually lay upon a speculative bubble, pumped up by the prospect of a bigger sucker who everyone believed could be found a little ways down the line.

A little earlier in 1999, Summers had made the cover of *Time* magazine, along with Greenspan and Rubin, as a part of what the magazine called the "Committee to Save the World," a swashbuckling team of professional class superheroes who intervened all around the globe when economies were in danger of blowing up. The story is one of the all-time great examples of just how bad journalism can get when a scribe is encouraged to express his love for the powerful and his deep respect for ideas that every member of his socioeconomic cohort agrees upon. *Time* described Summers as a "rocket scientist"; the sagacious Greenspan was said to understand that "markets are an expression of the deepest truths about human nature"; and Rubin was a wizard who had "remade the Treasury into an organization that is 'more like an investment bank.'" Together they were "a kind of free-market Politburo on economic matters," *Time* reported—the only people who mattered in President Clinton's inner circle.[37]

Today we also know what kind of person didn't matter.

Brooksley Born, who was the chair of Clinton's Commodities Futures Trading Commission, had seen many ominous signs of impending disaster in certain reaches of the derivatives industry; in 1998 she dared to propose that this rapidly growing market be brought under some kind of regulatory scrutiny. Born's suggestion turned out to be the opposite of a no-brainer: the three members of the Committee to Save the World came together not only to crush her proposal but to do the reverse—to ensure the elimination of the weak regulation that did exist. The ultimate result of their efforts, the Commodity Futures Modernization Act, signed into law by Clinton a month before he returned to private life, was a deregulatory debacle to which we can chalk up both the activities of Enron as well as the credit-default swaps that brought the entire world economy to the brink of collapse in 2008.[38]

Things ended badly for Brooksley Born, but Robert Rubin left the Treasury Department in glory just a few days after the measure repealing Glass-Steagall had passed the Senate. Four months later, he took up work at Citigroup, which by coincidence was the largest beneficiary of the repeal (it allowed the giant bank to merge with a giant insurance company). Rubin had come from Wall Street, delivered enormous bailouts and long-sought deregulation to his old colleagues, and then returned to the top ranks of an industry enjoying its most prosperous years in history. The goo-goos complained about the appearance of a conflict of interest; nobody listened to them.* The spot where policy making and self-interest intersected, it

---

*In fact, there were numerous Clinton appointees who went on to take jobs on Wall Street. But in *Bull Run* Daniel Gross described this as virtually a form of charity: "The New Moneycrats [Gross's term for financiers who support Democrats] have also helped provide jobs for another class of needy people: burned-out Democrats." (p. 160)

seemed in those happy times, was a place of wisdom and prosperity.

It's striking that so many of the great economic initiatives of the Clinton presidency led eventually to catastrophe. But what really makes this story poisonous is that liberals by and large convinced themselves for many years that nothing had gone wrong at all. Everything Clinton's team had done was an act of professional-class consensus. Because most of the fuses lit by Clinton and Co. didn't actually detonate until after he had left office—and by then some science-denying Republican was in the Oval Office—they found it easy to absolve the Democrat from blame. When a Rhodes scholar was the one deregulating and cutting taxes, why, those were good times; when some idiot from Texas tried his hand at it, the world crashed and burned. Just another demonstration of the importance of a good education, I guess.

So the world missed out on the lessons of deregulation and tax cuts until it was too late. But another teaching of the Clinton years came through loud and clear. This one instructed us on social class: which cohort had a future and which one did not; which was the right one to be in, which was the wrong one. "What were we saying to the country, to our young people, when we lowered capital gains taxes and raised taxes on those who earned their living by working?," asked Joseph Stiglitz: "That it is far better to make your living by speculation than by any other means."[39]

5

It Takes a Democrat

Let me suggest a different framework for understanding the Clinton years, something even grander than *The Clinton Wars*, or *Nasdaq!*, or even *Bill's Postpartisan Journey to Self-Discovery.* Here is what I propose: How the Market Order Got Cemented into Place.

It wasn't Ronald Reagan alone who did it. What distinguishes the political order we live under now is consensus on certain economic questions, and what made that consensus happen was the capitulation of the Democrats. Republicans could denounce big government all they wanted, but it took a Democrat to declare that "the era of big government is over" and to make it stick. This was Bill Clinton's historic achievement. Under his direction, as I wrote back then, the opposition "ceased to oppose."[1]

THE SECRET HISTORY

For those who are interested in the economic well-being of average Americans and in the political system's failure to protect them, one of the most telling episodes of the Clinton years is something that went largely unreported at the time: the series of secret negotiations with House Speaker Newt Gingrich that Clinton held in 1997. Liberals saw the Republican Gingrich back then as Clinton's unappeasable nemesis—as a berserk hater—but in fact the two men came from similar class and generational backgrounds and saw eye to eye on a number of things: NAFTA, deficit reduction, welfare reform, and the great overarching sophistries about "change" and the "New Economy."

The object of Clinton's outreach to Gingrich in 1997 was Social Security privatization, a hunk of legislative dynamite that would have blown apart the welfare state once and for all. According to Steven Gillon, the historian who uncovered this episode in his 2008 book, *The Pact*, privatization in some form had become attractive to politicians in both parties at that time; the word he uses to describe this growing attitude is "consensus," as in: the "growing consensus on both sides of the aisle in favor of having Social Security tap into the stock market to increase the rate of return on retirement funds."[2]

Gillon doesn't spend much time describing the lobbying campaign mounted by the mutual fund industry in the late 1990s to encourage Social Security privatization—a memorable effort driven by the brutally simple fact that requiring every American to have a brokerage account would have meant billions in administrative fees for mutual fund companies. But the historian does provide a fine account of the sensibility in the air in professional-class circles in the late Nineties. Describing the members of an Advisory Council on Social Security in 1996, Gillon writes that

> All agreed that the program needed to be reformed. All accepted that some portion of Social Security revenue should

> be placed in investments other than low-paying U.S. Treasury bonds. They agreed that benefits must be trimmed, that the retirement age should be pushed back, and that state and local government workers should be required to participate.[3]

"All agreed"; "all accepted." It's difficult for outsiders to understand the kind of hypnotic appeal such invocations of consensus hold for Washington and the prosperous, well-educated fellows who inhabit it. Every one of them knows that the real problem with government is what they call entitlement spending, meaning Social Security and Medicare; that the obvious solution is some sort of privatization; and also that every other responsible, professional-class person either agrees on this matter or else is a charlatan or demagogue of some species or other.

I have heard some expression of this consensus since the day I met my first congressional staffer back in the Eighties. I've heard it from certain kinds of Democrats as well as Republicans; from losers as well as winners. As with free trade and welfare reform, there is no amount of reporting or argument that will budge this idée fixe; people of a certain educational background simply know it to be true. Which brings us to the second thing everyone agrees upon: that ideology merely gets in the way—that if educated people from both parties could just get together and put partisanship aside, some great understanding on this matter of entitlements could quickly be reached. This is the Holy Grail, the high-minded act of privatization that would terminate the New Deal's most popular achievement and bring to a close the era of activist government. This is the true Grand Bargain our leaders have chased from the Nineties up to the age of Obama.

In 1997 the deal evaded Bill Clinton's grasp, but only barely. According to Gillon, Clinton and Gingrich had come to an agreement on how private accounts would be incorporated into the Social Security system; in exchange, the Republicans would stop pushing to blow the federal surplus on a tax cut. Like the New Democrats in our story, Gingrich claimed this was the right thing to do because of change: "We were trying to think through the necessary reforms to modernize America to move into the twenty-first century," he told the historian.[4]

The two leaders knew this would mean building "a new center/right political coalition" to get the deed done, because many Democrats could be counted on to oppose the deal. Indeed, as Gillon notes, on numerous issues "the president was closer to Gingrich than he was to the leadership of his own party," a description that could have been accurately applied to each of Clinton's great accomplishments—NAFTA, welfare reform, and bank deregulation, all of them made into law by cooperation between the Democratic president and the Republicans in Congress.

The schedule on which the two men agreed went as follows: Clinton would start hinting at the privatization proposal in January 1998. Various groups would then spend the year conducting a Social Security "dialogue" whose conclusions can be easily guessed.* Incredibly, the two leaders would somehow contrive to "keep the issue off the table in the 1998 congressional elections," and then get it enacted during the lame-duck session in December 1998, when nobody could hold either of them responsible.[5]

---

* Commissions pursuing predetermined conclusions and building fake consensus seem to have been something of a specialty of the Clinton White House. Hillary Clinton famously set up a great host of them during her push for health care reform in 1993.

Clinton actually went through with the first step in the plan, demanding in his 1998 State of the Union address that Congress use the federal surplus to "save Social Security first," a vague but noble-sounding demand that appears to have been his way of opening the privatization discussion.* As it happened, Social Security was already safe—safe from Clinton, that is—thanks to a certain Oval Office dalliance. The week before his speech, the media frenzy over Monica Lewinsky had begun, and it was all polarization and impeachment after that.

The day of the speech itself, Hillary Clinton went on TV and accused a "vast right-wing conspiracy" of coming together in an effort to bring her husband down. This was true enough as regards the sex scandal, but the conspiracy that really mattered was the one between her husband and his putative right-wing rival, Newt Gingrich.

Here's why the D.C. pundits came to love Bill Clinton: He almost did it. He almost achieved that great coalescence of the professional and business classes.

This was a Democrat, remember. And him being a Democrat was important. For the party that invented Social Security and defended it with a kind of gleeful zeal over the years—for this party even to contemplate turning the thing over to Wall Street was a concession of enormous significance.

---

* Any scheme for Social Security privatization will be very expensive. Once the transition to a private system has been made, the contributions of younger workers will go into individual investment accounts rather than the existing system. But the obligations of the existing system to the already retired will continue, requiring some other source of funding. Although I don't know for sure, my guess is that the shortfall from such a transition would probably have eaten up the budget surplus of the late 1990s and then some, and that this is what Clinton was referring to when he spoke of using the surplus to "save" Social Security.

CAPTIVE NATION

A few years ago, I read an article claiming that the United States is the first society ever to record more rapes of men than of women, a distinction attributable to the vast numbers of men we have seen fit to imprison.[6]

Another disturbing fact: According to the legal scholar Michelle Alexander, author of *The New Jim Crow*, there are now more black adults in some kind of "correctional control"—meaning under the restraint of some arm of the criminal justice system—than there were slaves in 1850. Naomi Murakawa, author of *The First Civil Right*, adds that fully "one in three black men" passes his life "under probation, parole, or prison on any given day."[7] Not only does the United States have the largest population of people incarcerated of any country, but we are the only nation that routinely hands out life sentences to children.

Anyone inquiring how an obscenity like this came to pass—how it is that the home of the free outstripped what we used to call "captive nations" as well as countries philosophically dedicated to wholesale imprisonment like apartheid South Africa—anyone looking into these things soon realizes that this cannot be laid simply and neatly at the doorstep of the Republican Party and Those Awful Wingers. It is true that the Republican Richard Nixon started the war on drugs, and that the Republican Ronald Reagan escalated it. But the Democrat Bill Clinton—the buddy of Bono and Nelson Mandela, the man repeatedly nominated for the Nobel Peace Prize—easily bested both of these Republicans as well as all other presidents in his zeal to incarcerate.[8] Alexander writes as follows of Clinton's 1994 crime law:

> Far from resisting the emergence of the new caste system, Clinton escalated the drug war beyond what conservatives had imagined possible a decade earlier. As the Justice Policy Institute has observed, "the Clinton Administration's 'tough on crime' policies resulted in the largest increases in federal and state prison inmates of any president in American history."[9]

If anything, Alexander is soft-pedaling her indictment. The Big Clampdown was a massive exercise in prison-building and mandatory sentencing. Clinton himself went before the eyes of the nation to promote this great new tactic called "Three Strikes," where triple offenders of certain kinds got to spend the rest of their lives in prison. His 1994 crime bill coerced state governments to enact what were called "Truth in Sentencing" provisions—which meant, essentially, a crackdown on parole. In 1995, as I mentioned above, Clinton signed his name to the bill stopping the U.S. Sentencing Commission from abolishing the notoriously racist 100-to-1 difference in penalties for crack and powdered cocaine.

Not everything lousy that happened in the country in the 1990s was Bill Clinton's fault. But with criminal punishment as well as with Social Security and free trade, the say-so of the left party in the system completely changed the balance of the situation. It was as though every kind of cruelty was suddenly permitted. The nation descended into a punitive frenzy, with state legislatures inventing ways to lock up their citizens with a kind of demonic glee. The state of Virginia, under the leadership of Republican governor George Allen, abolished parole altogether in 1995. "Zero tolerance" entered the lexicon and universal surveillance became part of the urban environment. In 1994 and '95, numerous states passed their own three-strikes laws, with

"Truth in Sentencing" provisions trotting along behind, as encouraged by Bill Clinton's law.

Historians of the Clinton presidency generally skip over the imprisonment craze into which he led the country in the mid-Nineties. It is hard to account for if the framework you're applying to those years is one in which Clinton was the victim of right-wing persecution. Those who do acknowledge Clinton's part in the Big Clampdown either depict it as a great success in the fight against crime—which it was not*—or else describe it in superficial Washington terms: He got a great big law passed through Congress, thus proving that he could be an effective bipartisan leader.

Besides, in rhetorical terms, Bill Clinton has always been a steadfast opponent of mass incarceration. In 1991, he said he thought it was awful that "we are now the number one nation in the world in the percentage of people we put in prison." In 1995, two weeks before he signed the crack/cocaine law, he declared that

> blacks are right to think something is terribly wrong . . . when there are more African American men in our correction system than in our colleges; when almost one in three African American men in their twenties are either in jail, on parole or otherwise under the supervision of the criminal system.

---

* According to a 2014 study of the age of mass incarceration, big increases in sentence length have "no material deterrent effect" on crime and do not reduce the crime rate. See *The Growth of Incarceration in the United States: Exploring Causes and Consequences*, a study by the National Research Council of the National Academies, 2014, p 140. Additionally, the violent-crime rate peaked in 1991 and was already on its way down by 1994.

In an interview with *Rolling Stone* in 2000, Clinton said, "the disparities are unconscionable between crack and powdered cocaine. I tried to change that." In 2008, he said he was sorry for the crack/cocaine law.[10] And then, when every presidential candidate began talking up prison reform in 2015, he apologized again, this time saying that the 1994 crime bill was "overdone" and thus implying that he hadn't really meant to throw so many people in prison.*

And maybe that's what really matters. Maybe that will suffice to get Clinton off the hook on the day when some future Truth and Reconciliation Commission finally starts parceling out the blame for the generation-destroying policies of those years.

But I doubt it. Someday we will understand that the punitive hysteria of the mid-1990s was not an accident; it was essential to Clintonism, as essential as his vaunted repeal of the welfare

---

* A Black Lives Matter activist, confronting Hillary Clinton about her husband's crime policies in August of 2015, used the unfortunate words "unintended consequences" to describe mass incarceration. In fact, it was widely known at the time that the consequence of the crack/cocaine sentencing disparity was the mass incarceration of black drug users. This was one of the reasons the U.S. Sentencing Commission tried to abolish the disparity in 1995, an action that Clinton and the Republican Congress overruled. It was also why the Congressional Black Caucus begged Clinton not to overrule it—and why prison riots erupted when it became clear Clinton was going to sign the bill overruling the recommendations of the Sentencing Commission. In October of 1995, the syndicated columnist Cynthia Tucker wrote a column on the crack/powder sentencing disparity. "Let's be clear about what these policies have done," she wrote:

> They have filled the nation's prisons with hundreds of thousands of young black and Latino men whose greatest crime is drug addiction. It is no wonder that one-third of black men in their 20s are under the jurisdiction of the criminal justice system. If we treated alcoholics and abusers of powdered cocaine this way, the nation's prisons would be bulging with white inmates.

system. Clinton treated different groups of Americans in radically different ways—crushing some in the iron fist of the state just as others were getting bailouts, deregulation, and a frolicking celebration of Think Different business innovation.

There is really no contradiction between these. Lenience and forgiveness and joyous creativity for one group while the other gets a biblical-style beatdown—these things actually fit together quite nicely. Indeed, the ascendance of the first group requires that the second be lowered gradually into hell. When you take Clintonism all together, it makes sense, and the sense it makes has to do with social class. Think of it as a slight variation on Stiglitz's observation about the superiority of speculation to all other occupations: What the poor get is discipline; what the professionals get is endless indulgence.

THE CARROT AND THE STICK

In the summer of 2015, Hillary Clinton briefly criticized the Republican presidential candidate Jeb Bush for saying that "people need to work longer hours." It's a shame she didn't stay with the subject. She might have recalled that, when she and her husband were reforming welfare in their White House days, pushing the poor into the workforce was administration policy. In fact, Bruce Reed, the Clinton aide who helped to craft the '96 welfare reform measure, once wrote that "The real Clinton legacy on the poor comes down to one word: work."[11]

On the financiers, the real Clinton legacy came down to four words: *Grab what you can.* For them, there were bailouts and trade deals that protected their interests and tax cuts and a timely shot of "liquidity" whenever stock markets seemed to be flagging. And a little deregulation should the laws of the land not meet with their favor.

But the poor needed to learn discipline. That seems to have been one of the ideas behind NAFTA: People employed in manufacturing had to accept working harder for less or else watch their jobs depart for Mexico. Discipline was the point of the '94 crime bill, too: The poor were to live in a state of constant supervision where there was "zero tolerance" for those who stepped out of line. Mercy was to be a luxury item now, a thing reserved for those who could make big donations to the Clinton presidential library.

Discipline was most emphatically the point of Clinton's 1996 welfare reform. This measure, as I said, deleted the longstanding federal guarantee to the people at society's lowest rung and shifted the obligation to care for them to the states, which were permitted to go about the task however they wanted. States could outsource the program, turn applicants away, give them whatever amount they thought was right, and so on. The only requirement was that no one could stay on the rolls beyond a certain length of time. The new law made no provision for job training or anything similar, even though the man who signed it was the same person who loved to repeat that "what you earn depends on what you can learn." For these people it was different: just get out there and work.

Some got the carrot; others got the stick. "Once the Democratic party had adopted this theology," Christopher Hitchens pointed out in 1999, "the poor had no one to whom they could turn. The immediate consequence of this was probably an intended one: the creation of a large helot underclass disciplined by fear and scarcity, subject to endless surveillance, and used as a weapon against any American worker lucky enough to hold a steady or unionized job."[12]

Welfare reform is almost always spoken of these days as a policy triumph, usually because of the single data point that there are fewer people now who collect welfare than there were before the law went into effect. This reasoning has always perplexed me: Of course fewer people are going to use a program if you cut the number of people allowed to use it.

The reason liberal pundits find this single data point convincing, I think, is because they want to be convinced. One object of welfare reform, remember, was to erase an embarrassing issue for Democrats, and if welfare recipients happened to disappear from the conversation along with it, well, that was just a bonus. There was no immediate burst of homelessness or desperation when AFDC was repealed, largely because the economy was just then expanding with the big bubble of the late 1990s. And, so: success! Problem solved!

But deleting welfare didn't eliminate poverty itself. We might as well have expected to conquer aging by overturning Social Security.

The poor are still with us, although the program that helped them is not. And once the flush times of the late Nineties receded, matters played out in exactly the dire way you'd expect: Neediness exploded in the United States. Thanks to Bill Clinton's welfare reform, there has been a large increase in the number of people living in what the sociologists call "extreme poverty," meaning living on less than two dollars per day. Studies of people in merely "deep poverty," meaning at a level half the official poverty line, noted that this particular stratum of the wretched reached its all-time high point in the years just after the Great Recession. The number of people on food stamps in 2014 was double what it had been in 1997.[13]

Another goal of welfare reform was reducing what used to be called the "illegitimacy rate." By removing society's guarantee for single moms, its proponents used to say, we would change the incentives and give people a nudge, and soon everyone would get married before they had kids. That's not what happened, though. In 1995, 32 percent of American children were born to unmarried mothers; today that number is 40 percent.[14]

Even the political aspect of welfare reform has proven illusory. Repealing AFDC was supposed to inoculate Democrats against predictable right-wing attacks on the party of moochers; this is what made it the crowning glory of Clintonism, the change that had to come before the New Dems could get started on "transforming politics." But today it's as though nothing changed at all. Conservatives still routinely blast the clueless generosity of the welfare state, which supposedly coddles the 47 percent and rocks the lazy to sleep in a comfy government-issue hammock.

But what I want to focus on here are the economic effects of welfare reform. Plunging our society's weakest and most vulnerable into economic desperation triggered a domino effect of misery right down the line, with the slightly better-off now feeling the competition of the utterly hopeless. The effect was to make all of us a little more precarious. On its own, welfare reform was a meanspirited thing to do—"one of the most regressive social programs promulgated by a democratic government in the twentieth century," in the words of the sociologist Loïc Wacquant, who has studied the subject in depth.

Considered as part of a grander economic architecture, however, it makes an awful kind of sense. As Wacquant continues, welfare reform "confirmed and accelerated the gradual replacement of a protective (semi) welfare state by a disciplinary state mating the stinging goad of workfare with the dull hammer of prisonfare, for which the close monitoring and the punitive containment of derelict categories stand in for social policy toward the dispossessed."[15] Toil hopelessly or go to prison: that is life at the bottom, thanks to Bill Clinton.

THE DISASTROUS SUCCESS OF THE CLINTON PRESIDENCY

One of the first exhibits you encounter when you visit the Clinton presidential museum in Little Rock is a vivid pink neon light representing the ever-growing number of jobs in America during Bill's White House years. There's also a Dow Jones zipper sign to remind you of the miraculous way the stock market ascended in the 1990s, but it's that disembodied, glowing pink line that keeps catching your eye as you wander among the exhibits.

If the former president had a little less modesty, his museum would probably find a way to trace that upward-trending pink line in the sky over Little Rock every night with a laser beam. They would trademark it, print it on T-shirts, baseball caps, and bags of New Economy potato chips. After all, this line demonstrates President Clinton's one real accomplishment.

Let us give Bill Clinton his due: This was a fine thing. When he was president, America came close to full employment. As a result, wages grew for several years—and for real, not just in nominal dollars.

But it was prosperity buoyed up by an investment bubble. It did not reverse the long-term trend toward inequality that Clinton liked to talk about in 1992. It did the opposite. The share of the national income taken by the top 1 percent zoomed upward along with the Nasdaq during Clinton's time in office. Financialization marched in step, with Wall Street accounting for an ever-greater percentage of GDP. Average CEO compensation at big companies hit twenty million dollars in 2000, the most ever recorded—some 383 times as much as average workers made during that final year of the bubble.[16]

Today, numbers like that make Americans furious; they send us raging onto the comments pages of our dying local newspapers, where we fume about our stunted lives. Back in the nineties, however, those developments fueled a steamy climate of market celebrationism the likes of which we will probably never see again. In 2000 I myself filled a whole book with samples of this stuff, like the commercials for a telecom outfit that hollered, "Is This a Great Time or What?"*

It wasn't all bubbly Internet fantasy. There was something else driving the New Economy ebullience in the Nineties, something that went beyond all the modish rhetoric about business rules being repealed and CEOs as supermen. Disagreements over how an economy worked or in which direction social policy was to be steered were being brushed aside. From entitlement reform to free trade, it was an age of harmony and understanding. "The United States has arrived at a new consensus," wrote Daniel Yergin and Joseph Stanislaw in an influential 1998 book on (what they believed to be) the eternal battle between markets and government: in their minds, markets had won a complete victory.[17]

It wasn't the microchip that brought us this togetherness, or optical fiber, or the Internet. The economics department of the University of Chicago didn't win this victory, nor did the fall of the Berlin Wall bring it about. Not even the election of Ronald Reagan was sufficient, on its own, to make the market consensus happen. It required something else—it required the capitulation of the other side.

That the triumph of Clinton marked the end of the Democrats as a party committed to working people and egalitarianism is not some perverse conviction held by out-of-touch

* The book was called *One Market Under God*. The telecom was MCI; thanks to the 1996 deregulation measure, it was permitted to merge with WorldCom, which a few years later blew up in the largest bankruptcy the country had ever seen.

eggheads like me. Clinton's admirers used to be quite open about it; for many of them, it was precisely what they liked about the guy. Clinton biographer Martin Walker, for example, found hope in "the degree to which [Clinton] explicitly repudiated the traditions of the Democratic Party" and noted that it wasn't until Clinton was seated in the Oval Office and the Democrats in Congress had gone down to defeat that "the old New Deal and Great Society consensus on domestic matters finally collapsed."[18]

Let us now apply what we have learned from our study of the Clinton era to the modern-day Democratic Party and the way it interacts with people concerned about inequality—the great mass of voters who can see what has happened to the middle class and who hold out hope that some modern FDR will come and save them. As we know, many Democratic leaders regard such voters as people who have nowhere else to go. Regardless of how poorly Democrats perform on inequality matters, they will never be as awful as those crazy Republicans.

People do find other places to go, of course—they stay home, they join the Tea Party, whatever. But my purpose here is to scrutinize the tacit Democratic boast about always being better than those crazy Republicans. In truth, what Bill Clinton accomplished were things that no Republican could have done. Thanks to our two-party system, Democratic politicians carry a brand identity that inhibits them in some ways but allows them remarkable latitude in others. They are forever seen as weaklings in the face of the country's enemies, for example; but on basic economic questions they are trusted to do the right thing for average people.

That a Democrat might be the one to pick apart the safety net is a violation of this basic brand identity, but by the very structure of the system it is extremely difficult to hold the party accountable for such a deed. This, in turn, is why *only* a Democrat was able to do that job and get away with it. Only a Democrat was capable of getting bank deregulation passed; only a Democrat could have rammed NAFTA through Congress; and only a Democrat would be capable of privatizing Social Security, as George W. Bush found out in 2005. "It's kind of the Nixon-goes-to-China theory," the conservative Democrat Charles Stenholm told the historian Steven Gillon on this last subject. "It takes a Democrat to do some of the hard choices in social programs."[19]

To judge by what he actually accomplished, Bill Clinton was not the lesser of two evils, as people on the left always say about Democrats at election time; he was the greater of the two. What he did as president was beyond the reach of even the most diabolical Republican. Only smiling Bill Clinton, well-known friend of working families, could commit such betrayals.

But prosperity meant that Clinton would not be judged on these grounds. Prosperity was the ultimate political trump card. Played the right way, prosperity could negate any concerns, could override any objections, could even make policies seem like their opposites.

Prosperity meant that, for years, Clinton associates like Hillary and Rahm Emanuel could pose as mystic prophets of affluence—they had worked with Bill, after all. They knew what it took to make a country rich. Prosperity made Clinton himself into a respected elder statesman, a champion of the little guy, and a towering economic success whose every move needed to be emulated by future Democrats.

Prosperity could even transform the traditional demands of Wall Street into the politics of people who worked. You could give the rich every last item on their bill of particulars and still present yourself to the public as a champion of the average citizen. Thus, in the summer of 2000, an article appeared in *Blueprint*, the magazine of the Democratic Leadership Council, insisting that thanks to the deeds of Bill Clinton, we now knew how to reduce inequality. All that America needed to end the gap between the rich and everyone else was growth brought on by "fiscal discipline, global competition, flexible labor markets, transparent capital markets, deregulated businesses, rapid communications, and limited government interference in markets."[20]

And these were Democrats. Over the years to come, their mantra would become a liberal version of the right's "voodoo economics." Just as Ronald Reagan's Republicans claimed to be able to bring down the federal deficit by cutting taxes, so Clinton's Democratic heirs were able to pass off virtually any favor to the rich as an act of concern for the poor. How, you might ask, does deregulating the banks help those who work? Well, that's what Bill Clinton did, and just look at what happened. Just look at how that glowing pink line went up and up.

6

The Hipster and the Banker Should Be Friends

In Chapter Two we reviewed the many questionable ideas professed by the Democratic Party's various reform movements back in the day. We learned how some of them saw profundity-for-the-ages in the Sixties counterculture, how others pretended to speak for the forgotten middle class, but how all of them ultimately came together in rejecting the New Deal order and anticipating the imminent dawning of the postindustrial society.

And then, one day, the damn thing actually dawned. It happened in the waning years of the Clinton administration, when the brilliant sunshine of a booming tech sector finally and permanently overcame the dusty tales of old-fashioned woe that used to emanate from places like Decatur, Illinois. The name Americans gave to this rising order was "the New Economy," a regime of tech-based prosperity unfolding into the future as far as the eye could see. The phrase and the idea behind it had once been popular among conservatives—Ronald Reagan himself used it in a famous speech in 1988[1]—but now Democrats rushed to claim it as their own. In 1999, the think tank run by the Democratic Leadership Council—the onetime champion of conservative Southern Democrats, remember—began issuing a "State New Economy Index," ranking the states according to how dedicated they were to education, venture capital, and the retention of "managerial/professional jobs," among other things. President Clinton himself hosted a White House Conference on the New Economy in April of 2000, claiming the marvelous new era to be the product of a balanced federal budget and the deregulatory program he had enacted during his time in office.[2]

The protagonists of this economic story were our familiar friends: the "learning class," the "wired workers," the "symbolic analysts." Innovation was the driving force behind this new era, sometimes personified by Wall Street, on other occasions by Silicon Valley. The place where the magic happened was "the ideopolis": the postindustrial city, where highly credentialed professionals advised clients, taught college students, wrote software, crafted mortgage-backed securities—and were served in turn by an army of retail greeters and latte foamers who were proud to share their betters' values.

This vision of what we were becoming was a specifically political one—a specifically Democratic one. The influential 2002 book that sketched it all out was called *The Emerging Democratic Majority*, the same title as Lanny Davis's 1974 effort, and it predicted an era of Democratic domination for the same reasons as its predecessor had: we were becoming a postindustrial society in which professionals, as a class, were increasing explosively in number. The authors of this new iteration, John Judis and Ruy Teixeira, still urged Democrats to try to win back the working-class voters they had lost to Nixon and Reagan and, now, George W. Bush, but the task wasn't quite as urgent this time around. Because the groups that had come together to back McGovern in 1972—meaning women, minorities and professionals—had become so much more important over the intervening years, Democratic triumph was now basically assured, in an electoral reversal the authors called "George McGovern's Revenge."

Look more closely at these prosperous ideopolises and the picture becomes even more familiar. The symbolic embodiment of all this innovative postindustrial economic activity was none other than Frederick Dutton's countercultural hero, hymned now as the very embodiment of the New Economy. Youth radicalism became the language in which the winners assured us that they cared about our individuality and that all their fine new digital products were designed strictly to liberate the world. Remember? "Burn down business-as-usual," screamed a typical management text of the year 2000 called *The Cluetrain Manifesto.*

> Set up barricades. Cripple the tanks. Topple the statues of heroes too long dead into the street. . . . Sound familiar? You bet it does. And the message has been the same all along, from Paris in '68 to the Berlin Wall, from Warsaw to Tiananmen Square: Let the kids rock and roll![3]

The connection between counterculture and corporate power was a typical assertion of the New Economy era, and what it implied was that rebellion was not about overturning elites, it was about encouraging business enterprise. I myself mocked this idea in voluminous detail at the time. But it did not wane with the dot-com crash; indeed, it has never retreated at all. From Burning Man to Apple's TV commercials, it is all over the place today. Think of the rock stars who showed up for Facebook billionaire Sean Parker's wedding in Big Sur, or the rock 'n' roll museum founded by Microsoft billionaire Paul Allen in Seattle, or the transformation of San Francisco, hometown of the counterculture, into an upscale suburb of Silicon Valley. Wherever you once found alternative and even adversarial culture, today you find people of merit and money and status. And, of course, you also find Democrats.

It is, in a way, the telos of everything I have been describing so far. It is as though the enlightened youth of the Sixties had stepped straight from battling the pig in Chicago '68 to a panel discussion on crowdfunding at this year's South by Southwest, the annual festival in Austin, Texas, that has mutated from an indie-rock get-together into a tech-entrepreneur's convention; a place where the hip share the streets with venture capitalists on the prowl. This combination might sound strange to you, but for a certain breed of Democratic politician it has become a natural habitat. At SXSW 2015, for example, Fetty Wap performed "Trap Queen," the Zombies played hits from the '60s, Snoop Dogg talked about his paintings—and Commerce Secretary Penny Pritzker swore in the new director of the U.S. Patent and Trademark Office, Michelle Lee. In case you're keeping track, that's a former subprime lender swearing in a former Google executive, before an audience of hard-rocking entrepreneurship fans.[4]

THE MARRIAGE OF MONEY AND MORALS

In the Democrats' vision of the postindustrial society, and up until very recently, one industry in particular always stood out as an object of liberal-class admiration: high finance. For liberal thinkers, Wall Street was the place where money, merit, and morality came together.

Once upon a time, the suggestion that Democrats might align themselves with investment banking would have sounded preposterous. This is the party that made hating Wall Street its prime passion in William Jennings Bryan's crusade against the gold standard in 1896 . . . that won its great historic triumph in the aftermath of Wall Street's failure in 1929 . . . that launched the Securities and Exchange Commission in 1934 . . . that eventually raised the marginal tax rate paid by the country's highest earners to more than 90 percent.

To the leaders of the liberal class, however, the ambition is not so fantastic. For them, the transfer of the party's affections from the middle class to the banker was not a strategic blunder but a necessary step up. It made deep ethical sense as well. In fact, each new moment in the courtship of the Democrats and the rich convinced them that they were witnessing a natural union for the postindustrial, post-partisan age. Wealth and righteousness, the two traditional poles of American goodness, would finally be as one.

This romantic story has many points of origin, but let us return, for the sake of convenience, to the administration of Bill Clinton. You will recall that Clinton won the presidency after running as a populist alternative to the aristocratic George H. W. Bush; almost immediately after being elected, however, he chose to make financial markets his number one constituency. To satisfy those markets, he made reducing the federal deficit his top priority; he cut capital-gains taxes; he deregulated the banking industry; he ensured that derivatives would face no government scrutiny; and he cheered for the bull market as though it were an achievement of the average citizen: "How can any American, of any station in life, not be proud of the financial markets we have built," he said in 1997.[5]

Remember also Clinton's personal obsequiousness to the class of Americans who actually built the financial markets—the way he fundraised among them, invited them for coffee in the White House, and partied with them in the Hamptons. "The people of the Hamptons want desperately for Clinton to be safe," said one representative of that gilded region when impeachment proceedings drove the president into its sheltering embrace. "He is the spirit of the bull market."[6]

Clinton's achievement was to make Democrats an equal competitor with Republicans for Wall Street's affections—a momentous accomplishment in the eyes of some. *Bull Run*, a book published near the apex of the Nasdaq bubble in 2000, excitedly listed all the prominent bankers who were Democrats, all the former Wall Streeters who worked in the Clinton administration, and all the former Clinton administration hands who worked on Wall Street. In fact, so relentlessly did its author, Daniel Gross, unfurl this long roll of honor that the reader is, finally, convinced of his thesis: The Democrats essentially became the party of finance in those years. "[B]y 1996," Gross announces, "being a responsible Democrat, and one interested in prosperity and opportunity for people at all levels in society, meant being concerned about the fate of the stock and bond markets."[7]

Wall Street was an ideal constituency for a party reorienting itself as a representative of the professional class. The industry in question was supremely wealthy, of course. And financiers tended to be well-graduated people of a certain cultural liberalism; the prospect of gay marriage, for example, never seemed to send them into a moral panic the way it did so many others. Wall Street didn't pollute either, at least not in a way that cameras can see. The industry's operations were always coated in a thick patina of expert-talk, which (as we saw in Chapter One), the professional mind finds irresistibly beguiling. Furthermore, any distasteful results of Wall Street's operations could be easily ignored and were always far removed from the thrilling precincts of lower Manhattan.

In 2004 the journalist Matt Bai discovered a clique of earnest venture capitalists who were pouring money into liberal activist groups. It seems these public-minded tycoons were concerned about the Democrats losing elections and losing their way, and thankfully they were able to diagnose the party's malady as a case of being "maddeningly slow to adapt their message to the postindustrial age." Thirty-three years after Frederick Dutton said just about the same thing, these investors had realized that "progressive politics [was] a market in need of entrepreneurship"; that the country's left was "still doing business in an old, Rust Belt kind of way."[8]

In 2007, the business world was startled to learn that John Mack, the CEO of Morgan Stanley and a prominent fund-raiser for George W. Bush, had declared himself ready for Hillary Clinton, hosting a fund-raiser for the former first lady's presidential campaign in the investment bank's offices. The financier's conversion was so startling that it made the cover of *Fortune* magazine, with the words "Business Loves Hillary!" printed over a photograph of Ms. Clinton.[9]

The Democrat who would really pitch the Wall Street woo in 2008, however, was not Hillary Clinton but her rival, Illinois Senator Barack Obama. He became in that year not only the first Democratic presidential candidate in modern times to badly out-fund-raise his Republican opponent, but the first to prevail in campaign contributions from the financial industry specifically, traditionally a Republican bulwark.

As for the reasons the financiers chose Obama over his Republican opponent, we know surprisingly little. One motive, certainly, was that business likes to back winners, and 2008 looked like a Democratic year, what with the economic collapse and the backlash against the incompetent Bush administration. But let us not discount the professional-class admiration the financiers themselves expressed to the press. "My goal is not to pay less taxes," the Obama donor and hedge fund boss William Ackman told Reuters in July of 2008. "My goal is to elect an incredibly smart and capable guy."[10] In the days before the crash, perhaps that was enough of a reason. Financiers were smart people. Obama was a smart person. Nuff said.

BLUE BILLIONAIRES

And so it was that during the Aughts the media made its great discovery: a substantial number of rich people were in fact pretty liberal. There were precedents for this, of course—think of the many WASP Brahmins over the years who have been interested in protecting endangered species—but what was happening now was different. Not only were there said to be many more rich liberals than in the past, but they were separated from rich conservatives by a rift greater than personal taste. The divide between rich liberals and rich conservatives was supposed to be something essential, something engraved in the very structure of our society—and, needless to say, something upon which you could safely build the Democratic party.

Some saw the split between the two factions of the wealthy in quasi-moral terms. For Daniel Gross, writing in 2000, it all came down to "arrogant" capital versus "humble" capital—meaning that selfish and stuck-up investment bankers were Republicans while modest and unpretentious ones were Democrats. For the journalist David Callahan, it was (among other things) a matter of the "dirty rich" versus the "clean rich"—meaning that industrialists who polluted were conservatives while those who purchased carbon offsets were liberals.[11]

Every now and then, one of these rich liberals was moved to write a manifesto handing down his own personal wisdom on the matter. John Sperling, the billionaire behind the for-profit University of Phoenix, made a notable splash in 2004 when he published a work of political theory called *The Great Divide: Retro vs. Metro America*. Like every other liberal-class reformer to take up the pencil over the preceding thirty years, the billionaire Sperling* advised Democrats to give up immediately on the class-based politics of the New Deal; what the party needed to adopt instead was an industry-based approach. Instead of understanding voters in terms of their place in the social hierarchy, in other words, the way to think about them was by what industry dominated their state or region. Democrats had to understand that places where people embraced "economic modernity" and worked in "manufacturing, finance, insurance, and services in general" were now what made up the liberal base. Places where "extraction industries" dominated, on the other hand, were the heart of red-state backwardness, closed to science and entrepreneurship, and given (thanks to their weird fundamentalist religions) to racism and low taxes.

So spake the liberal billionaire. The country had polarized itself into "two nations," he declared—two incompatible cultural-economic systems. One of these Americas, the "Retro" one, was "rooted in the past"; the other America, which Sperling

---

* *The Great Divide* actually had five authors, a pollster, and two researchers. Sperling's name came first and was given typographical prominence over the others, however, and the book is customarily attributed to him.

dubbed "Metro," was "modern and focused on the future." The obviously superior "Metro" America consisted of "vibrant" cities where people appreciated fine things like ballet and believed in "rational discourse" and birth control. "Retro" America, however, was a place of ugly pursuits like oil and farming, a land of white supremacy where people have "chosen irrationality" along with lowbrow religions in which pudgy men bellow feral slogans at giant rallies.[12]

Another failing of the "Retro" areas, the billionaire charged, was that they were hostile to the spirit of enterprise, suffering from "a dearth of scientists, inventors, innovators, entrepreneurs, and captains of industry—the people who build modern economies." Those fine people were only to be found in the "Metro" regions, places where thrived admirable institutions like the Massachusetts Institute of Technology, which (Sperling wanted you to know) owned a highly creative Frank Gehry building under whose wildly zigzagging roof transpired all manner of juicy "research-focused collaboration."

THE MARX OF THE MASTER CLASS

Creative buildings, creative innovation, creativity in general—who doesn't love these things? Creativity is self-evidently good; it is beyond controversy, and in the years of the last decade it also began to seem like the defining virtue of liberalism, the quality that brought together all its different constituencies among the affluent.

During the Aughts, Democratic officials and administrators across the country were wowed by the idea that conspicuous public counterculture was a thing to be encouraged, because it appealed to members of the professional-managerial class.

Making such people feel welcome, in turn, was the way to achieve prosperity, as we could clearly see from successful cities like Austin and San Francisco.

This idea, which raged through the Bush years and which rages still, was given memorable expression by a professor of economic development named Richard Florida, specifically in his 2002 bestseller, *The Rise of the Creative Class*.

Yes, the "creative class." We've heard several flattering ways of describing the professional cohort, and now we come to the most obsequious designation of them all. According to Richard Florida, "creatives" were "the dominant class in America," because the thing they controlled—"creativity"—had become "the *decisive* source of competitive advantage"; "new technologies, new industries, new wealth and all other good economic things flow from it."[13]

In Florida's reasoning, this "creative class" included traditional artists and intellectuals, but the creatives who really mattered were people who worked in tech, people who worked in offices, people with advanced degrees. The same people, as it happened, with whom Democrats had been infatuated since the days of McGovern, only with one new detail: professionals were now described as the class that *creates*, like farmers were in the imagination of Thomas Jefferson or like the proletariat was in the dreams of the 1930s.

Cities and regions across the country heeded the guru's advice and swung immediately into the work of ingratiating themselves with the creative class. The hard-bitten state of Michigan launched a "Cool Cities Initiative," which, in the words of the state's governor, established numerous "local commissions on cool that are uncorking the bottle of creativity." Dayton, Ohio, decided it needed a film festival as well as a

"Dayton Creative Incubator," a performance hall called "C{space," and an art exhibit called "Creative Soul of Dayton." Tampa, Florida, appointed what *USA Today* called a "manager of creative industries" and "Creative Tampa Bay" dedicated itself to "synergizing the community's assets to cultivate an environment that encourages innovation, expands the economy and is a magnet for creative people," as its website used to say.

The ones who ingratiated the most were Democrats, who saw in the "creative class" strategy a way to revitalize struggling cities that were left behind when manufacturing departed for other climes. The many, many bike paths that were built in hopes that professionals would show up and ride upon them? By and large, those were built by Democrats. All those art districts and street fairs? Democrats. Indeed, Republicans were excluded from competing for the favor of the new dominant class almost by definition, since one of Richard Florida's requirements was that cities perform well on what he called the "Gay Index." Sure, those vulgar Republicans could offer crass inducements like low taxes, but in the age of creativity it was supposed to be your town's theatrical performances and its carefully handmade cupcakes that truly opened the door to prosperity.

Prosperity was a laudable goal, of course, and supporting culture was a laudable means. But that doesn't mean the one is necessarily connected to the other. In fact, the creative-class theory was based on a colossal blurring of cause and effect: An art scene isn't something that springs up before a city becomes affluent; generally speaking, it follows the money. This didn't stop political officials all over the country from adopting the creative-class strategy, however; in the absence of any concrete development policies, it must have seemed like a quick and affordable way to tackle civic decline. Florida himself would later back away from certain aspects of his original theory, admitting that "we can't stop the decline of some places, and that we would be foolish to try."[14]

I bring all this up not because I want to refute it—it refutes itself—but because its eager adoption by liberal politicians tells us something important about the modern Democratic Party and its attitudes toward equality. In its quest for prosperity, the Party of the People declared itself wholeheartedly in favor of a social theory that forthrightly exalted the rich—the all-powerful creative class. For many cities and states, this *was* the economic strategy; this was what our leaders came up with to revive the urban wastelands and restore the de-industrialized zones. The Democratic idea was no longer to confront privilege but to flatter privilege, to sing the praises of our tasteful new master class. True, this was all done with an eye toward rebuilding the crumbling cities where the rest of us lived and worked, but the consequences of all this "creative class" bootlicking will take a long time to wear off.

Working by then as a consultant to governments around the country, Florida himself ventured into politics in 2004, when he took to the pages of *Washington Monthly* to denounce the Republican Party and the science-doubting administration of George W. Bush as enemies of capitalism—or of modern, "creative" capitalism, anyway. The red states the Republicans represented were lands of economic backwardness, according to Florida, while Democratic areas, with their tolerance and love of learning, were zones of thrusting modernity. During the great years of the New Economy, Florida reminisced, these liberal-led places

> became hothouses of innovation, the modern-day equivalents of Renaissance city-states, where scientists, artists, designers,

> engineers, financiers, marketers, and sundry entrepreneurs fed off each other's knowledge, energy, and capital to make new products, new services, and whole new industries: cutting-edge entertainment in southern California, new financial instruments in New York, computer products in northern California and Austin, satellites and telecommunications in Washington, D.C., software and innovative retail in Seattle, biotechnology in Boston.[15]

Let us be clear about the political views Florida was expounding here. The problem with, say, George W. Bush's administration was not that it favored the rich; it was that it favored the *wrong rich*—the "old-economy" rich. Similarly, the problem with the intense Republican partisanship of those years was that it turned a deaf ear to the voices of the country's most important and creative industries (such as Wall Street and Silicon Valley), since such places chose Democrats as a matter of course.

Richard Florida wept for unfairly ignored industries, but he expressed little sympathy for the working people whose issues were now ignored by both parties. In fact, he sometimes seemed to regard these people as part of the problem. In the summer of 2008, Florida told a British newspaper that "the creative class anticipates the future, while the working class tends to seek protection from it." The only lesson we really needed to learn from the working-class experience was how they pulled off their political triumph in the 1930s, which Florida thought the creative class now needed to replicate: "Just as Franklin Delano Roosevelt forged a new majority on the swelling ranks of blue-collar workers, so must the party that hopes to win this presidential election earn the enthusiastic support of today's ascending economic and political force—the creative class."[16]

Florida spoke those words in June of 2008. The collapse of the ultra-creative Lehman Brothers investment bank came a scant three months later, and I would like to be able to say that these dreams of prosperity-through-tastefulness followed—right down the drain with the hedge funds and subprime lenders of the world. After all, one of the greatest deeds of the creative class was . . . financial innovation—meaning, among other things, the poisoned mortgage-backed securities that brought the global economy so close to death.

But the ideas I have described in this chapter did not suffer the same fate. As with free trade and welfare reform, there seems to be no refutation that can dissuade their supporters. Indeed, with the election of the young and innovative challenger, Barack Obama, they got a second wind. Under his administration they became more vigorous than ever, and with their flourishing our modern Democrats wandered ever further from their egalitarian traditions.

7

How the Crisis Went to Waste

Having spent decades assuring the public that their renunciation of the New Deal was genuine, in 2008 Democrats suddenly decided that the New Deal was back and that Franklin Roosevelt was more relevant than ever.

It took a global financial catastrophe to make them reverse themselves in this way—a recurrence of the Great Depression complete with Wall Street swindles, a burst financial bubble, and weeks of panic as unemployment spiked, assets tumbled, and the economy's foundations quivered. The confident days of the free-market consensus seemed to be shuddering to a close. The promise of a universally affluent postindustrial era now looked as empty and forlorn as a row of abandoned McMansions on some lonely cul-de-sac in the Nevada desert.

It wasn't merely Barack Obama's singular identification with "Hope" and "Change" that made him seem like the reincarnation of Franklin Roosevelt; in contrast to every other candidate, he recognized how political convention had given us economic disaster. In March of 2008, he gave his speech at Cooper Union in New York City appraising the crisis even as it developed; he understood the parallel with the bubble and burst of 1929; he knew how deregulation had contributed to our present predicament; and he blamed Wall Street for giving us an economy in which ordinary people never got a chance to prosper. It was a complete break with the school of Democratic Party thinking I have described in these pages.

His adversaries also did their part to make the parallel complete. President George W. Bush basically checked out for the crisis, leaving matters to his Treasury secretary, Hank Paulson. This official, in combination with Fed Chairman Ben Bernanke, proceeded to infuriate the public with a series of massive bank bailouts. Nor was the Republican presidential candidate, Senator John McCain, really up to the shocking turn of events; in his desperation and muddlement he announced that "the fundamentals of our economy are strong" on the very day of the Lehman Brothers collapse.

Obama, by contrast, seemed capable, youthful, vigorous, and intelligent. The volunteers who fuelled his run were so organized and enthusiastic that they appeared, to quote a team of scholars who have studied them, "more like a social movement than an electoral campaign." As the economic crisis deepened, Obama's greatness seemed to intensify; 100,000 listeners showed up at a rally for the candidate in St. Louis that October; another 100,000 turned out in Denver. There were an estimated 240,000 people on hand in Chicago on election night when Obama swamped McCain; the largest crowd ever to attend a presidential inauguration showed up to witness his swearing-in on January 20, 2009.[1]

The Democratic landslide carried away years of crusted ideas about the benevolence of high finance, and it also seemed to herald the end of decades of panicky Democratic capitulations to the right. Obama appealed to many of the fought-over demographic groups, and he did it without the concessions that party orthodoxy said he needed to make. He wasn't a Southerner; he wasn't mired in the culture wars; he hadn't tried to prove he was tough by supporting the Iraq war; he didn't triangulate and split hairs and cater in some nonverbal way to the white backlash; hell, he wasn't even white himself. For good measure, he snubbed the Democratic Leadership Council when they met in Chicago in 2008.

The connection between the confident new president and the hero of the 1930s was noted again and again by newspaper and magazine journalists. That a period of activist, FDR-style government should of necessity follow the collapse of capitalism seemed to be a truth universally acknowledged; writers on the left were enthusiastic about the prospect while conservatives trembled at the imminent reversal of everything they had achieved over the decades. "Roosevelt-mania" had seized America, declared the *Economist* magazine; Obama himself was reading books about the Depression, and on an episode of *60 Minutes* in November 2008 he said "what you see in FDR that I hope my team can emulate is not always getting it right, but projecting a sense of confidence, and a willingness to try things. And experiment in order to get people working again."[2]

Obama's $800 billion stimulus program, introduced in Congress six days after his inauguration, was said to be so sweeping it constituted nothing less than a "New New Deal," to quote the title of a book by *Time* magazine's Michael Grunwald. Another frequent comparison concerned Roosevelt's famous "brain trust," the group of professors and intellectuals the president called together in 1933 to help him plan the nation's economic recovery; Obama, it was said, needed to do exactly the same. The incompetents of the Bush Administration had run the country into the ground; perhaps what we needed most of all was government by the capable. Brains would find the way out of this crisis.

That was certainly what I myself thought at the time. Another journalist who seemed to feel this way was Jacob Weisberg, whom we last met calling attention to Clinton-era "Clincest" and who now called for a "Brilliant Brain Trust" in *Newsweek*.[3] Obama needed to "pick the smartest people he can find for his cabinet," to "give greater weight to intellectual acumen and subject-specific knowledge." The embodiment of such an approach, Weisberg went on to claim, was the economist Larry Summers, formerly the president of Harvard University and "the outstanding international economist of his generation." Summers had his problems, Weisberg admitted; he could be arrogant and contemptuous toward the less intelligent. "But these are the defects of a superior mind," Weisberg wrote, the unavoidable price you pay for having such a gifted individual on your team.

The professorial Obama proceeded to fill his administration in precisely this way. According to *Newsweek* reporter Jonathan Alter—who has written books on both Obama and FDR—some 90 percent of the new administration's staffers had professional degrees of some kind, and some 25 percent had either graduated from Harvard or taught there. Obama's team included a Nobel Prize winner, a Pulitzer Prize winner, a MacArthur "genius grant" winner, numerous Rhodes Scholars, and Summers, who presided over his National Economic Council. "It's merit-based," Claire McCaskill, senator of Missouri, is reported to have said of the president's hiring strategy. "It's getting the best people and best ideas."[4]

The process by which "the best people" were chosen is hinted at by an episode Chris Hayes describes in *Twilight of the Elites*. It was 2009, the president was picking a new Supreme Court justice, and pundits and presidential advisers alike were carefully weighing the qualifications of the well-graduated individuals under consideration. One attribute in particular commanded their attention: Which candidate was the "smartest"? On and on the wise ones reasoned, deducing somehow that one candidate was "smarter" than a second, who was, in turn, smarter than a third, who was, sadly, "not as smart as she seems to think she is." Of all the controversies before the nation and the many nuances of legal thought, this is what it came down to for the liberal class: smartness. For them, the Supreme Court was like a really selective institution on the far side of some cosmic SAT test.

Putting "the best people" in charge takes us to the essential battleground of American politics, as some people see it. This is what so many believe the war between Ds and Rs comes down to: intellect versus ignorance; science versus faith; Harvard versus wherever it was that Sarah Palin went to collidge. Summers himself was a forceful exponent of this point of view, saying in the first months of the new administration, "We've gone from a moment when we've never had a *less* social-science-oriented group"—meaning the philistine government of George W. Bush—"to a moment when we've never had a *more* social-science-oriented group. So . . . we'll see what happens."[5]

SAME-DOT-GOV

It has now been seven years since the Day Change Came, and we can indeed see what happened. On the most urgent issue facing the nation—what to do about the banks—the intelligence quotient of the president's team turned out to matter almost not at all. The erudite Obama administration used its mandate to continue the policies of the crude and tasteless Bush administration essentially unchanged, at least for the first few years. The bank bailouts proceeded as before. Tim Geithner, who had helped to run the Bush administration's bailouts from his seat at the New York branch of the Federal Reserve, now ran the Obama administration's bailouts from his seat at the Treasury Department. Ben Bernanke was re-upped at the Federal Reserve Board in Washington. Summers himself went on TV to defend the Policy of Same at its very worst juncture, the time in 2009 when bonuses went out to the executives of the failed insurance company/hedge fund AIG.[6]

For the new administration, as for the old, an obliging consideration toward banker confidence took precedence over everything else. For fear of frightening the men of lower Manhattan, the Obama team dared undertake none of the serious measures the times obviously called for. No big Wall Street institutions were put into receivership or cut down to size. No important Wall Street bankers were terminated in the manner of the unfortunate chairman of General Motors.

As a result, the situation continued as follows: The Wall Street banks, being "too big to fail," enjoyed a more-or-less explicit government guarantee against bankruptcy, but in order to enjoy that protection they were not required to stop doing the risky things that had got them in so much trouble in the first place. It was the perfect outcome for them, with the taxpayers of an entire nation essentially staking them to endless turns at the roulette wheel.* Writing of this awful period, Elizabeth Warren (who worked then as a bailout oversight official) concluded that "the president chose his team, and when there was only so much

* The Dodd-Frank banking reform law, which the president signed in 2010 and which I shall describe in Chapter Eight, was supposed to remedy this intolerable situation.

time and so much money to go around, the president's team chose Wall Street."[7]

The classic and most direct solution to an epidemic of corrupt bank management and fraudulent bank lending is to use the authority that comes with rescuing failed banks to close those banks down or to fire those banks' top managers. This was evidently never seriously considered by Obama's team of geniuses.

Another landmark Thirties policy option—requiring banks to separate their investment operations from their commercial banking services—was ultimately taken up by Democrats, and a version of it was even written into the Dodd-Frank bank reform measure. Whether and how it will actually be enforced is unknown as of this writing, since the law's provisions and loopholes are still being written and hollowed out by lawyers and regulators. We do know this: the too-big-to-fail banks are bigger than they were before the crisis, having swallowed up other banks as part of the rescue scheme. We also know that people who work in securities still make far more than those who toil in other industries—the average salary for people in that line of work in New York City was $404,000 in 2014—and their bonuses have almost returned to the levels achieved in the days before the crash.

On the second-most-urgent issue facing the nation—what to do about the recession and the unemployed—the administration's "New New Deal" program of deficit spending proved to be insufficient for what the ailing nation required. In an uncanny replay of the episode with which the Clinton administration had started, Obama's economic brain trust instructed him not to frighten markets by spending too much and expanding the federal deficit too greatly.[8] It was exactly the wrong advice for the moment, as less orthodox economists like Paul Krugman spent those years insisting.

But Obama's stimulus package *did* get through Congress, and it *was* larger in nominal dollars than any stimulus had ever been before. Unfortunately, the biggest single part of it was wasted on tax cuts designed to lure Republican votes. Another chunk was wasted on coaxing state governments to embrace charter schools and to open their education systems to consultants and entrepreneurs. The Big Stimulus also contained many good things: subsidies for clean-energy projects, a push to update medical record-keeping, billions for high-speed rail projects, and support for a long list of state and local construction schemes—the famous "shovel ready" projects about which everyone was talking in 2009. If you can name just one of them today without going to Wikipedia, you have my respect.[9]

What the sprawling stimulus measure did not include was the obvious thing, the most effective thing, the thing Americans of all ages remember that Franklin Roosevelt did—direct federal job-creation in the WPA manner. Obama was careful to avoid such things, because they would have expanded the federal workforce. Instead, his New New Deal merely sent money to others; on its own it built no tunnels in national parks, constructed no Art Deco county courthouses, painted no murals on post office walls, published no guidebooks to the states. As a result, it missed out on another achievement of the Roosevelt era: the creation of spectacular and unmistakable monuments to activist government.[10]

Unemployment did eventually come down, of course, as the economy healed from the bursting of the housing bubble. But the process was slow, it somehow didn't bring rising wages, and eventually the president came to believe that it couldn't be otherwise. According to the journalist Ron Suskind, President Obama convinced himself in late 2009 that there wasn't much he could do about the problem anyway; that, thanks to productivity growth, a high-unemployment economy was "the way it was supposed to be," in Suskind's words.[11] It was on the basis of this fatalistic illusion, Suskind continues, that Obama instructed his team not to push for another round of stimulus spending.

A NEW DEAL FOR WHOM?

If this was a modern-day New Deal, it was a timid iteration that was not particularly concerned with the big-picture deterioration of average people's economic situation—the wages that never grew, the rising incomes that always went to someone else. In terms of rhetoric, Barack Obama could be an eloquent champion of these people and their problems; it is thanks in part to his speeches that "inequality" became a mainstream political issue at all. But in terms of deeds, the Obama administration repeatedly sacrificed working people's interests in the service of some greater goal, or for what Washington called "optics," or for no discernible reason at all.

Things didn't go down this way because helping average citizens during hard times is a utopian dream, but rather because those citizens' interests conflicted with the interests of the upper strata. A choice between the two had to be made, and Obama made it.

The most notorious example was a Democratic proposal that would have allowed judges to modify homeowners' mortgage debt when they filed for bankruptcy—a process called "cramdown" that would have been extremely helpful to millions of homeowners but would also have had unpleasant consequences for whoever it was who owned the mortgages. In 2008, Obama had announced he was in favor of cramdown, but when it came up in the Senate in April of 2009, the president and his team, in the concise description of Obama biographer Jonathan

Alter, "wouldn't lift a finger to help."[12] With the banks lobbying energetically against it, the measure naturally failed.

Fortunately, the original bank-bailout measure that had passed Congress under President Bush included a component that was supposed to assist homeowners who were underwater on their mortgages; unfortunately, it was implemented in such a way as to become another costly fiasco, sometimes actually worsening the homeowners' situation. Neil Barofsky, one of Elizabeth Warren's colleagues in overseeing the bailouts, met with Treasury Secretary Geithner in the fall of 2009 to talk it over. Here is how the meeting went, according to Barofsky's memoir:

> In defense of the program, Geithner finally blurted out, "We estimate that they can handle ten million foreclosures, over time," referring to the banks. "This program will help foam the runway for them."
>
> A lightbulb went on for me. Elizabeth had been challenging Geithner on how the program was going to help home owners, and he had responded by citing how it would help the *banks*.[13]

Workers got the same treatment. As a presidential candidate, for example, Obama had loudly denounced the still-unpopular NAFTA; as president, he let such talk drift away. In Obama's early days, labor's highest priority in Washington was a legislative proposal called the Employee Free Choice Act, which would have made it easier for workers to bargain collectively with management, and might even have reversed the long slide in the unionized percentage of the workforce. Again, Obama declared himself in support of the measure; he had even voted for it as a U.S. senator. Again, though, as Wal-Mart and the Chamber of Commerce mobilized their lobbyists against the measure, the president's audacity seemed to disappear. The White House simply chose to let it go. One detail that caught my eye at the time was the amazing number of erstwhile liberals that business interests had hired to do their lobbying on this matter: former assistants to John Kerry, to Rahm Emanuel, to several Democratic senators, even to the secretary of labor.[14]

When the president *did* take a bold stand, it sometimes came at the expense of those same working Americans. I am referring to the 2015 debate over the Trans-Pacific Partnership treaty, which aimed to extend the NAFTA pattern to many countries on the Pacific Rim. Predictably, the phrase "no-brainer" made its appearance again, most notably from the pencil of an economist who thought the question before us was not the treaty's particulars but whether trade was a good thing. Obama himself, having spun a full one-eighty since his days criticizing NAFTA, accused the treaty's opponents of stupidly wanting to "pull up the drawbridge and build a moat around ourselves."[15]

The enlightened ones who knew better than to pull up the drawbridge were the industry groups—representatives of Big Pharma and Silicon Valley, for example—who got to advise the officials negotiating the partnership. Unsurprisingly, the treaty they produced will serve these industry groups well: like NAFTA, it is mainly designed to protect their investments abroad. For example, the TPP will help to obstruct trade in cheap generic pharmaceuticals and push people toward buying the expensive brand names. American workers will receive no such protections, of course; for them, it's to be competition to the death. Their employers, on the other hand, will be further empowered to move operations at will, traveling to low-wage, nonunion locales as they see fit and suing countries for adopting policies that disrupt their profits.

Treating workers and owners in these sharply different ways

has been the rule of the Obama years, but there have also been exceptions to it—big ones. The one great achievement of Obama's presidency, the health insurance reform known as "Obamacare," has many flaws, but it also subsidizes the purchase of coverage by people who otherwise can't afford it. This detail was an important victory for the poor—and also a measure without which Obamacare could not accomplish the other things it does, such as stopping insurers from cancelling sick people's insurance. Another triumph was the establishment of a Consumer Financial Protection Bureau in 2010, a much-needed regulatory agency that is supposed to keep an eye on predatory practices by payday loan shops, credit card companies, and the like. The CFPB is especially interesting to the historian of modern liberalism because its mission statement denounces debt products of the past that were "overly complicated" as well as "loans that [Americans] did not fully understand"—qualities that some well-graduated Democrats often think of in positive terms.[16]

One place where workers definitely came first was Obama's 2012 reelection campaign. Economic conditions were still terrible for ordinary people, even though the recession was over by then, and while the Republican nominee, the wealthy venture-capitalist Mitt Romney, tried to blame Obama for this state of affairs, the Democrats had a reply that was simpler still. They played the class card. Obama gave the first of his many speeches deploring inequality in December of 2011 in the small town of Osawatomie, Kansas—symbolically important as John Brown's hometown and as the place where Theodore Roosevelt announced his conversion to progressivism—and over the course of the next year populist rhetoric came to suffuse his party's talk. All of it pointed to one single conclusion: rich-kid Romney, blue-ribbon fat cat, doesn't get people like you. He "may get the economy, he may know how to make money, he may have made hundreds of millions for him and his investors," an Obama adviser told journalist Dan Balz. "But every time he did, folks like you lost your pensions, lost your jobs, jobs got shipped overseas."[17]

That's how the campaign of 2012 came to feature the starkest proletarian appeals in many years. That's how the Democratic convention became a long exercise in lighthearted class animus. And that's how a Democratic Super PAC came to air a shattering TV commercial in which a worker at a paper company that had been taken over by Bain Capital, Romney's firm, recalled how his new bosses instructed him to build a stage; when he had finished the job, those bosses climbed up on that stage and fired that worker and everyone else at the company. The commercial was so shockingly maudlin that, according to Balz, voters in Ohio could recall "specific details" about the spot even after it had not aired for seven weeks.[18]

Talk aside, the situation of working people has continued to deteriorate. Since the recession ended in June 2009, the country's gross domestic product has grown by 13.8 percent; in that same period, salaries and wages have gone up a mere 1.8 percent. The economic clout of labor unions has continued to shrink, as the percentage of private sector workers who were members of a union has dwindled from 7.2 percent in 2009 to 6.6 percent in 2014. The "labor share" of the nation's income, as I mentioned in the Introduction, declined sharply from its old postwar average; during the Obama presidency it has stumbled along at or near its all-time lows.[19]

The "profit share," meanwhile, has hit all-time highs, as has the Dow Jones Industrial Average, the NASDAQ, and Wall Street compensation. There's been another novel factor as well. In the past, administrations taking office after a wave of corporate crime would often use high-profile prosecutions to signal that a tough new sheriff was on the job. Obama chose not to. Instead, his Justice Department let slide nearly every bit of bank misbehavior to make headlines, from the countless apparent frauds of the housing-bubble days to the huge LIBOR-fixing scam to the "robo-signing" mass-foreclosure scandal of 2010. All these outrages—and yet, according to one study, Federal prosecutions for white-collar crimes hit a twenty-year low in 2015.[20]

In a 2012 speech, the head of Obama's Criminal Division, Lanny Breuer, announced that he was sometimes persuaded when banks and corporations asked him not to prosecute on the grounds that it might cause the company in question to fail and thus hurt the economy. "We must take into account the effect of an indictment on innocent employees and shareholders," Breuer said, describing a courtesy that American prosecutors extend to no other group and that, by its nature, makes a joke of the idea of equality before the law.[21]

This was Clintonism on monster-truck tires. Not only is it more profitable to make your living by speculation than by working, but it puts you above the law as well.

THE OCEAN-LINER PRESIDENCY

Democrats lost control of the House of Representatives in 2011 and of the Senate in 2015. Although Obama was resoundingly reelected in 2012, he did little on equality issues once the Tea Party tidal wave hit the Washington beach.

By then he had already veered off in pursuit of a "Grand Bargain" in which Democrats would offer up their once-sacred social insurance programs to the budgetary knife if Republicans would consider tax increases. To co-chair the commission charged with hammering out the budget agreement, Obama even chose Erskine Bowles, the man who had been Clinton's emissary to

Newt Gingrich in the secret negotiations over privatizing Social Security.

The Bowles-Simpson Commission failed in its unsavory budget-balancing mission. So did all the other similar efforts of those years. No one outside Washington could really follow the two sides' complicated budget battles, though they dragged on year after year. But Obama's determination to win some great Clintonian victory over the federal deficit grew so strong that for a while it cancelled out nearly everything else that had once animated his hopeful supporters.

Obama still had his remarkable skill with words, but at some point the eloquent president reportedly lost his faith in persuasion.[22] His presidency had its great moments, of course: the Osama bin Laden raid, the diplomatic recognition of Cuba, the deal with Iran. But on inequality he was reduced to making speeches.

To the dismal record of the later Obama years, leading liberal-class thinkers have responded in an entirely characteristic manner: by constructing a theory of American politics in which inactivity was the best anyone could hope for. Obama has not really disappointed at all. On the contrary, they've claimed, the powerlessness of the presidency has been one of the great determining facts of American history—a truth established by political science itself—and Obama has grappled with it as best he could. Presidents, wrote *New York Times* columnist Frank Bruni in 2015, are "not always mighty frigates parting the waters"; sometimes they're "buoys on the tides of history, rising and falling with the swells." The true problem, liberal thinkers concluded, were the whining, unrealistic idealists who expected so much from Obama—and of course those diabolical Republicans in Congress, constantly outmaneuvering the poor, powerless man in the Oval Office.[23]

By June 2015, Obama himself had taken to saying the same thing, relating to the comedian Marc Maron how he often had to tell his disappointed supporters that "you can't get cynical or frustrated because you didn't get all the way there immediately." A little later he offered the classic metaphor for U.S. government inflexibility:

> Sometimes the task of government is to make incremental improvements, or try to steer the ocean liner two degrees north or south, so that ten years from now, suddenly we're in a very different place than we were. But at the time, at the moment, people may feel like, we need a 50 degree turn, we don't need a two degree turn. . . . And you *can't* turn 50 degrees.
>
> And it's not just because of corporate lobbyists, it's not just because of big money, it's because societies don't turn 50 degrees. Democracies certainly don't turn 50 degrees.[24]

It is easy to understand why pundits want to write apologetics for the president, and it is even easier to understand why Obama wants to describe his presidency in such a way. Having put so much faith in his transformative potential, his followers need to come to terms with how nontransformative he has been.

OCEAN LINERS WERE MEANT TO FLY

If our goal is to rescue the reputation of a hero who turned out to have clay feet, this is surely the way to go. Ocean liners are hard to turn. Presidents don't have a lot of power. Republicans are in league with the devil.

If what we are concerned with is inequality, however, it

would behoove us to admit the obvious forthrightly: that Obama could have done many things differently, that the Republicans aren't superhuman, and that the presidency is in fact a powerful office.

It is so powerful that, even in Obama's worst period, with Congress entirely in the hands of intransigent Republicans, it would still have been possible for the president to use the executive branch to do big and consequential things about inequality. To name just one: He might have resumed Franklin Roosevelt's legacy on antitrust enforcement.

Allow me to explain. Not too long ago, monopolies and oligopolies were illegal in America. This was because our ancestors understood that concentrated economic power was incompatible with democracy and equality in all sorts of ways. Since the days of Ronald Reagan, however, every administration has chosen to drop the enforcement of the antitrust laws except in rare cases. This has come to mean that mergers and takeovers are permitted in nearly all instances, and achieving monopoly has once again become the obvious objective of every would-be business leader. From Big Pharma to Silicon Valley, everyone in the C-suites knows that this is the path to success today. "Competition is for losers," they say. Unless your startup has a plan for cornering and using market power, you can forget about interest from venture capital.[25]

Tolerating such practices has had obvious consequences, both in our everyday economic lives—where citizens face unchallengeable economic power everywhere from beer to bookselling—and in terms of the gradual plutocratization of society. Unrestrained corporate power has naturally yielded unrestrained wealth for corporate leaders and their Wall Street backers.

Barack Obama could have changed this, and by extension, changed the political climate of the country merely by deciding to enforce the nation's laws in the same way that administrations before Reagan did. The antitrust laws themselves were written a century ago and are still on the books. The current Republican Congress would have had little say in the matter. It would have been almost entirely up to the executive branch.

On this front and many others* Obama was completely free to act, especially before 2010, and even after the Republicans took Congress. The times certainly called for it, with Amazon, Google, and AB InBev romping the globe. Still, he did next to nothing. In fact, anti-monopoly investigations conducted by Obama's Justice Department went from a barely breathing four in 2009 to a flat zero in 2014.[26] (By way of contrast: In 1980, under a different Democratic administration, there were 65 such investigations.)

Let us return again to the financial crisis and the Wall Street bailouts—the episode that will define our politics for generations, that captured everything that is going wrong with the country, that ensured Obama's election as president in the first place. To say that Obama fumbled this most critical issue is to understate the matter pretty dramatically. More to the point is the great question of *why* he fumbled it so dramatically. Was it because the ocean liner couldn't be turned?

---

* High-profile prosecutions of financial-industry fraudsters would have been healthy and were entirely within Obama's power even after the Democrats lost Congress. Using Education Department funding to encourage universities to reconsider their out-of-control tuition inflating would also have been transformative. Obama's Federal Trade Commission could have cracked down on the pharmaceutical companies that have been raising so dramatically the price of certain prescription drugs. On this last topic, see David Dayen, "Why Are Drug Companies Running Amok?," *The Intercept,* December 16, 2015.

On the contrary. It was *fully within Obama's power* to react to the financial crisis in a more aggressive and appropriate way: laws were in place, there was ample precedent, he wasn't forced to pick the men whom Democrat Senator Byron Dorgan plaintively called "the wrong people" for his economic team.[27] It wasn't the Republicans who made Obama choose Tim Geithner to run the bailouts or Attorney General Eric Holder to (not) prosecute dishonest bankers or Ben Bernanke to serve another term at the Fed.

It would have been *good policy* had Obama reacted to the financial crisis in a more aggressive and appropriate way—by which I mean, the economy would have recovered more quickly and the danger of a future crisis brought on by financial fraud or concentrated economic power would have been reduced.

It would have been *massively popular* had Obama swung the wheel of the ocean liner and reacted to the financial crisis in a more aggressive and appropriate way. Everyone admits this at least tacitly, even the architects of Obama's bailout policies, who like to think of themselves as having resisted the public's mindless baying for banker blood.[28] Acting aggressively might also have countered the sham populism of the Tea Party movement and prevented the Republican *reconquista* of Congress.

There were countless opportunities for the kind of decisive action I am describing: Obama could have questioned or even unwound Bush's bailouts; he could have fired the bad regulators who let it all happen; he could have stopped the AIG bonuses instead of having his team go on television to defend them; he could have pushed to allow bankruptcy judges to modify mortgages; he could have put the "zombie banks" into receivership; he could have shifted FBI agents back to white-collar crime; and so on.

Obama did none of it.

This is a critical point. On the matter of dealing with Wall Street, there was no conflict between idealism and pragmatism. The high-minded and Jeffersonian move, in this case, would have also been the practical move, the policy that would have been healthiest for the nation, the one that would have paid off best in the crude terms of public opinion polls.

And still he didn't do it. He didn't even try. In fact, Obama's team did the opposite. They did everything they could to "foam the runways" and never showed any real interest in confronting the big banks.

Obama didn't play the greatest of all issues the way he did because getting tough with Wall Street would have looked bad or because the presidency lacks sufficient power. Everything I just mentioned was eminently doable in 2009. Putting banks into receivership is a common and even sometimes necessary legal procedure. The country was begging Obama to do it. But he chose not to.

Once we acknowledge this, we must acknowledge the possibility that Obama and his team didn't act forcefully to press an equality-minded economic agenda in those days and in the years that followed because they didn't want to. That he and they didn't do many of the things their supporters wanted them to do because they didn't believe in doing those things. It wasn't because the ocean liner would have been too hard to turn, or because those silly idealists were unrealistic; it was because *they didn't want to do those things.*

8

The Defects of a Superior Mind

Let us now examine in detail each of President Obama's three big legislative victories, which he won in the two years before the Democrats lost control of Congress in the 2010 elections: The big stimulus package of 2009, the Dodd-Frank banking measure, and the landmark Affordable Care Act. In certain remarkable ways, each of these legislative achievements followed the same characteristic pattern—one that diminishes their effectiveness but allows Democrats to pursue the professional consensus they crave.

THE ENDS OF COMPLEXITY

All of them, for starters, chose complexity over straightforwardness. The virtue of the old Glass-Steagall Act, which regulated the banking industry from 1933 until its final repeal in the Clinton era, was its simplicity: It structurally separated investment banking from commercial banking and forced those parts to compete with one another. The 2010 Dodd-Frank Act, which was supposed to re-regulate the business, uses a different method—it instructs federal agencies to make detailed new rules for the industry. As I write this, the agencies have finished about two-thirds of that task, with their regulatory work now running to a staggering 22,000 pages of rules, loopholes, and exceptions.

This intricacy does not make Dodd-Frank an outlier among Obama-era reforms; this makes it typical. The Affordable Care Act is even more profoundly dizzying. On the matter of reforming the country's health care system, there were in 2009 two admirably straightforward proposals on the table: a Canadian-style single-payer system and the briefly popular "public option," in which the government itself would provide competition to existing health insurance companies. President Obama had publicly declared his support for both these choices over the years. Neither won the favor of Obama's all-important proxy on this issue, however, by which I mean former Senator Max Baucus, Democrat of Montana, a notable friend of the lobbyist and (as of this writing) the U.S. ambassador to China.

Instead we got Obamacare, with its exchanges, its individual and employer mandates, its Cadillac tax, its subsidies to individuals and to the insurance industry, and its thousands of other moving parts, sluicing funding this way and that. Complexity is its most striking characteristic. No one is really certain how it operates, whether it is a tax or a mandate (OK, the Supreme Court has determined that it's the former), or whether it will truly make health care more affordable. In a video clip accessible on YouTube, Democratic Senator Jay Rockefeller can be seen describing Obamacare as "the most complex piece of legislation ever passed by the United States Congress"; a former state health-insurance official in Massachusetts, whose health care system was Obama's model, moaned that "We took the most complex health care system on God's green earth, and made it 10 times more complex."[1]

Why did Team Obama choose to go this route? One explanation is suggested by the infamous remarks of Obamacare consultant Jonathan Gruber, an MIT economist who was videotaped telling an academic conference in 2013 that the law was deliberately "written in a tortured way" with a "lack of transparency" that was meant to confuse evaluators and thus get it past the clueless and bewildered public. (Gruber's exact phrase was "the stupidity of the American voter."[2]) This is repugnant, but it seems plausible. We know that complexity serves exactly this purpose in other branches of professional practice—think of the baffling opacity of Wall Street's technical dialect, which is designed to make outside scrutiny difficult if not impossible. Why not here, too?

Had fairness and greater equality been the primary goals of either Obamacare or Dodd-Frank, they would no doubt have been far more straightforward. But complexity allowed Obama to square the circle of modern liberalism. It allowed him to achieve the double mandate of making health care more affordable while preserving existing players at the same time. A single-payer system would obviously have done grave damage to the insurance industry, while a public option would have given it unwelcome competition. But Obamacare did the opposite—it made those insurers into a permanent feature of the economic landscape. Their enthusiasm for the measure was obvious and much discussed at the time, as was that of Big Pharma: Obamacare essentially made our patronage of these industries mandatory.

A forgotten school of left-wing historians used to argue that the regulatory state began not with public-minded statesmen cracking the whip and taming big biz, but just the opposite—with business leaders deliberately inviting federal regulation as a way to build barriers to entry and give their cartels the protection of law. Long-ago giants of steel, tobacco, telephones, and meatpacking all welcomed federal regulation because of the effects it would have on smaller competitors. That old style of regulation brought ancillary benefits to the public, of course: better food, a standardized phone system. But its main objects were stability for existing businesses and guaranteed profits in perpetuity.[3]

Certain events surrounding the advent of Obamacare have resurrected this scary hypothesis. In the summer of 2009, PhRMA, the lobby of the big pharmaceutical companies, aggressively supported the president's health care proposal. In exchange for their support, the administration had made a deal barring any possibility of drug reimportation from Canada, a country with a sane health care system.

Nevertheless, in July of that year, President Obama chose to describe opponents of his reform as people desperate to preserve "a system that works for the insurance and the drug companies." This gave the proceedings an air of populist drama that they otherwise lacked, but it hurt the feelings of the PhRMA lobbyists. It seems they were sensitive souls. Didn't the president know they were on his side? Thanks to emails later released by the House Energy and Commerce Committee, we know that the folks from PhRMA visited the White House and demanded an explanation. As a PhRMA lobbyist described the scene,

> Then Rahm came in. Among other things, said very positive things about what we were doing and said "I know you are swimming in different waters. I take personal responsibility for that error. As you know, this is out of character for what the President has been saying since we made our deal."[4]

This is not to say that the "deal" Obama made with PhRMA was altogether without merit, only that it was a deal, a deliberate swap in which a chance for a truly democratic health care system was parlayed into the opposite.

The deal that the financial industry secured from the Democrats wasn't quite as rich, but in it we can see traces of the same impulse. In the Obama administration's early years, you will recall, the Wall Street banks were regarded as "too big to fail," their health essentially guaranteed by the federal government even though many of them appeared to have been neck-deep in fraudulent activity during the bubble days. Dodd-Frank was supposed to change this: being a "systemically important financial institution" now carried special regulatory obligations with which lesser banks did not have to comply.

The objective of the law's tortuous complexity was again to allow us to have it both ways—to leave the big banks intact and to render them harmless at the same time. Dodd-Frank goes about reforming the banks by outlawing many of the specific practices that were implicated in the housing bubble and the financial crisis, thus generating the tens of thousands of pages of rules and exceptions that are the law's most remarkable feature. At the same time, however, Dodd-Frank leaves the banks themselves standing, and it does little to alter the more fundamental conventions of modern banking—like ballooning compensation—that gave rise to the madness in the first place. As the regulatory expert Bill Black says, it is like trying to achieve gun safety by banning the specific caliber of ammunition that was used in the latest massacre. It won't be difficult for the villains to find a different way to get what they want.

Structural reform would actually have been much simpler, since much of it could have been accomplished by carefully rolling back the deregulations of the Clinton and Reagan years. Such a reform would have been far-reaching, too. But as it stands, Dodd-Frank does little to tackle the greater problem of the financial sector swallowing the real economy, although that was obviously what the times called for and although taking the banks apart would no doubt have done much to reverse the ever-growing wealth of the One Percent. Instead, Wall Street executives are still among the wealthiest people in the land; their lobbyists are still like a small army besieging Capitol Hill; and with their campaign contributions and their friendly persuasiveness they are industriously writing loopholes and exceptions into the fiendishly complicated and yet still unfinished new law.

AMONG THE SERIOUS

In the early days of the Obama administration, as we have seen, there was a healthy Ivy League delegation in the executive branch; as the years went on, the administration grew even more selective, even more closely focused on professional status as it is defined by a tiny group of institutions. As of this writing, fully two-thirds of President Obama's cabinet-level officers are products of these elite schools; all but three of them have graduate degrees.[5] For the rest of us, this should serve as a cue to inquire a little more carefully into the phenomenon of genius-in-government. Of what does these people's brilliance really consist?

It is not book-learning alone. Consider Larry Summers: during the two years when he worked at D. E. Shaw, the hedge fund that is thickly populated with chess champions and math Olympians, he is known to have made some $5.2 million. In exchange for this, he reportedly worked one day a week at tasks that have been described as standing somewhere between trivial and ornamental. Do the math and that comes out to about $52,000 a day—more than the average American household earns in an entire year.[6]

Stints like this turn out to be a frequent item on the résumés of Obama's leadership clique, almost as common as the Ivy League educations and advanced degrees that so impressed the nation's pundits in the administration's early days. Rahm Emanuel, the president's first chief of staff, had also spent a brief period in investment banking, during which he amassed a sum several times greater than Summers's. Bill Daley, the man who replaced Emanuel, had passed many years at JPMorgan, while Jack Lew, who eventually replaced Daley (before going on to run the Treasury Department), had previously directed a Citibank group that invested in hedge funds. Michael Froman, the president's trade representative, also came from Citibank.

Other Obama officials worked the equation in reverse. Tim Geithner, the Treasury secretary during the crisis years, serves today as president of Warburg Pincus, a private equity firm. Obama's first director of the Office of Management and Budget, Peter Orszag, left government for a job at Citibank. Gene Sperling, a director of the National Economic Council, signed up with PIMCO, as did Ben Bernanke, Obama's first Fed Chairman; White House Counsel Gregory Craig opted for Goldman Sachs; and the incorrigible Daley worked it at both ends, choosing post–White House to join Argentière Capital, a hedge fund based in the Swiss city of Zug.

Thus did the Party of the People turn the government over to Wall Street in the years after Wall Street had done such lasting damage to . . . well, the People. The classic explanation for this perverse act is the donations the banks made to Obama's campaign in 2008. But there's another, and it takes us deep into the shared predilections of the liberal class: Obama deferred to Wall Street in so many ways because investment banking signifies professional status like almost nothing else. For the kind of achievement-conscious people who filled the administration, investment bankers were more than friends—they were fellow professionals; people of subtle minds, sophisticated jargon, and extraordinary innovativeness. They were the "creative class" that Democrats revere.

What I am suggesting is that the liberal class's unquestioning, reflexive respect for professional expertise was an impediment to thinking rationally about Wall Street. It blinded the Democrats to the problems of megabanks, to the need for structural change, and to the epidemic of fraud that overswept the business.

Washington's professional deference to Wall Street comes up again and again in accounts of the Obama era. Neil Barofsky, for example, found it at work in the Treasury Department, where no one would question the industry's basic assumptions about merit and compensation:

> The Wall Street fiction that certain financial executives were preternaturally gifted supermen who deserved every penny of their staggering paychecks and bonuses was firmly ingrained in Treasury's psyche. No matter that the financial crisis had demonstrated just how unremarkable the work of those executives had turned out to be, that belief system endured at Treasury across administrations. If a Wall Street executive was contracted to receive a $6.4 million "retention" bonus, the assumption was that he must be worth it.[7]

Thus did meritocracy subvert reform. Jargon also helped. Elizabeth Warren tells how Wall Street's simulation of professional expertise helped to bamboozle members of Congress:

> Financial reform was complicated, and the bank lobbyists used a clever technique: They bombarded the members of

> Congress with complex arguments filled with obscure terms. Whenever a congressman pushed back on an idea, the lobbyists would explain that although the congressman *seemed* to be making a good point, he didn't *really* understand the complex financial system. . . . It was the ultimate insider's play: *Trust us because we understand it and you don't.*[8]

Then there was the aura of financial worldliness with which liberal groupthink surrounded itself. As with trade issues, which always seem to come down to a clash between the educated against the ignorant, the administration's policymaking professionals regarded the demand for breaking up too-big-to-fail banks as hopelessly unsophisticated—even when the argument was made by no less an authority than former Fed Chairman Paul Volcker. Jonathan Alter captures this feeling exactly when he writes, "To the policy mandarins, who believed from the beginning of their academic training in the merits of financial engineering, Volcker's argument wasn't serious."[9]

And seriousness is the coin of the realm in Washington, a city that finds Wall Street's simulation of professional solemnity to be highly convincing, what with its impenetrable technical dialect and its advanced financial instruments. So complex are the latter, one deputy U.S. attorney general complained in 2014, that when examining them, "we are dealing with financial rocket science."[10]

The economic expertise of Wall Street's analysts, strategists, and traders is taken for granted in Washington. This belief seeps into all corners of life in the capital. Consider the words of White House Press Secretary Jay Carney, who advocated for a payroll tax cut in 2011 by referencing "responsible economists," by which he meant "not adjuncts of one party or the other, or people from partisan think tanks, but economists on Wall Street, economists out in the country and academic economists who are not affiliated with a party or a position. . . ."[11] What is interesting here is Carney's assumption, three years after the financial crisis, that "Wall Street" shares the high ground of respectability with academia. It is not a synonym for "criminal," but the opposite: a signifier of legitimacy.

Public officials aren't supposed to wreck this highly creative industry by regulating its operations or capping its compensation scales or putting its great institutions into receivership; they are supposed to respect it. To forgive its peccadilloes. To nurture its innovations. To let it know that it need never fly to London or Zurich. This is professional courtesy on a level so elementary it shouldn't even require thought.

CONSENSUS OF THE WILLING

All the things I have mentioned so far—the fascination with complexity, the desire to preserve existing players, the genuflection before expertise—all of them arise from one of the deepest wellsprings of liberal thought and action: the longing for a grand consensus of the professional class that never seems to come. We saw an earlier version in Bill Clinton's presidency, but Barack Obama displayed a passion for reaching an understanding with his foes that was at times embarrassing to behold. The president borrowed big chunks of his health care reform plan, for example, from the conservative Heritage Foundation and from a plan proposed by Republicans back in the 1990s. He struck deals with the insurance companies, the medical profession, and Big Pharma. He and his team then sat vainly for months waiting for a Republican to sign on to the plan and thus certify it as "bipartisan." In the very speech that so affronted the thin-skinned men of PhRMA, Obama also boasted that "we've forged a level of consensus on health care that has never been reached in the history of this country."[12]

That Obama would be more interested in consensus than in confrontation was something we should have seen coming; after all, the magical healing properties of consensus had been one of the great themes of Obama's pre-presidential career. It was the motif of his bestselling 2006 book, *The Audacity of Hope*, a long salute to bipartisanship that is distinguished from the hundreds of other titles in that genre by the intellectual pirouettes that then-Senator Obama performed around this deeply boring topic. Americans have "a common set of values that bind us together despite our differences," he proclaimed in Chapter One of that work, just before telling us "we need a new kind of politics, one that can excavate and build upon those shared understandings that pull us together as Americans." Ideology, which is the opposite of consensus, cannot possibly "meet the challenges we face as a country." And so tritely on.

As president, Obama worked hard to signal continuity with Bush administration policy and then, in 2010, to lend his gravitas to the worldwide push for austerity. This was the low point of the Obama years, when the president made his "pivot" to deficit reduction even though the slump continued and unemployment was intolerably high. "Families across the country are tightening their belts and making tough decisions," he said in his State of the Union Address in 2010. "The federal government should do the same." As a matter of fact, the federal government *shouldn't* do the same; as many pointed out at the time, it should do the opposite—that's the wisdom of countercyclical spending, which the world learned at such great cost during the Great Depression.

This may have put Obama on the wrong side of history, but it put him squarely in the center of Beltway culture. The editorial page of the *Washington Post*, for example, kept up its endless war against deficits and entitlements right through the financial crisis and the economic slump that followed; any occasion was a good one for getting tough about the deficit. This was the context in which the capital embarked on its years of deficit-reduction measures, each of them chasing the president's dream of a "Grand Bargain" in which the war between the political parties would be forever resolved: the Spending Freeze, the Bowles-Simpson Commission, the Congressional "Supercommittee," the "fiscal cliff" that was reached when the Supercommittee failed, the Sequester of 2013, and so on. They were, each of them, the product of a self-assured culture of D.C. professionalism that Paul Krugman has lampooned with the phrase, "very serious people."

"Serious" is exactly the right word. One of the timeless characteristics of rule-by-experts is the belief that informed and "serious" people know the answers to our problems, and that ideology and politics are pointless distractions keeping us from putting solutions in place.[13] But never has the connection between professionalism and this post-ideological faith been more obvious than in the career of Barack Obama. For him, all the issues are already settled; all the answers are known; all the serious people are in agreement. Everyone in D.C. knows that entitlements have to be reformed and that the deficit has to be brought under control.

For Obama and his supporters, there seems to be something elemental, something basic in the many showdowns between his cool, technocratic style and the raging, wailing, senseless defiance of the Republicans in Congress. Surely they believe that it's mind against sentiment, ego against id, civilization against barbarism.

For us, however, what needs to be pointed out is that, with

their sonorous warnings about deficits, Obama's "very serious people" turned out to be completely wrong. The expertise of the experts was, in this case, worthless.

THE HORROR OF THE UNPROFESSIONAL

I was surprised to learn that when Secretary of Defense Ashton Carter wanted to scold Russia for its campaign of airstrikes in Syria in the fall of 2015, the word he chose to apply was "unprofessional." Given the magnitude of the provocation, it seemed a little strange—as though he thought there were an International Association of Smartbomb Deployment Executives that might, once alerted by American officials, hold an inquiry into Russia's behavior and hand down a stern reprimand.

On reflection, slighting foes for their lack of professionalism was something of a theme of the Obama years. An Iowa Democrat became notorious in 2014, for example, when he tried to insult an Iowa Republican by calling him "a farmer from Iowa who never went to law school." Similarly, it was "unprofessionalism" (in the description of Thomas Friedman) that embarrassed the insubordinate Afghan-war General Stanley McChrystal, who made ill-considered remarks about the president to *Rolling Stone* magazine. And in the summer of 2013, when National Security Agency contractor Edward Snowden exposed his employer's mass surveillance of email and phone calls, the aspect of his past that his detractors chose to emphasize was . . . his failure to graduate from high school.[14] How could such a no-account person challenge this intensely social-science-oriented administration?

But it was public school teachers who made the most obvious target for professional reprimand by the administration. They are, after all, pointedly different from other highly educated professions: Teachers are represented by trade unions, not proper professional associations, and their values of seniority and solidarity conflict with the cult of merit embraced by other professions. For years, the school reform movement has worked to replace or weaken teachers' unions with remedies like standardized testing, charter schools, and tactical deployment of the cadres of Teach for America, a corps of enthusiastic graduates from highly ranked colleges who take on teaching duties in classrooms across the country after only minimal training.

Team Obama joined the fight against teachers unions from day one: the administration supported charter schools and standardized tests; they gave big grants to Teach for America. In Jonathan Alter's description of how the administration decided to take on the matter, it is clear that professionalism provided the framework for their thinking. Teachers' credentials are described as somewhat bogus; they "often bore no relationship to [teachers'] skills in the classroom." What teachers needed was a more empirical form of certification: they had to be tested and then tested again. Even more offensive to the administration was the way teachers' unions had resisted certain accountability measures over the years, resulting in a situation "almost unimaginable to professionals in any other part of the economy," as Alter puts it.[15]

As it happens, the vast majority of Americans *are* unprofessional: they are the managed, not the managers. But people whose faith lies in "cream rising to the top" (to repeat Alter's take on Obama's credo) tend to disdain those at the bottom. Those who succeed, the doctrine of merit holds, are those who deserve to—who race to the top, who get accepted to "good" colleges and get graduate degrees in the right subjects. Those who don't sort of deserve their fates.

"One of the challenges in our society is that the truth is

kind of a disequalizer," Larry Summers told journalist Ron Suskind during the early days of the Obama administration. "One of the reasons that inequality has probably gone up in our society is that people are being treated closer to the way that they're supposed to be treated."[16]

Remember, as you let that last sentence slide slowly down your throat, that this was a *Democrat* saying this—a prominent Democrat, a high-ranking cabinet official in the Clinton years and the man standing at the right hand of power in the first Obama administration.*

The merit mind-set destroyed not only the possibility of real action against inequality; in some ways it killed off the hopes of the Obama presidency altogether. "From the days of the 2008 Obama transition team offices, it was clear that the Administration was going to be populated with Ivy Leaguers who had cut their teeth, and filled their bank accounts, at McKinsey, Goldman Sachs and Citigroup," a labor movement official writes me.

> The President, who was so impressed with his classmates' intelligence at Harvard and Columbia, gave them the real reins of power, and they used those reins to strangle him and his ambition of being a transformative President. The overwhelming aroma of privilege started at the top and at the beginning. . . . It reached down deep into the operational levels of government, to the lowest-level political appointees. Our members watched this process unfold in 2009 and 2010, and when it came time to defend the Obama Administration at the polls in 2010, no one showed up.

---

*I am pleased to report that, like other characters in our story, Summers seemed to change his thinking on inequality after he left government.

THE RACE IS NOT TO THE SWIFT

All these brilliant people, all these honored professionals and Ivy League PhDs, and yet one of the most striking features of the Obama administration has been its timidity, its leaden lack of originality. The situation of 2009 called for daring and imagination, but what we got were half-measures in all things.

It didn't have to be this way. In fact, none of the lamentable episodes I have described in these chapters—not even the technocratic longing for consensus—are built-in defects of expertise-in-government. Nations have found ways to have genius and daring at the same time; indeed, before the "ocean liner" experience of the Obama years taught me otherwise, I used to believe that these qualities went hand-in-hand. For example, the original New Deal, which set the standard for an administration of intellectuals, was creative and experimental above all else. Programs would be conjured out of nothing overnight. And when one of them failed, Roosevelt's Brain Trust would try something else.

Obama's team, by contrast, was "smart." They were often people of dazzling credentials as scholars but not necessarily as reformers, regulators, and law enforcers. They had successfully internalized mainstream thinking in their respective disciplines, maybe, but that was not enough for the challenges of the moment. Reform often comes from the margins of American life, but marginal is not a term anyone would use to describe the satisfied, conventionally minded people of the Obama administration. This team was limited by its excellence, restrained by its orthodoxy.

Professional correctness also fetched the Obama administration a beating in the arena of partisan combat. In their guileless search for Grand Bargains and bipartisan comity, it seems never to have dawned on Team D that their Republican opponents might do exactly what Newt Gingrich and Tom DeLay taught them to do in the 1990s: dedicate themselves completely to obstruction, drag the conversation always to the right, and refuse to confer even the slightest bit of legitimacy on the Democratic administration. Failing to guess that this extremely likely eventuality might come to pass cost our pack of geniuses many months of wasted time as they fruitlessly pursued Republican votes for their health care bill. Worse: the Affordable Care Act that Obama ultimately signed into law relies in numerous ways on the cooperation of state-level politicians—many of them Republicans who, we now know, are just as enthralled by the obstruction game as are their national leaders.

Worst of all was the administration's ideological assumption that Democrats simply owned economic discontent. Those upset because Team Obama didn't get tough with Wall Street would have nowhere else to go, they thought. It was science, *political* science: move to the center, and you can take such people's votes for granted.

That the liberals' failures might expose them to deadly flanking fire from the right is something the administration appears not to have seen coming; for all their subtle learning, many members of the liberal class still don't believe it really happened—what did them in, they think, was just the recrudescence of some boorish reflex in the minds of an unenlightened public. And this brings us to perhaps the most crucial indictment of them all: these Democrats don't seem really to care about winning elections. Even that, the most fundamental political act, takes a back seat to professional vanity.[17]

9

The Blue State Model

When you press Democrats on their uninspiring deeds—their lousy free trade deals, for example, or their incomprehensible Wall Street reform legislation—when you press them on any of these things, they reply automatically that this is the best anyone could have done. After all, they had to deal with those awful Republicans, and those awful Republicans wouldn't let the really good stuff get through. They filibustered in the Senate. They gerrymandered in the congressional districts. And, besides, it's hard to turn an ocean liner. Surely you don't think the tepid-to-lukewarm things Clinton and Obama have done in Washington really represent the fiery Democratic soul.

So let us go to a place that does. Let us choose a locale where Democratic rule is virtually unopposed, a place where Republican obstruction and sabotage cannot taint the experiment.

This chapter owes a big debt to John Summers, who encouraged me to explore this subject and who wrote a groundbreaking essay on the innovation cult in Cambridge, Massachusetts, called "The People's Republic of Zuckerstan." See *Baffler* 24 (2014).

THESE ARE DEMOCRATS

The map offers several possibilities. The deep-blue state of Rhode Island, for example, where the Party of the People controls both houses of the state's General Assembly and where voters in 2014 chose as their governor the Democrat Gina Raimondo, who was endorsed for the job by President Obama as well as by Hillary Clinton.

"[I]ncome inequality is the biggest problem we face," Raimondo once told the admiring *New York Times* columnist Frank Bruni, and by the standards of the liberal class, she has much to recommend her for tackling that problem. She has degrees from both Harvard and Yale and, like others in our story, was a Rhodes Scholar to boot. She came up through the greatest of the creative industries—by which I mean venture capital—and as Rhode Island's treasurer, she spent the last several years fighting with state employees over retirement issues, reducing their benefits and entrusting the management of their pensions to hedge funds.

Perhaps this doesn't sound to you like much of a way of tackling income inequality, and perhaps it isn't one. But Raimondo also assures the world that when she talks about inequality she means it. She told Bruni that she has confronted investment bankers with these words: "You're some of the smartest, richest people in the world, and you need to be a part of fixing America." Somehow, this rebuke did not frighten them off. Investment bankers were among Raimondo's greatest campaign contributors.[1]

Perhaps they were just showing their enthusiasm for Raimondo's economic plan, which is to enthrone "innovation" as her state's guiding purpose. She has proposed to build a "Rhode Island Innovation Institute"; to guide the young with "entrepreneurial training"; to set up what her economic plan calls a "concierge service" for startups; to take all the great ideas bubbling up in the state and "commercialize" them by "partnering our world-class colleges and universities with the private sector and philanthropic ventures."[2]

Another blue zone that might be worth studying is the extremely Democratic city of Chicago under its current mayor, Rahm Emanuel, who was a close adviser to Presidents Obama and Clinton. Emanuel followed a similar trajectory to Raimondo's: a fancy education, a brief but lucrative spell at an investment bank, conspicuous battles with public employees (in his case, teachers), and various feats of privatization, such as turning over the cleaning of public schools and the collecting of bus fares to contractors.

Just like other leading Democrats, Emanuel did it all in service of the beleaguered middle class, whose vanished job security and fallen standard of living he loves to mourn. His passion for the little guy was rewarded, just as it was in Raimondo's case, with lavish campaign donations from hedge fund managers and then donations from still other hedge fund managers. Like Raimondo, Rahm has made a fetish of innovation, building an Innovation Delivery Team and announcing that the equality-minded city of Chicago today seeks "innovation for all." "When it comes to innovation," Emanuel writes, "Chicago is open for business."[3]

This is a curious pattern, is it not? Blue-state Democrats, with transparent connections to high finance, who have deliberately antagonized public employees, and whose chief economic proposal has to do with promoting "innovation," a grand and promising idea that remains suspiciously vague. None of them can claim that their hands were forced by Republicans. They came up with this program all on their own.

Once we start looking, we see this pattern everywhere. In New York State, for example: Governor Andrew Cuomo's alliance with hedge funds and investment banks is legendary. Financiers support him in his various campaigns; he shows them the love with tax cuts; and they all work harmoniously together on a campaign to reform public education in New York State. The main target of this reform effort, by the way, is that mighty foe, the New York public school teacher, a figure Cuomo has assailed and berated in numerous ways over the years.*

Is there anything toward which the stern-faced, discipline-minded Andrew Cuomo feels tenderly? Why, yes, there is: innovation. Chapter Five of his 2014 campaign book, *Moving the New NY Forward* (throughout which Cuomo refers to himself in the third person), is entirely dedicated to the subject. It tells how his policies have been "encouraging the key collaborations that help innovation clusters grow and deepen." Collaborations such as "Startup NY," a program that uses public universities and tax breaks as entrepreneur bait; it is, Cuomo tells us, "a game-changing initiative" that works by making public universities "into tax-free communities that attract new businesses, venture capital, start-ups, and investments from across the world."[4]

There is also a version that comes from sky-blue Delaware, where Democratic governor Jack Markell—a man much beloved of the East Coast banking and telecom communities—has tried to privatize the Port of Wilmington, has done battle

* Among other things, the Democrat Cuomo has said that his program for teacher evaluation is "the single best thing that I can do as governor that's going to matter long-term to break what is in essence one of the only remaining public monopolies—and that's what this is, it's a public monopoly." See Valerie Straus, "Cuomo Calls Public School System a 'Monopoly' He Wants to Bust," *Washington Post*, October 29, 2014.

with public workers, and has fashioned a role for himself as an info-age thought-leader. Toward the end of 2014, Markell traveled to Stanford University, the center of the knowledge economy, to speak about "Disruptive Innovation," meaning, in this case, web-based companies that displace an existing personal service. The question before policymakers like him, Markell said (according to his prepared text) was "how we can facilitate the success of these innovations." He further wondered how Delawareans might "switch our schools" in order to produce the kind of workforce that innovative companies want and even how they might consult with the "business community to make curricula relevant."[5]

If you think this is about bowing down before the One Percent, you've got Markell all wrong. Writing for the *Atlantic* magazine a few months after his Stanford speech, he called on Americans to recognize "the synergy, rather than the contradiction, between economic growth and economic justice." What he means is that economic justice only comes about through economic growth, and therefore the primary duty of anyone who wants to tackle inequality is "to create a nurturing environment where business leaders and entrepreneurs want to locate and expand."[6]

SHINING CITY ON A HILL

The real spiritual homeland of the liberal class is Boston, Massachusetts. As the seat of American higher learning, it seems unsurprising that it should anchor one of the most Democratic of states, a place where elected Republicans are highly unusual. When other cities and states, made desperate by the advance of deindustrialization, set up fake bohemias and implore their universities to generate profitable ideas, Boston is the place they are trying to emulate, the city where it all works, smoothly and successfully. This is the city that virtually invented the blue-state economic model, in which prosperity arises from higher education and the knowledge-based industries that surround it.

As of 2010, some 152,000 students lived in the city of Boston, making up 16.5 percent of the total population. Boston's metro area encompasses eighty-five private colleges and universities, the greatest concentration of higher-ed institutions in the country—probably in the world. The Boston area has all the ancillary advantages to show for it: a highly educated population, an unusually large number of patents, and more Nobel laureates than any other city in the country.[7] Harvard University, the country's oldest institution of higher learning, is actually mentioned in Massachusetts's 1780 constitution, a document which quaintly declares the commonwealth's interest in promoting "the republic of Letters."

These days, all Americans are interested in higher ed, but not because we want better poets and theologians. We love our universities because we believe they carry a straight-up payoff in dollars. Here, too, Massachusetts is the model. The Boston area has prospered fabulously as knowledge workers have become the country's dominant cohort. In every sort of lab-coat and starched-shirt pursuit the city is well-represented: it has R&D; it has law firms; it has investment banks; it has management consulting; it has a remarkable concentration of life-science businesses.

The coming of post-industrial society* has treated this most ancient of American cities extremely well. Massachusetts routinely occupies the number one spot on the previously

---

* "The coming of post-industrial society" is a phrase that was coined, incidentally, by Daniel Bell, a professor at Harvard.

mentioned State New Economy Index, a measure of how "knowledge-based, globalized, entrepreneurial, IT-driven and innovation-based" a place happens to be. Massachusetts also ranks high on most of Richard Florida's statistical indices of approbation—in 2003, it was number one on the "creative class index," number three in innovation and in high tech[8]—and his many books marvel at the city's concentration of venture capital, its allure to young people, or the time it enticed some firm away from some unenlightened locale in the hinterlands.

Boston's knowledge economy is the best, and it is the oldest. The city's Route 128 corridor was the original model for a suburban tech district, lined ever since it was built with defense contractors and computer manufacturers. The suburbs situated along this golden thoroughfare are among the wealthiest municipalities in the nation, populated by engineers and lawyers and aerospace workers. Their public schools are excellent, their downtowns are cute, and their socially enlightened residents were the prototype for the figure of the "suburban liberal"—the kind of people who voted enthusiastically for McGovern in 1972.[9]

Another prototype: the Massachusetts Institute of Technology, situated in Cambridge, is where began our modern conception of the university as an incubator for business enterprises. According to a report on MIT's achievements in this category, the school's alumni have started nearly 26,000 companies over the years, including Intel, Hewlett Packard, and Qualcomm; if you were to take those 26,000 companies as a separate nation, the report tells us, its economy would be one of the most productive in the world.[10]

Then there are Boston's many biotech and pharmaceutical concerns, grouped together in what is known as the "life sciences super cluster," which, properly understood, is part of an "ecosystem" in which PhDs can "partner" with VCs and in which big pharmaceutical firms can acquire small ones. While other industries shrivel, the Boston super cluster grows, with the life-sciences professionals of the world lighting out for the Athens of America and the massive new "innovation centers" shoehorning themselves one after the other into the crowded academic suburb of Cambridge.[11]

To think about it slightly more critically, Boston is the headquarters for two industries that are steadily bankrupting middle America: big learning and big medicine, both of them imposing costs that everyone else is basically required to pay and yet which increase at a pace far more rapid than wages or inflation. A thousand dollars a pill, thirty grand a semester: the debts that are gradually choking the life out of people where *you* live are what has made *this* city so very rich.

Perhaps it makes sense, then, that another category in which Massachusetts leads the nation is inequality. Once the visitor leaves the brainy bustle of Boston, he discovers that this state is filled with wreckage—with former manufacturing towns, with workers watching their way of life drain away, with cities that are little more than warehouses for people on Medicare.[12] According to one survey, Massachusetts has the eighth-worst rate of income inequality among the states; by another metric it ranks fourth. However you choose to measure the diverging fortunes of the Ten Percent and the rest, Massachusetts always seems to finish among the nation's most unequal places.[13]

SEETHING CITY ON A CLIFF

You can see what I mean when you visit Fall River, an old mill town fifty miles south of Boston. Median household income in that city is $33,000, among the lowest in the state; unemployment is among the highest, 15 percent in March 2014, nearly five years after the recession ended. Twenty-three percent of Fall River's inhabitants live in poverty. The city lost its many fabric-making concerns years ago and with them it lost its reason for being. People have been deserting the place for decades.[14]

Many of the empty factories in which their ancestors worked are still standing, however. Solid nineteenth-century structures of granite or brick, these huge boxes dominate the city visually—there always seems to be one or two of them in the vista, contrasting painfully with whatever colorful plastic fast-food joint has been slapped up next door.

Most of these old factories are boarded up, unmistakable emblems of hopelessness right up to the roof. But the ones that have been successfully repurposed are in some ways even worse, filled as they often are with enterprises offering cheap suits or help with drug addiction. A clinic in the hulk of one abandoned mill has a sign on the window reading, simply, "Cancer & Blood."

The effect of all this is to remind you with every prospect that this is a place and a way of life from which the politicians have withdrawn their blessing. Like so many other American scenes, this one is the product of decades of deindustrialization, engineered by Republicans and rationalized by Democrats. Fifty miles away, Boston is a roaring success, but the doctrine of prosperity that you see on every corner in Boston also serves to explain away the failure you see on every corner in Fall River. This is a place where affluence never returns—not because affluence for Fall River is impossible or unimaginable, but because our country's leaders have blandly accepted a social order that constantly bids down the wages of people like these while bidding up the rewards for innovators, creatives, and professionals.

Even the city's one real hope for new employment opportunities—an Amazon warehouse that is in the planning stages—will serve to lock in this relationship. If all goes according to plan, and if Amazon sticks to the practices it has pioneered elsewhere, people from Fall River will one day get to do exhausting work with few benefits while being electronically monitored for efficiency, in order to save the affluent customers of nearby Boston a few pennies when they buy books or electronics.[15]

But that is all in the future. These days, the local newspaper publishes an endless stream of stories about drug arrests, shootings, drunk-driving crashes, the stupidity of local politicians, and the lamentable surplus of "affordable housing." Like similar places, the town is up to its eyeballs in wrathful bitterness against public workers. As in, Why do they deserve a decent life when the rest of us have no chance at all? It's every man for himself here in a "competition for crumbs," as a Fall River friend puts it.

For all that, it is an exemplary place in one respect: as a vantage point from which to contemplate the diminishing opportunities of modern American life. This is the project of Fall River *Herald News* columnist Marc Munroe Dion, one of the last remaining practitioners of the working-class style that used to be such a staple of journalism in this country. Here in Fall River, the sarcastic, hard-boiled sensibility makes a last stand against the indifference of the affluent world.

Dion pours his acid derision on the bike paths that Fall River has (of course) built for the yet-to-arrive creative class. He cheers for the bravery of Wal-Mart workers who, it appears, are finally starting to stand up to their bosses. He watches a 2012 Obama-Romney debate and thinks of all the people he knows who would be considered part of Romney's lazy 47 percent—including his own mother, a factory worker during

World War II who was now "draining our country dry through the twin Ponzi schemes of Social Security and Medicare."[16]

"To us, it looks as though the city is dissolving," Dion wrote in late 2015. As the working-class apocalypse takes hold, he invites readers to remember exactly what it was they once liked about their town. "Fall River used to be a good place to be poor," he concludes. "You didn't need much education to work, you didn't need much money to live and you knew everybody." As that life has disappeared, so have the politics that actually made some kind of sense; they were an early casualty of what has happened here. Those who still care about the war of Rs and Ds, Dion writes, are practicing "political rituals that haven't made sense since the 1980s, feathered tribesmen dancing around a god carved out of a tree trunk."[17]

THE GREAT ENTREPRENEURIAL AWAKENING

Back in Boston, meanwhile, there is meaning and exciting purpose wherever you look. When I visited, in the spring of 2015, I found a city in the grip of a collective mania, an enthusiasm for innovation that I can only compare to a religious revival, to the kind of crowd-passion that would periodically sweep through New England back in the days when the purpose of Harvard was to produce clergymen, not startups.

The frenzy manifests itself in countless ways. The last mayor of Boston was mourned on his passing as a man who "believed in innovation"; who "brought innovation to Boston." The state's Innovation Institute issues annual reports on the "Massachusetts Innovation Economy"; as innovation economies go, they brag, this one is "the largest in the U.S. when measured as a percent of employment." And of course there are publications that cover this thrumming beehive of novelty: "BostInno," a startup website dedicated to boosting startups, and "Beta Boston," which is a project of the more established but still super-enthusiastic *Boston Globe*.[18]

Fall River is pocked with empty mills, but the streets of Boston are dotted with facilities intended to make entrepreneurship easy and convenient. In my brief time there, I toured innovation center after innovation center, each one featuring brightly colored furniture, open workspaces, inspiring quotations about inventiveness, ping-pong tables and Guitar Hero sets and other instruments of break-time levity (not one of which I ever saw actually being used), and walls that were covered with high-gloss paint meant to be written upon with dry-erase markers.

In addition to these many designated centers of business creativity, I discovered that Boston boasts a full-blown Innovation District, a disused industrial neighborhood that has actually been zoned creative—a projection of the post-industrial blue-state ideal onto the urban grid itself. The heart of the neighborhood is a building called "District Hall"—"Boston's New Home for Innovation"—which appeared to me to be a glorified multipurpose room, enclosed in a sharply angular façade, and sharing a roof with a restaurant that offers "inventive cuisine for innovative people." The wi-fi was free; the screens hung here and there displayed still more famous quotations about inventiveness; and of course the walls were writable; but otherwise it was not much different from an ordinary public library. Aside from not having anything to read, that is.

This was my introduction to the innovation infrastructure of the city, much of it built up by entrepreneurs shrewdly angling to grab a piece of the entrepreneur craze. There are "co-working" spaces like "Workbar" and "WeWork," shared offices for startups that can't afford the real thing. There are startup "incubators" and startup "accelerators," which aim to ease the innovator's eternal struggle with an uncaring public: the Startup Institute, for example, and the famous Mass-Challenge, the "World's Largest Startup Accelerator," which runs an annual competition for new companies and hands out prizes at the end.

The keystone of the inno-structure is the university; indeed, some people in this city of universities have come to believe that the starting-up of companies and the launching of professional careers is the very purpose of higher education. The one equals the other. It is the reason MIT has two associate deans for innovation rather than just one and that its president writes op-eds instructing the nation about the right way "to deliver innovation." It is the reason Northeastern University has a "venture accelerator" it calls IDEA; that Harvard has the famous Innovation Center; that Boston University's business school has a Department of Strategy and Innovation; that its College of Engineering has a Product Innovation Center; and that one of its colleges offers a certificate in Innovation and Entrepreneurship.

At Harvard, where I met innovation guru Clayton Christensen ambling across a parking lot, the dream of being the next Mark Zuckerberg or Bill Gates is almost palpable. As well as the usual incubators and accelerators, the school boasts a $100 million venture capital fund that is focused on commercializing the ideas of former students.[19] One of this fund's press releases quotes a Harvard professor on how this heap of money advances the school's "mission," which today (apparently) includes "marshaling significant resources to help create thrilling companies." The fund holds campus events too, and at the one I attended, at a Harvard dormitory called Eliot House, an audience of undergraduates listened as a professor from a nearby university talked about his many patents in the medical and pharmaceutical fields.

Sometimes the theology of the innovation cult is stated plainly: We know what makes an economy work, and it is *university-driven innovation.* The state's own Department of Housing and Economic Development says it flatly on its website: "The foundation of the Massachusetts economy is the innovative and entrepreneurial capability of its residents to transform existing technologies and industries and create new ones." This is the state government speaking, remember. It continues:

> The pillars of this innovation economy are the state's universities and research institutions, the rich cluster of innovation-based companies, and the sophisticated angel, venture capital and financial services communities that help fund and mentor the pipeline of entrepreneurs. At the heart are the skilled and creative people who choose to make Massachusetts their home.

More typical, however, are tail-chasing proclamations like this one, which can be found on the website of the MIT Innovation Initiative: "The MIT Innovation Initiative is an Institute-wide, multi-year agenda to transform the Institute's innovation ecosystem—internally, around the globe and with its partners—for accelerated impact well into the 21st century."[20]

This sounds distinctly like bullshit, but if MIT wants to think of itself in such a way, that's their business. The problem arises when we enshrine innovation as a public philosophy—

when we look to it as the solution to our economic ills and understand it as the guide for how economies ought to parcel out rewards. To put it bluntly, it is not clear that cheering for innovation in the bombastic way we see in the blue states actually improves the economic well-being of average citizens. For example, the last fifteen years have been a golden age of financial and software innovation, but they have been feeble in terms of GDP growth. In ideological terms, however, innovation definitely works: as a way of excusing soaring inequality and explaining the exalted status of the rich, it is the best we've got.

TRIUMPH OF THE INNO-CRATS

Massachusetts's identification with the Democratic Party is profound and well-known. The home state of the Kennedy family, it has produced two other Democratic presidential nominees in recent decades—Governor Michael Dukakis and Senator John Kerry—and was, as we know, the only state won by George McGovern in 1972. Mitt Romney, the Republican leader in 2012, also hailed from the Bay State, but Massachusetts was none too enthusiastic about his candidacy. When that year's results were in, Romney didn't carry a single county of the state he had once served as governor.

Even when Massachusetts has had Republican governors, it hasn't really mattered. Not only do these lonesome GOPers tend to be just as dedicated as their rivals to the blue-state model, but the Mass legislature remains lopsidedly Democratic no matter what, capable of passing whatever it chooses over the governor's veto. In the time I was writing this book, for example, the state's senate included only six Republican members out of forty—a lopsided normal that is, among other things, an almost perfect mirror image of the Kansas state senate.

Politically speaking, the cult of the knowledge economy goes back a long way in Massachusetts. Many, if not all, of the state's leading politicians have done their part boosting for it over the years, celebrating startups and professing their admiration for the creative class.

Among this honor roll of innovation Democrats, former Governor Deval Patrick, who presided over the Massachusetts government from 2007 to 2015, takes pride of place. He is typical of liberal-class leaders; you might even say he is their most successful exemplar. Everyone seems to like him, even his opponents. He is a witty and affable public speaker as well as a man of competence, a highly educated technocrat who is comfortable in corporate surroundings. Thanks to his upbringing in a Chicago housing project, he also understands the plight of the poor, and (perhaps best of all) he is an honest politician in a state accustomed to wide-open corruption. Patrick was also the first black governor of Massachusetts and, in some ways, an ideal Democrat for the era of Barack Obama—who, as it happens, is one of his closest political allies.[21]

"Our government is incredibly enlightened," said John Harthorne, the head of the MassChallenge startup incubator, in a 2010 TED talk in which he explained why he chose Massachusetts for his planned entrepreneurial utopia. "I would wager a bet that Deval Patrick could go head-to-head on an intelligence test with any other governor."[22]

Patrick's oft-told life story follows the classic Democratic trajectory. A young man with loads of intelligence but no money, Patrick was lifted from nowheresville by an academic scholarship to a fancy prep school. A few years after that, he got into Harvard and, in exactly the manner of the Clinton and Obama stories, the doors to a previously unknown world swung open for him.

He climbed effortlessly through the meritocracy. Law school was also Harvard and, after working for the NAACP for a number of years, Patrick went to Washington and ran the Civil Rights Division of the Justice Department, an important job. In 1994, he won a $54 million settlement in a memorable discrimination suit against Denny's restaurants—among other things, the chain had once refused service to black members of the president's Secret Service unit—and shortly afterward Patrick took up a case that had to do with the subprime real estate lender Long Beach Mortgage. The charge this time was discriminatory lending; eventually Patrick settled this case, too, although for a less impressive sum.

In the Aughts, Deval Patrick became a corporate lawyer, and before long he took the customary next step for Democrats of a certain kind: he went to work for the very corporate outfit he had once sued, taking a seat in 2004 on the board of the parent company of the subprime lender that was now calling itself Ameriquest.

Yes: Ameriquest. In 2004, the company was the country's largest subprime lender and, we now know, a pioneer in the kinds of practices that, after being adopted by many others, came close to destroying the world's financial system.[23] For Ameriquest insiders, packaging up "stated-income" loans and sending them down the Wall Street pipeline was a highly profitable business—an "innovative"[24] business, even; for everyone else on the planet, it was like chugging arsenic. Bankers profited and the world paid—the world is *still* paying. Any politician associated with this sleazy outfit should have had his career terminated immediately and unconditionally.

Patrick dodged that particular bullet, however. He was elected governor of Massachusetts in November of 2006, the year before the first tremors of the coming economic earthquake would be felt. The controversies arising from his service on Ameriquest's board were easily contained.

As governor, Patrick became a kind of missionary for the innovation cult. "The Massachusetts economy is an innovation economy," he liked to declare, and he made similar comments countless times, slightly varying the order of the optimistic keywords: "Innovation is a centerpiece of the Massachusetts economy," et cetera.[25] The governor opened "innovation schools," a species of ramped-up charter school. He signed the "Social Innovation Compact," which had something to do with meeting "the private sector's need for skilled entry-level professional talent."[26] In a 2009 speech called "The Innovation Economy," Patrick elaborated the political theory of innovation in greater detail, telling an audience of corporate types in Silicon Valley about Massachusetts's "high concentration of brainpower" and "world-class" universities, and how "we in government are actively partnering with the private sector and the universities, to strengthen our innovation industries."[27]

What did all of this inno-talk mean? Much of the time, it was pure applesauce—standard-issue platitudes to be rolled out every time some pharmaceutical company opened an office building somewhere in the state.

On other occasions, Patrick's favorite buzzword came with a gigantic price tag, like the billion dollars in subsidies and tax breaks that the governor authorized in 2008 to encourage pharmaceutical and biotech companies to do business in Massachusetts. Lesser achievements included the million dollars Patrick spent "to provide assistance, mentoring and advice to startups and innovation companies" and the other million-and-a-half spent to support startups at the University of Massachusetts at Lowell.[28]

On still other occasions, favoring inno has meant bulldozing the people in its path—for instance, the taxi drivers whose livelihoods are being usurped by ridesharing apps like Uber. When these workers staged a variety of protests in the Boston area, Patrick intervened decisively on the side of the distant software company; apparently convenience for the people who ride in taxis was more important than good pay for people who drive those taxis. It probably didn't hurt that Uber had hired a former Patrick aide as a lobbyist, but the real point was, of course, innovation: Uber was the future, the taxi drivers were the past, and the path for Massachusetts was obvious.

No surprise, then, that the first recipient of the Deval Patrick Commonwealth Innovation Award was none other than Deval Patrick. The prize was bestowed on him in 2014 by MassChallenge's Harthorne, joined by the CEO of Uber, Travis Kalanick, who showed up in order to add some entrepreneurial gravitas to the moment. "I wanted to be here to thank the governor for his leadership, his vision around innovation, around technology, and creating that innovative spirit here in Massachusetts," Kalanick said on that solemn occasion.[29]

Eric Schmidt, the chairman of Google, was also on hand to salute Massachusetts for an "explosion of startups." "We need more entrepreneurs because they create jobs, they solve every known problem," he intoned.

That was a bold claim to make for any social cohort, but John Harthorne went even further: "MassChallenge is an attempt to remind us and refocus as a community and a society on creating value," he declared. "We designed it to help entrepreneurs win because entrepreneurs are the value creators of society."[30]

This was not a political event, strictly speaking, but that last comment was most definitely a political statement, as blunt a justification of class hierarchy as anything I've heard this side of the Tea Party movement.

Three months after the prize ceremony, the Democrat Deval Patrick's second term as governor came to an end. A short while later, he won an even bigger prize: a job as a managing director of Bain Capital, the private equity firm founded by Mitt Romney—and that had been so powerfully denounced by Democrats during the 2012 election. Patrick spoke about the job like it was just another startup: "It was a happy and timely coincidence I was interested in building a business that Bain was also interested in building," he told the *Wall Street Journal*. Romney reportedly phoned him with congratulations.[31]

ENTREPRENEURS FIRST

Another thing that Google's Eric Schmidt said on the occasion of the Deval Patrick Commonwealth Innovation Award was that "if you want to solve the economic problems of the U.S., create more entrepreneurs." That sort of sums up the ideology in this corporate commonwealth. But how has such a doctrine become holy writ in a party dedicated to the welfare of the common man? And how has all this come to pass in the liberal state of Massachusetts?

The answer is that I've got the wrong liberalism. The kind of liberalism that has dominated Massachusetts for the last few decades isn't the stuff of Franklin Roosevelt or the United Auto Workers; it's the Route 128/suburban-professionals variety. Professional-class liberals aren't really alarmed by oversized rewards for society's winners; on the contrary, this seems natural to them—because they *are* society's winners. The liberalism of professionals just does not extend to matters of inequality; this is the area where soft hearts abruptly turn hard.

While Massachusetts is a liberal place—the state that sent Elizabeth Warren to the Senate even—equality issues do not necessarily go over smoothly here. The state's income tax, to mention a particularly egregious example, is a flat tax, with the same rate paid by rich and poor alike. When the Massachusetts legislature raised the minimum wage in 2014, it was only after a huge grassroots campaign made it clear that the issue would soon pass as a ballot initiative anyway. In 2012, the legislature enacted a three-strikes mandatory sentencing law a full twenty years after violent crime peaked in America. And when the legislature limited collective bargaining rights for public employees in 2011, causing columnists across the country to compare Massachusetts to Scott Walker's Wisconsin, Governor Deval Patrick eventually signed on. It was something the state had to do in order to cut costs, people said.

Innovation liberalism is "a liberalism of the rich," to use the straightforward phrase of local labor leader Harris Gruman. This doctrine has no patience with the idea that everyone should share in society's wealth. What Massachusetts liberals pine for, by and large, is a more perfect meritocracy—a system where everyone gets an equal chance and the truly talented get to rise. Once that requirement is satisfied—once diversity has been achieved and the brilliant people of all races and genders have been identified and credentialed—this species of liberal can't really conceive of any further grievance against the system. The demands of ordinary working-class people, Gruman says, are unpersuasive to them: "Janitors, fast-food servers, home care or child care providers—most of whom are women and people of color—they don't have college degrees."

And if you don't have a college degree in Boston—brother, you've got no one to blame but yourself.

10

The Innovation Class

In his 2011 State of the Union Address, President Obama addressed the plight of the country's working people—of Americans who used to be able to get a "job for life" without having a college degree. The president gave a powerful description of what had happened to them with deindustrialization: their shattered towns, their ruined lives, their piddling paychecks.

Ordinarily, this is the point where a Democrat would start laying out his plans to reverse this disaster—a public works program, an end to the exodus of manufacturing, and so on. But not this Democrat. Instead, using the following words, he told those working people that nothing could be done for them: "So yes, the world has changed. The competition for jobs is real." What has happened to working people was simply "real." It was reality. What you do about reality is you get used to it.

But then, a few moments later, Obama pivoted to a happier subject. It was 2011, the recession was technically over, his signature health care proposal had been enshrined in law, and it was time for him to outline the positive economic program that would define the rest of his presidency.

You guessed it: innovation was what we needed more of.

"The first step in winning the future," Obama announced, "is encouraging American innovation." On this matter the president showed no trace of fatalism or resignation before an unalterable reality. On this matter, government could act without any problem. We needed to subsidize innovators, he said, and generously, in order "to spur on more success stories." Since everyone knows that innovation is connected to higher learning, Obama called on students to study harder and for more people to go to college.

I remember listening to him talk about "innovation," and just tuning it out. At the time I thought of innovation as a cliché, a generic faith in progress. But Obama was serious about this stuff. Encouraging innovation was to be his great economic vision, his liberal utopia. Bill Clinton had become identified with the dot-com New Economy by accident; Barack Obama was going to do it deliberately. A month after that State of the Union speech, the White House made it official. "America's future economic growth and international competitiveness depend on our capacity to innovate," a policy document declared. "To win the future, we must out-innovate, out-educate, and out-build the rest of the world."[1]

WHAT'S GOOD FOR GOOGLE

I have described Barack Obama's commitment to traditional Democratic concerns as falling somewhere between indifferent and icy. The financial industry, however, has seen him as a red-hot radical since his first days in office. In 2008, they had sided with Obama over John McCain, but by 2012 Wall Street stood solid behind the Republican Romney.

No matter. By that time, the place once filled by finance in the Democratic imagination had begun giving way to Silicon

Valley, a different "creative-class" industry with billions to give in campaign contributions. Changes in the administration's personnel paralleled the money story: at the beginning of the Obama years, the government's revolving doors had all connected to Wall Street; within a few years, the people spinning them were either coming from or heading toward the West Coast. In 2014, David Plouffe, the architect of Obama's inspiring first presidential campaign, began to work his political magic for Uber. Jay Carney, the president's former press secretary, hired on at Amazon the following year. Larry Summers, for his part, became an adviser for an outfit called OpenGov. Back in Washington, meanwhile, the president established a special federal unit that used Silicon Valley techniques and personnel to revolutionize the government's web presence; starstruck tech journalists call it "Obama's stealth startup."[2]

The mutual attraction between the president and Silicon Valley had actually begun during Obama's first campaign, when he famously used Facebook to connect with the young; his reelection effort was the first to use big data and microtargeting to find swing voters. Some observers like to imagine the Obama campaigns as triumphant social movements; others see them as triumphs of quite a different nature: as electronic victories demonstrating the irresistible power of digital networks.

For people who take the latter view, the Obama presidency is another triumphant iteration of the story Silicon Valley loves to tell itself, the tale of the brilliant startup challenging the slow-moving incumbent, of the scrappy underdog who takes on the conservative dinosaur. Obama is thus said to be, in a typical bit of liberal-class narcissism, "the first tech president." The tech people themselves go further: a prominent Silicon Valley venture capitalist calls him "the greatest president of my lifetime." This is virtually the last surviving form of Obama idealism out there, still going strong in the president's final year in office.*

The administration's relationship with Silicon Valley has never caused the kind of controversy that his former closeness with Wall Street did—probably because Silicon Valley has never contrived to toss the world economy into a wood chipper. Also, it is hard to hate this industry, regardless of what they do. An aura of youthful lightheartedness seems to envelop every interaction between the president and the techies. After all, one notable manifestation of Obama's outreach to this powerful industry was his farcical 2015 interview with YouTube comedienne GloZell Green. Another was this famous exchange with Mark Zuckerberg, in the course of a "town hall" meeting at Facebook headquarters during which Obama proposed that the rich should pay higher taxes than they currently do:

> Zuckerberg: "I'm cool with that."
> Obama: "I know you're OK with that."[3]

In the 1980s and '90s, Silicon Valley was not a particularly Democratic industry. Its libertarianism was well-known and the subject of endless fascination; its leaders were among the richest people in the world; and its great chronicler and booster at the time, George Gilder, was a prominent conservative intellectual whose works had been influential in the Reagan admin-

---

*In truth, the "first tech president" was surely Herbert Hoover, a Stanford graduate who was one of the world's most prominent engineers before becoming president. As secretary of commerce in the 1920s, Hoover took an interest not only in radio but in the brand-new technology of television. The venture capitalist who regards Obama so highly is John Doerr of Kleiner Perkins Caufield & Byers, according to the *Silicon Valley Business Journal*, September 22, 2015.

istration. Gilder's take on Silicon Valley's politics went far beyond the partisan preferences of its leading figures; the primacy of market economics, Gilder said, was actually inscribed in the structure of the microchip itself. By its very architecture, tech was supposed to work against economic authority of the taxing and regulating kind.

Not anymore. Today, Silicon Valley's prosperity is supposed to be the ultimate demonstration of the worthiness of the liberal class. Just look at how the postindustrial society has singled out the educated and the creative, the engineers and the scientists; see how it has showered them with economic rewards beyond imagining. History itself has elevated this one industry over all others, and with it the Democrats have prospered as well, since they long ago positioned themselves as the party of the modern world's winners. You may be drowning, but the rising tide is lifting their boat very nicely.

When Democrats talk about tech, sooner or later they always go back to the search-engine giant Google. In *The Audacity of Hope*, Barack Obama tells how he made a pilgrimage to the company's headquarters as a senator, and as president, according to a *Wall Street Journal* story from 2015, he went on to name-check Google in fully half of his State of the Union speeches. Google employees made up the third-largest group of contributors to Obama's 2012 campaign, and Eric Schmidt pops up in the annals of modern liberalism with a curious regularity. He served on Obama's Transition Economic Advisory Board, for example, and even stood on stage with the president-elect and his economic advisers during Obama's news conference three days after the 2008 election. During the 2012 race, Schmidt advised Obama's team on its famous big-data strategy. In 2015 Schmidt launched a "political technology startup" that is supposed to deliver the latest techniques in digital voter identification to the

Hillary Clinton presidential campaign.[4] He is the liberal class's favorite billionaire.

Schmidt's own writing makes it obvious why he and Google appeal so strongly to the Democrats: the party and the company are traveling parallel cultural tracks. Schmidt begins his 2014 management book, *How Google Works*, by playing up the company's academic pedigree. After launching Google out of a dorm room, the two founders acted "like the professors in their Stanford computer science lab" and gave the smart young professionals they hired maximum freedom. The company they proceeded to build, according to Schmidt, is a "meritocracy," a place where the smartest prevail, where bias and prejudice count for nothing, where the best ideas win out.[5] The ideal economic actor in this context is the one Schmidt calls "the smart creative":

> In our industry . . . she is most likely a computer scientist. . . . But in other industries she may be a doctor, designer, scientist, filmmaker, engineer, chef, or mathematician. She is an expert in doing. . . . She is analytically smart. . . . She is business smart. . . . She is competitive smart. . . . She is user smart. . . . She is curious creative. . . . She is risky creative. . . . She is self-directed creative. . . . She is open creative. . . . She is thorough creative. . . . She is communicative creative.[6]

It is a little tiresome, is it not? We've heard about the learning class, the wired workers, the creative class, and now the "smart creatives." But always it means the same thing: the well-graduated professionals.

In a 2013 public conversation with journalist Walter Isaacson, Schmidt announced that everyone present in the audience was a faithful worshiper "in the church of the knowledge economy," a stage of the development of civilization in which wealth is created by "entrepreneurs and innovation." When Schmidt was asked what America might do to get its economy going again, the answer was predictable: "What we need to do is come up with policies which actually allow the creative people who can create value and invent new things" to do their stuff. If we put these people first, we will enjoy "huge new jobs, huge new choices of employment." As an example of the kind of thing these people might come up with, Schmidt mentioned driverless cars, a legendary Google project that, if it is ever perfected, might make redundant everyone who drives a taxi, limo, or semi-trailer truck. The short-term effect of such an efficiency would obviously be to increase unemployment, not reduce it.

In the bailout days, you might recall, people were outraged to learn that, thanks to the number of federal officials drawn from Goldman Sachs, one of its nicknames was "Government Sachs." Now, though, as the Obama years draw to a close, it's the "United States of Google" that should concern us more. I mean this not just in terms of the revolving door between Google and government or the weird ubiquity of Eric Schmidt in Democratic Party gatherings, but in a grander way as well. Google's vast ambitions often seem to aim at *replacing* government. Its core business, to begin with, is providing services that will be the public utilities of the twenty-first century: searching the Internet, for example, or communicating via email. In my fiscally challenged hometown of Kansas City, Google even got the rights to set up a local fiber-optic broadband system, making Google a public utility by definition, although one that is not obliged to provide service to everyone.[7]

Then there's the spying. In his important 2013 book, *Who Owns the Future?*, the tech writer Jaron Lanier describes the emerging Internet giants of our time as "third-party spy service[s]." Many of them, he argues, make their profits via "the creation of ultrasecret mega-dossiers about what others are doing";[8] everything else they offer—retail sales, connecting with friends, searching the Internet—is secondary.

Back to Google, the liberal class's favorite Internet company: they track your web searches to sell you stuff; they scan your emails to sell you more stuff. For those who are worried about the loss of privacy such practices seem to portend, Eric Schmidt tells us—in a book cowritten with a former adviser to Secretary of State Hillary Clinton—that it's all inevitable anyway, nothing we can do about it. In the future, they write, "by the time a man is in his forties, he will have accumulated and stored a comprehensive online narrative, all facts and fictions, every misstep and every triumph, spanning every phase of his life. Even the rumors will live forever."[9]

The aim of such a statement, obviously, is to make Google's scary business model seem like no big deal, just the future doing what comes naturally. Even so, the scary side keeps peeking through. Schmidt's single most famous statement, delivered to a CNBC talker in 2009, is a direct rationalization of surveillance-for-profit: "If you have something that you don't want anyone to know, maybe you shouldn't be doing it in the first place."[10] The way to react to a world in which you are under observation at all times, in other words, is simply to never step out of line.

INNO-QUALITY

What's wrong with liberals embracing tech and innovation? Surely it's not an expensive passion, like mass transit or Medicare or the hundreds of other things Democrats love to blow money on. Even if it seems like empty rhetoric, there's still a small chance that something good will come of it. Maybe a bunch of students with a really awesome idea will enter a contest at a startup incubator somewhere and win the eye of a friendly billionaire, and next thing you know we'll all be driving cars that don't pollute or something. It might happen. Why not give it a shot?

Besides, nobody is *against* innovation. It is the subject of an enormous literature, a literature that sells well and is almost entirely laudatory. President Obama says innovation is how to "win the future." Democratic governors across the country agree with him. It is as purehearted an undertaking as the liberal mind can conceive.

In fact, the culture of innovation is so pure and so stridently noble that it often sounds like advertising. You hear about the startup that is going to help with sanitation in African cities; the one that's going to print out prosthetic hands for disabled children; the one that's procuring clothes for homeless children. "We're with people who are curing cancer in a different way, and changing banking technology, and helping folks who can't see anymore," says a woman in a short YouTube video about MassChallenge. Inno is going to solve global warming. Inno is coming up with new treatments for autism. Inno is so inherently moral that there is even a UNICEF Innovation team; dial up its homepage and you will encounter the following introductory sentence: "In 2015, innovation is vital to the state of the world's children."

The fog of righteousness surrounding this concept is so thick it allows all manner of absurdly altruistic claims. "Can startups help solve Boston's Biggest Problems?" asked an email I received last spring. Of course they can! The group that sent it, CityStart Boston ("Leveraging the Innovation Community to Tackle Civic Issues"), announced plans to mobilize "the entire Boston startup ecosystem" to "collaborate to develop viable ventures designed . . ." Wait! Stop here for a moment, reader, and try to guess: in what way is the startup ecosystem going to collaborate to solve Boston's biggest problems? If you guessed "to enhance innovation in Boston's neighborhoods," you were right. Startups are going to collaborate to enhance startups.

This struck me as a pretty basic misunderstanding of the way capitalism works—as does, in fact, the whole notion of a nurturing "ecosystem" dedicated to "mentoring" and "incubating" other people's precious startups. (It's a basic misunderstanding of ecology, too, but we will let that pass.) Other than the chance to make some money, why would a capitalist participate in such a thing? If startups really were to encourage other startups, they would be contributing pretty directly to their own competition—and robust competition is precisely what today's thinking business person wants to avoid. The winning quality today is monopoly, not competition.

But this is not a literature given to subtlety or introspection. As the tech writer Evgeny Morozov points out in *To Save Everything, Click Here*, the cult of innovation holds every info-age novelty to be "inherently good in itself, regardless of its social or political consequences." Sure enough, as far as I have been able to determine, few of the people who write or talk about innovation even acknowledge the possibility that innovations might be harmful instead of noble and productive. And yet recent history is littered with exactly such stuff: Innovations that allow companies to spy on us. Innovations that allow terrorist groups to recruit online. Innovations that allowed Enron to do all the fine things it used to do. Come to think of it, the whole economic debacle of the last ten years owes its existence to the financial innovations of the Nineties and the Aughts—the credit default swaps, or the algorithms companies used to hand out mortgage loans—innovations that were celebrated in their day in the same mindlessly positive way we celebrate tech today.

Somehow that stuff never comes up, however. We know what

innovation is about, and it's righteousness and triumph. Success is all you'll find when you riffle through the inno-thoughts produced by the various foundations, institutes, websites, mentors, accelerators, incubators, and entrepreneurship competitions. You hear about startups that just raised $3.1 million in venture capital; startups that are partnering with some more established operation from California; startups that have made their starter-uppers into billionaires.

Inno is about egalitarianism as well. Indeed, as the preeminent expression of the endless American uprising against the entrenched and the powerful, how could it be otherwise? Inequality is, by definition, just one more problem our lovable entrepreneurs have set out to solve, and in the eyes of some, they have succeeded. Marc Andreessen, the famous venture capitalist, has described the vacation rental platform Airbnb as a solution for income inequality. Chris Lehane, a former assistant to Bill Clinton and Al Gore who now does public affairs for Airbnb, has said the same. Objecting to proposed regulation of the company, Lehane has said that cities "understand that in a time of economic inequality, this is a question of whose side are you on: do you want to be on the side of the middle class, or do you want to be opposed to the middle class?"[11]

David Plouffe, Obama's great people-mobilizer, now sells the freelance taxi app Uber with the same workerist pitch he once used to sell Obama: as the solution to the recession. "There are still too many people who aren't feeling the full effects of [the] recovery, and too many people who are still looking for work," he said in a speech at a Washington incubator in 2015. But Uber, for whom anyone could sign up and drive, is "making a real and growing difference when it comes to the challenges of wage stagnation and underemployment."[12]

During a talk at South by Southwest in 2014, Eric Schmidt

lamented the effects of growing inequality on places like San Francisco, where the cost of living has ascended out of most people's reach, but he declared that the solutions "all involve creating more fast-growing startups." The answer, he told the audience, was a society-wide acceptance of inno as a way of life. "Each and every one" of us must be "in favor of more education, more analytical education, more immigration, more capital formation, more creative areas, more areas that are allowed by regulation to be unregulated, so that startups can actually flourish in them, [and] we can get through this."[13]

ATOMIZED LABOR

This is the point where I am supposed to slap down Schmidt, Plouffe, Lehane, and company for suggesting that the solution to inequality is the very thing that is causing the problem. Technology is what has destroyed the livelihoods of so many, I am supposed to say: How can anyone suggest that more of it will make matters better?

But that's not really the question. Oh, it's easy to find people who say that technological advances are the root of inequality, that the massive efficiencies tech creates naturally shift wealth upward and put less-qualified people out of work. Indeed, this has been such a commonplace view for so long that Hillary Clinton herself repeated it in her 1996 book, *It Takes a Village*: "Changes in the economy, such as technological innovations and the globalization of commerce," she wrote, "have combined over the past two decades to produce what economists Robert H. Frank and Philip J. Cook call a 'winner-take-all society.' "[14]

When you think about it this way, it all seems inevitable. Inequality is a thing that is happening to us the way "globalization" or the weather happens to us: as an irresistible force of nature. That it also rewards the meritorious and bids down the lives of the unskilled and the poorly graduated makes it seem even more like an act of God.

In truth, however, nothing is inevitable and very little is new. And tech is no more the root of the problem than are trade or globalization. Many of our most vaunted innovations are simply methods—electronic or otherwise—of pulling off some age-old profit-maximizing maneuver by new and unregulated means. Sometimes they are designed to accomplish things that would be regulated or even illegal under other circumstances, or else they are designed to alter relationships of economic power in some ingenious way—to strip away this or that protection from workers or copyright holders, for example.

Consider the many celebrated business innovations that are, in reality, nothing more than instruments to get around our society's traditional middle-class economic arrangements. Uber is the most obvious example: much of its value comes not from the efficiencies in taxi-hailing that it has engineered but rather from the way it allows the company to circumvent state and local taxi rules having to do with safety and sometimes insurance.

The circumvention strategy is everywhere in inno-land once you start looking for it. Airbnb allows consumers and providers to get around various safety and zoning rules with which conventional hotels must comply.[15] Amazon allows customers in many places to avoid paying sales taxes. The circumvention strategy isn't restricted to software innovations, either. One of the great attractions of credit default swaps—a big financial innovation of the last decade—is that they were completely unregulated.

Monopoly is the telos of innovation, the holy grail fervently sought after by every young coder sweating away in the incubator.

The reason is plain enough: monopoly is the most direct road to profit, and the online world offers countless opportunities to achieve it. Jaron Lanier has described all the ways dominant digital networks can use market power to coerce customers, users, and advertisers; in his account the powerful players are all patterned after Wal-Mart, which so effectively dominates its suppliers and ruins its small-town competitors.[16]

With Amazon, the Wal-Mart comparison is obvious. The giant online retailer has used its position as the country's dominant bookstore to dictate terms to book publishers and to punish those who won't play ball. During its dispute with Hachette in 2014, the retailer actually singled out certain authors (namely, one Paul Ryan) for preferential treatment. Nice, friendly Google does similar things with its advertisers and was investigated for the practice by the Federal Trade Commission in 2012; the FTC's staff decided that Google's practices did "real harm to consumers and to innovation in the online search and advertising markets." No charges were filed in either case.[17]

The pharmaceutical industry, one of the great gushing sources of inno-worship, enjoys an even closer relationship with monopoly. They must be granted the power to charge whatever they want for their patented drugs, they insist, or else innovation will cease. This is the logic that has permitted Big Pharma to raise prices so emphatically in recent years, even on drugs that are many decades old. Monopoly is what makes innovation possible; take it away and the genius factory will close down.[18]

But it is in the endless conflict between management and labor that our innovation class has shown true genius. It is a matter of legal record that, for years, the CEOs of Apple, Intel, Google, Pixar, and other Silicon Valley firms operated something very much like a cartel against their own employees. In a scandal that journalists now call "the Techtopus," these worthies agreed to avoid recruiting one another's tech workers and thus keep those workers' wages down across the industry. In 2007, in one of the most famous chapters of the Techtopus story, the famous innovator Steve Jobs emailed Eric Schmidt, demanding that this CEO and friend of top Democrats do something about a Google recruiter who was trying to lure an employee away from Apple. Two days later, according to the reporter who has studied the case most comprehensively, Schmidt wrote back to Jobs to tell him the recruiter had been fired. Jobs then forwarded Schmidt's email around with this comment appended: ":)"[19]

Amazon, meanwhile, is famous for devising ways to goad its executives into fighting with one another—engaging in what the *New York Times* calls an "experiment in how far it can push white-collar workers"—while its blue-collar workers, often recruited through local temp agencies, are electronically tracked so that their efficiency is maximized as they go about assembling items in the company's enormous fulfillment centers.[20] For the rest of us, Amazon has come up with a nifty device for casual employment called "the Mechanical Turk," in which tasks that can't be done by computers are tossed to the reserve army of the millions, who receive pennies for their trouble.

This last is a good introduction to the so-called sharing economy—"sharing" because you're using your own car or apartment or computer, not your employer's—which has been one of the few robustly growing employment opportunities of the Obama years. The magic derives from the way just about anyone can sign up at one of these sharing companies and work as a sort of temp, only hooked up with the client and employer via software, which makes it all digital and innovative and convenient. In nearly every other way, however, the sharing economy is one of the most lopsided, antiworker employment schemes to come down the pike in many years. The costs and risks associated with this industry—insurance, owning a car, saving for sickness and retirement—are all loaded onto the shoulders of the worker, and yet the innovator back in California who has written the software still helps himself to a large cut of whatever the proceeds of your labor happen to be. It is "every man for himself" as a national employment strategy.

Organized labor was the great force of the Roosevelt years, but it is *atomized labor*, cheered for and pushed by Democrats like Plouffe and Lehane, that will forever shape American memories of the Obama years. Of the companies that are poised to profit on this coming war of all against all, Uber is the most famous; as I have mentioned, it invites each of us to spend our spare time as hacks for hire. But with the magic of innovation, virtually any field can join the race to the bottom. There's Law-Trades, a sort of Uber for lawyers, and HouseCall, an Uber for "home service professionals." Everyone's favorite is something called TaskRabbit, which allows people to farm out odd jobs to random day laborers, whom the app encourages you to imagine as cute, harmless bunnies.

"Crowdworking" is the most startling variation on the theme, a scheme that allows anyone, anywhere to perform tiny digital tasks in exchange for extremely low pay. This way, everyone can become part of the great "on-demand labor pool" of millions, coming together to parse data and make Silicon Valley's bottom line that much fatter. The CEO of a crowdworking company called CrowdFlower explains how the magic is done:

> Before the Internet, it would be really difficult to find someone, sit them down for ten minutes and get them to work for you, and then fire them after those ten minutes. But with technology, you can actually find them, pay them the tiny

> amount of money, and then get rid of them when you don't need them anymore.[21]

By the way, the CEO who reportedly spoke those lines—a young gentleman named Lukas Biewald—is an Obama donor who, according to a post on the CrowdFlower blog, was asked in 2012 to help out with the Big Data part of the president's reelection campaign.[22]

TECH AS CULTURE

Few of the innovations I have mentioned here were laudable—at least, not in the ecstatic UNICEF way people celebrate inno these days. The more important point is that *none of them were inevitable*. Government could easily have prevented or at least mitigated every single one of the developments I have described; it was fully within the power of Washington or our various state governments. Indeed, when a company's business strategy consists of some novel way to get around safety regulations, or antitrust statutes, or basic labor law, it is the government's duty to do something about it.

The Obama administration's Justice Department came into office promising stern action against corporate cartels that fixed prices, which is precisely what the Silicon Valley Techtopus seems to have been doing with tech workers; an official from the Antitrust Division had even announced in a 2009 speech that "the Division has long advocated that the most effective deterrent for hard core cartel activity, such as price fixing, bid rigging, and allocation agreements, is stiff prison sentences."[23]

Not this time. When the Justice Department learned about

the conspiracy to suppress tech workers' wages in 2010, it did just about the same thing it had done with the "Too Big to Jail" banks: it filed a civil suit and boldly extracted from the tech companies in question . . . a promise not to do it again, for five years. (The affected tech workers had more success on their own, filing a class-action lawsuit against four of the big Silicon Valley companies; it was settled for $415 million in 2015.)[24]

Let's look again at Uber, the machine for inequality, which has had a damaging effect on many people who drive taxis for a living. It also happens to be a clever innovation. This has made it a basic political test for Democrats: Should they support the company with its ingenious software, or the working people whose livelihoods it threatens?

Some cities in Belgium, Canada, Germany, and India have answered the question by banning Uber. France has declared certain Uber operations illegal and at one point arrested several Uber executives. In New York, Mayor Bill de Blasio chose to side with taxi drivers, calling for a cap on the number of Uber drivers allowed in the city. But Governor Andrew Cuomo got the last word, forcing de Blasio to back down and saluting Uber as "one of these great inventions, startups, of this new economy . . . it's offering a great service for people, and it's giving people jobs."[25]

Had Andrew Cuomo chosen to require Uber to play by the existing rules in New York, he could have done so. Had the Federal Trade Commission wished to rein in exorbitant price increases in certain prescription drugs, they could have done so. Had the FTC chosen to lower the boom on Google, that too appears to have been within its power. Why didn't the Party of the People try? Was that old ocean liner just too hard to turn?

I doubt it. That Google hired several of President Obama's former advisers probably had something to do with it. But a more basic reason is that many of our leading Democrats know you don't treat blue-state innovators in this way. They lead clean industries, virtuous industries—knowledge industries. They represent the learning class, the creative class. They are the future, and what you do with the future is you win it.

In reality, there is little new about this stuff except the software, the convenience, and the spying. Each of the innovations I have mentioned merely updates or digitizes some business strategy that Americans learned long ago to be wary of. Amazon updates the practices of Wal-Mart, for example, while Google has dusted off corporate behavior from the days of the Robber Barons. What Uber does has been compared to the every-man-for-himself hiring procedures of the pre-union shipping docks, while TaskRabbit is just a modern and even more flexible version of the old familiar temp agency I worked for back in the 1980s. Together, as Robert Reich has written, all these developments are "the logical culmination of a process that began thirty years ago when corporations began turning over full-time jobs to temporary workers, independent contractors, free-lancers, and consultants."[26] This is atavism, not innovation. It has not reversed the trends of the last thirty years; it has accelerated them. And if we keep going in this direction, it will one day reduce all of us to day laborers, standing around like the guys outside the local hardware store, hoping for work.

Technological innovation is not the reason all this is happening, just as the atomic bomb was not the cause of World War II: it is the latest weapon in an age-old war. Technological innovation is not what is hammering down working peoples' share of what the country earns; technological innovation is the excuse for this development. Inno is a fable that persuades us to accept economic arrangements we would otherwise regard as unpleasant or intolerable—that convinces us that the very particular configuration of economic power we inhabit is in fact a neutral matter of science, of nature, of the way God wants things to be. Every time we describe the economy as an "ecosystem" we accept this point of view. Every time we write off the situation of workers as a matter of unalterable "reality" we resign ourselves to it.

In truth, we have been hearing some version of all this innotalk since the 1970s—a snarling Republican iteration, which demands our submission before the almighty entrepreneur; and a friendly and caring Democratic one, which promises to patch us up with job training and student loans. What each version brushes under the rug is that it doesn't have to be this way. Economies aren't ecosystems. They aren't naturally occurring phenomena to which we must learn to acclimate. Their rules are made by humans. They are, in a word, political. In a democracy we can set the economic table however we choose.

"Amazon is not happening to bookselling," Jeff Bezos of Amazon likes to say. "The future is happening to bookselling." And what the future wants just happens to be exactly what Amazon wants. What an amazing coincidence.

As long as we continue to believe such statements, for exactly that long will the situation of average Americans continue to deteriorate and inequality to worsen.

11

Liberal Gilt

We have now observed several instances of the cycle of enthusiastic idealism that propels modern Democratic politics, as well as the lagging cycle of disappointment that invariably follows it. Both cycles are highly predictable given the economic desperation of ordinary Americans—and so is the next stage in the process: the transfer of this passionate idealism to Hillary Clinton. It is, as they say, her turn. After losing to Barack Obama in the Democratic primaries in 2008, she waited patiently for the years to pass, serving as his secretary of state, doing good works with the Clinton Foundation, and now she gets both to run for the presidency and to be the vessel of liberal hopes. It is to her that we will all soon look for our salvation.

As Hillary Clinton has no doubt noticed, the circumstances of 2016 present a striking similarity to the ones that put her husband in the White House in 1992. Again Americans are outraged at the way the middle class is falling to pieces and at the greed of the people on top. The best-seller lists are once again filled with books about inequality. Today Americans are working even harder for even less than when Bill Clinton made "working harder for less" his campaign catchphrase. The way

Hillary Clinton—the way any Democrat—will play such a situation is extremely easy to guess.

"You see corporations making record profits, with CEOs making record pay, but your paychecks have barely budged," Hillary declared in June 2015, launching her presidential campaign. "Prosperity can't be just for CEOs and hedge fund managers." On she talked as the months rolled by, pronouncing in her careful way the rote denunciations of Wall Street that were supposed to make the crowds roar and the financiers tremble.

That those financiers and hedge fund managers do not actually find Hillary's populism menacing is a well-established fact. Barack Obama's mild rebukes caused Wall Street to explode in fury and self-pity back in 2009 and 2010; the financiers pouted and cried and picked up their campaign donations and went home. But Hillary's comments provoke no such reaction. Only a few days before she launched her campaign, for example, John Mack, the former CEO of Morgan Stanley, was asked by a host on the Fox Business channel whether her populist talk was causing him to reconsider his support for her. On the contrary: "To me, it's all politics," he responded. "It's trying to get elected, to get the nomination."[1]

"None of them think she really means her populism," wrote a prominent business journalist in 2014 about the bankers and Hillary. The Clinton Foundation has actually held meetings at the headquarters of Goldman Sachs, he points out. He quotes another Morgan Stanley officer who believes that "like her husband, [Hillary] will govern from the center, and work to get things done, and be capable of garnering support across different groups, including working with Republicans."[2]

How are the bankers so sure? Possibly because they have read the memoirs of Robert Rubin, the former chairman of Citibank, the former secretary of the Treasury, the former co-head of Goldman Sachs. One of the themes in this book is Rubin's constant war with the populists in the Party and in the Clinton administration—a struggle in which Hillary was an important ally. Rubin tells how Hillary once helped him to get what he calls "class-laden language" deleted from a presidential speech and also how she helped prevent the Democrats from appealing to "class conflict" in a general election—on the grounds that it "is not an effective approach" to the "swing voters in the middle of the electorate."[3]

Trying to figure out exactly where Hillary Clinton actually stands on political issues can be crazy-making. As a presidential candidate, for example, she says she deplores the revolving door between government and Wall Street because it destroys our "trust in government"—a noble sentiment. When she ran the State Department, however, that door spun on a well-lubricated axis. As a presidential candidate, she opposes Obama's Trans-Pacific Partnership treaty, as do I; as secretary of state, however, she helped negotiate it. As a presidential candidate in 2008, she claimed to oppose NAFTA, the first great triumph of the (Bill) Clinton administration; not only had she supported it earlier, but as a U.S. senator, she had voted for numerous Bush administration free-trade treaties.[4]

The same is true nearly wherever you look. The great imprisonment mania of the 1990s, for example: As first lady, Hillary's appetite to incarcerate was unassuageable. "We need more and tougher prison sentences for repeat offenders," she said in 1994, kicking off a bloodthirsty call for more three-strikes laws. On another day, seven years later, Senator Hillary Clinton could be found urging law students to "Dare to care about the one and a half million children who have a parent in jail."[5] Even the well-being of poor women and children, Hillary's great signature issue in her youth, had to hit the bricks when the time arrived in

1996 for welfare reform, a measure she not only supported but for which she says she lobbied.[6]

As a presidential candidate in 2008, Hillary liked to identify herself with working-class middle Americans; as a lawyer in Arkansas in the Eighties, however, she was a proud member of the board of directors of Wal-Mart, the retailer that has acted on middle America like a neutron bomb. As a student leader in the Sixties, she opposed the Vietnam War; as a senator in the Bush years, she voted for the Iraq War; as a presidential candidate, she has now returned to her roots and acknowledges that vote was wrong.

On the increasingly fraught matter of the sharing economy—the battle of Silicon Valley and Uber versus the workers of the world—Hillary actually tried to have it both ways in the same speech in July 2015. She first said she approved of how these new developments were "unleashing innovation," but also allowed that she worried about the "hard questions" they raised. That was tepid, but it was not tepid enough. Republicans pounced; they harbored no reservations at all about innovation, they said. Hillary's chief technology officer was forced to double down on her employer's wishy-wash: "Sharing economy firms are disrupting traditional industries for the better across the globe," she wrote, but workers still needed to be protected. This dutiful inhabitant of Hillaryland then rushed to remind "the tech community" of the ties that bound them to the Democrats: immigration, environment, and gay marriage. Republicans? Ugh: "very few technologists I know stand with them."[7]

Times change. Politicians compromise. Neither is a sin. The way Hillary herself puts it is that while her principles never waver, "I do absorb new information."[8] Still, her combination is unique. She is politically capricious, and yet (as we shall see) she maintains an image of rock-solid moral commitment. How these two coexist is the mystery of Hillary Rodham Clinton.

"I'M GOOD, I'M GOOD, I'M GOOD"

The one thing about Hillary that everyone knows and on which everyone agrees is how smart she is. She is an accomplished professional, a brilliant leader of a brilliant generation, a woman of obvious intelligence.

Rather than investigate her record, biographies of Hillary Clinton read like high-achieving résumés. They tell us about her accomplishments in high school in the Chicago suburbs, how she was student-body president at Wellesley College, what she said in her bold graduation speech in 1969, and how that speech was covered by *Life* magazine, which was in turn excited by the "top students" around the country who were rebelling even as they graduated. Then: the fine law schools into which Hillary was accepted, her deeds at the Yale law review, how she made the shortlist of lawyers invited to work on the Nixon impeachment inquiry, and how she could easily have bagged a partnership at a prestigious law firm but—in a risky gambit marveled at by everyone who writes about her—how she chose instead to move to Arkansas and join forces with that other prominent leader of the Sixties generation, Bill Clinton, who had managed to compile an impressive résumé in his own right.

Her biographers write about Hillary this way because her successes in the upper reaches of the meritocracy are what make her a leader. Indeed, Hillary talks this way herself. In 2001, when she was a U.S. senator from New York, she was still telling the story of how she made the hard choice between Yale and Harvard law schools. The theme of her 2008 presidential campaign was opening the most important job in the world to talent. As secretary of state in the Obama years, she repeated many times her belief that "talent is universal, but opportunity is not." It is her motto, her credo, her innermost faith: that smart people are born free but everywhere they are in chains, prevented by unfair systems from rising to the top.[9] Meritocracy is simply who she is.

The other persistent refrain in accounts of Hillary Clinton's life is her dedication to high principle. Again, all her biographers agree on this, everyone knows it is true. The way Hillary negotiates between high-minded principle and the practical demands of the world is a theme that weaves itself into her story just as growth and self-actualization flavor biographies of her husband. It comes naturally to everyone who thinks about her, and it has since the very beginning, since her college commencement speech in 1969 rebuked those who thought of politics as "the art of the possible" rather than "the art of making what appears to be impossible, possible."

"Hillary always *knew* what was right," declares biographer Gail Sheehy. "Over the long haul," observes biographer David Brock, "she had no intention of conceding the substantive issues or bedrock principles to the other side." Her 2008 campaign adviser Ann Lewis once described Hillary's political philosophy with this inspirational-poster favorite: "Do all the good you can, by all the means you can, in all the ways you can, in all the places you can, at all the times you can, to all the people you can, as long as ever you can."[10]

"Hillary's ambition was always to do good on a huge scale," writes biographer Carl Bernstein of her college years, "and her nascent instinct, so visible at Wellesley, to mediate principle with pragmatism—without abandoning basic beliefs—seemed a powerful and plausible way of achieving it."[11]

That's some slippery stuff right there, but you get the feeling that Bernstein is doing his best. After all, describing someone's "ambition to do good on a huge scale" is like analyzing the harmonies of the spheres: it's not easy. And it gets even less easy when Bernstein's heroine goes to Yale Law School. There, the journalist writes, "she was a recognizable star on campus, much discussed among the law school's students, known as politically ambitious, practical, and highly principled."[12]

As first lady in the 1990s, Hillary Clinton went on to enthuse about some respectable something called the "Politics of Meaning" and was profiled in the *New York Times Magazine* as "Saint Hillary," a woman who "would like to do good, on a grand scale, and she would like others to do good as well." In a presidential primary debate in 2015, she announced, "I'm not taking a back seat to anybody on my values [and] my principles."*

If you're like me, all this talk of rock-solid principles makes you immediately wonder what those principles are. Young Hillary was "known" for them; she had no intention of ever conceding them; she takes second place to nobody in honoring them; but what they actually *were* is always left unspoken. The "politics of meaning," yes, we remember hearing that phrase, but meaning *what?* What did it all mean?

---

*Maintaining her façade of goodness and moral principle has also brought Hillary Clinton occasional distress. One such instance, according to her biographer Carl Bernstein, was the matter of the misplaced billing records from her lawyer days, which became such a sought-after object during the Whitewater investigation of the mid-1990s. Hillary didn't want the billing records made public, Bernstein suggests, because they were—to repeat the words of the unnamed Clinton administration lawyer whom Bernstein quotes—"professionally embarrassing" to her. The reason: They showed what an ordinary life she led. "Her law practice, for example," Bernstein's source continues. "The billing records are embarrassing, maybe for what they show about how she spent her time, which was not in any kind of high-minded or incredibly intellectual pursuit of the law, which is sort of her reputation, but [these were] small-potatoes deals." (Bernstein, *A Woman in Charge*, p. 454, brackets in original.)

NO CEILINGS

Nothing is more characteristic of the liberal class than its members' sense of their own elevated goodness. It is a feeling that overrides any particular inconsistency or policy failing—the lousy deeds of Bill Clinton, for example, do not reduce his status in this value system. Still, it is not merely the shrill self-righteousness that conservatives love to deplore. Nor is it simply the air of militant politeness you encounter in places like Boston or Bethesda. It is more rarefied than that, a combination of virtue and pedigree, a matter of educational accomplishment, of taste, of status . . . of professionalism.

When this value system judges Hillary to be a woman of high idealism, what is being referenced might more accurately be called the atmosphere of acute virtue—of pure, serene, Alpine propriety—through which her campaign and, indeed, her person seems to move at all times.

I myself got a whiff of this intoxicating stuff the day after International Women's Day in March 2015, when I attended a Clinton Foundation production at the Best Buy theater in New York City called "No Ceilings." The happening I am describing wasn't a campaign event—the 2016 race had not started at that point—nor was it a panel discussion, as there were no disagreements among participants or questions from the audience. Instead, it was a choreographed presentation of various findings having to do with women's standing in the world. But if you paid attention, it provided a way to understand Hillary's genuine views on the great social question before the nation—the problem of income inequality.

Onto the stage before us came Hillary Clinton, the Democratic Party's heiress apparent; Melinda Gates, the wife of the richest man in the world (the event was a coproduction with the

Bill & Melinda Gates Foundation); various NGO executives; a Hollywood celebrity; a Silicon Valley CEO; a best-selling author; an expert from Georgetown University; a Nobel Prize winner; and a large supporting cast of women from the third world. Everyone strode with polished informality about the stage, reading their lines from an invisible teleprompter. Back and forth, the presenters called out to one another in tones of gracious supportiveness and flattery so sweet it bordered on idolatry.

In her introduction to the event, for example, the TV star America Ferrera, who has appeared at many Clinton events both philanthropic and political, gave a shout-out to the "incredible women who have brought us all here today" and the "amazing girls" whose conversation she had been permitted to join. Then Chelsea Clinton, who announced herself "completely awed" by the "incredible swell of people and partners" who had participated in some event the previous day, invited us to harken to the "inspiring voices of leaders, of communities, of companies, of countries."[13]

Those were just the first few minutes of the event. It kept on like that for hours. When someone's "potential" was mentioned, it was described as "boundless." People's "stories" were "compelling," when they weren't "inspiring," or "incredible," or "incredibly inspiring." A Kenyan activist was introduced as "the incomparable." A man thanked the Clinton Foundation for its leadership, and Hillary Clinton thanked someone for saying that women were harmed more by climate change than were men.

The real star of this show was the creative innovator, the figure who crops up whenever the liberal class gets together to talk about spreading the prosperity around more fairly. In this case, the innovations being hailed were mainly transpiring in the third world. "Every year, millions and millions of women everywhere are empowering themselves and their communities by finding unique, dynamic, and productive ways to enter the workforce, start their own businesses and contribute to their economies and their countries," said Chelsea Clinton, introducing an "inspiring innovator and chocolatier" from Trinidad.

Melinda Gates followed up the chocolatier's presentation by heaping up even more praise: "She was an amazing businesswoman, you can see why we all find her so inspiring." Then, a little later on: "Entrepreneurship is really vital to women. . . . It's also their ability to advance into leadership roles in corporations. And corporations play such a big role in the global economy."

They sure do. The presence of Melinda Gates should probably have been a clue, but still I was surprised when the rhetoric of idealistic affirmation expanded to cover technology, meaning social media. Participants described it as one of the greatest liberators of humanity ever conceived. Do I exaggerate? Not really. Hear, again, the words of America Ferrera:

> We're hearing these stories for the first time because of a new thing called social media. . . . Twenty years ago, in many communities across the world, women and girls were often virtually silenced, with no outlet and no resources to raise their voices, and with it, themselves. And that's huge. One out of every two people, 50 percent of the world's population, without a voice. Social media is a new tool to amplify our voices. No matter which platform you prefer, social media has given us all an extraordinary new world, where anyone, no matter their gender, can share their story across communities, continents, and computer screens. A whole new world without ceilings.

"Techno-ecstatic" was the term I used to describe rhetoric like this during the 1990s, and now, two crashes and countless tech scandals later, here it was, its claims of freedom-through-smartphones undimmed and unmodified. This form of idealism had survived everything: mass surveillance, inequality, the gig economy. Nothing could dent it.

Roughly speaking, there were two groups present at this distinctly first-world gathering: hard-working women of color and authoritative women of whiteness. Many of the people making presentations came from third-world countries—a midwife from Haiti, a student from Afghanistan, the chocolate maker from Trinidad, a former child bride from India, an environmental activist from Kenya—while the women anchoring this swirling praise-fest were former Secretary of State Hillary Clinton and the wealthy foundation executive Melinda Gates.

What this event suggested is that there is a kind of naturally occurring solidarity between the millions of women at the bottom of the world's pyramid and the tiny handful of women at its very top. The hardship those third-world women have endured and the entrepreneurial efforts they have undertaken are powerful symbols of the struggle of American professional women to become CEOs of Fortune 500 companies (one of the ambitions that was discussed in detail at the event) or of a woman to be elected president.

GOOD THINGS ARE GOOD

That was my first experience of the microclimate of virtue that surrounds Hillary Rodham Clinton. The mystic bond between high-achieving American professionals and the planet's most victimized people, I would discover, is a recurring theme in her life and work.

But it is not her theme alone. Regardless of who leads it, the professional-class liberalism I have been describing in these pages seems to be forever traveling on a quest for some place of greater righteousness. It is always engaged in a search for some subject of overwhelming, noncontroversial goodness with which it can identify itself and under whose umbrella of virtue it can put across its self-interested class program.

There have been many other virtue-objects over the years: people and ideas whose surplus goodness could be extracted for deployment elsewhere. The great virtue-rush of the 1990s, for example, was focused on children, then thought to be the last word in overwhelming, noncontroversial goodness. Who could be *against kids*? No one, of course, and so the race was on to justify whatever your program happened to be in their name. In the course of Hillary Clinton's 1996 book, *It Takes a Village*, the favorite rationale of the day—think of the children!—was deployed to explain her husband's crime bill as well as more directly child-related causes like charter schools.

You can find dozens of examples of this kind of liberal-class virtue-quest if you try, but instead of listing them, let me go straight to the point: This is not politics. It's an imitation of politics. It *feels* political, yes: it's highly moralistic, it sets up an easy melodrama of good versus bad, it allows you to make all kinds of judgments about people you disagree with, but ultimately it's a diversion, a way of putting across a policy program while avoiding any sincere discussion of the policies in question. The virtue-quest is an exciting moral crusade that *seems* to be extremely important but at the conclusion of which you discover you've got little to show for it besides NAFTA, bank deregulation, and a prison spree.

This book is about Democrats, but of course Republicans do

it too. Over the years, the culture wars unfolded in precisely the same way as the liberal virtue-quest: as an exciting ersatz politics that seemed to be really important but at the conclusion of which voters discovered they had little to show for it all besides more free-trade agreements, more bank deregulation, and a different prison spree.

CHAMPION OF THE ONE TRUE INTERNET

The Clinton Foundation event gives us context in which to understand Hillary's most important moment as a maker of policy—her four years as Barack Obama's secretary of state. Although her purview was foreign policy, we can nevertheless see from her deeds at State how she thinks and the ways she intends to tackle inequality. The themes should be familiar by now: the Internet, innovation, and getting everyone hooked up to the financial industry.

In emphasizing these aspects of her tenure at the State Department, I do not mean to brush off the better-known diplomatic triumphs that Hillary Clinton engineered, like the international effort to isolate Iran. Nor do I mean to soft-pedal her better-known diplomatic failures, like the cataclysmic civil war in Libya, a conflict Clinton worked so hard to stoke that the *Washington Post* in 2011 called it "Hillary's War."[14]

The concern of this book is ideas, not diplomacy, and one of the biggest ideas Hillary Clinton proposed at State was what she called "Internet Freedom." This was to be the very "cornerstone of the 21st century statecraft policy agenda," according to a State Department press release, and Secretary Clinton returned to the principle frequently. In a high-profile speech in January of 2010, she declared that, henceforth, the United States "stand[s] for a single internet where all of humanity has equal access to knowledge and ideas." Committing ourselves to defending this unified Internet from all who would censor it, she continued, was a logical extension of what Franklin Roosevelt had been after with his Four Freedoms; it wasn't all that much different from the UN's Universal Declaration of Human Rights, either. To Clinton it was a matter of direct moral simplicity: open expression on the Internet equals freedom; evil regimes are those that try to suppress that freedom with things like "a new information curtain."[15]

Understanding the Internet as a force of pure nobility is a revered pundit tradition in the United States, and in the days when Clinton declared humanity's Internet Freedom, those ideals were on the lips of every commentator. In the summer of 2009, the Iranian regime had violently suppressed a series of enormous street protests—protests that, the American pundit-community immediately determined, had been as much a testament to the power of Twitter as they were about any local grievance having to do with Iran itself. The so-called Twitter Revolution fit neatly into the beloved idea that new communications technologies—technologies invented or dominated by Americans, that is—militate by their very nature against dictatorships, a market-populist article of faith shared everywhere from Wall Street to Silicon Valley.[16]

Then there was the economic side of the single, unified Internet, and it, too, was all about liberation. For the "people at the bottom of the world's economic ladder," Hillary Clinton averred on that day in 2010, the Internet was a savior. She declared that a connection to it was "an on-ramp to modernity." The fear that the Internet might create "haves and have-nots" was false, she continued; she knew of farmers in Kenya who were using "mobile banking technology" and of "women entrepreneurs" somewhere else in Africa who were getting "microcredit loans" and she also knew about a doctor who used a search engine to diagnose a disease.[17] I guess she hadn't heard about what was happening to journalists or musicians or taxi drivers in her own country, but I quibble; as long as this technology was free, anyone could see that it pushed in one direction only, and that was up.

Clinton spent much of her time as secretary of state leading the fight for this noble cause. "States, terrorists, and those who would act as their proxies must know that the United States will protect our networks," she said in 2010. At a conference in The Hague in 2011, she took the stage to warn against evil regimes that "want to create national barriers in cyberspace" and to sympathize with business leaders facing tough questions like "Is there something you can do to prevent governments from using your products to spy on their own citizens?" She was introduced on that occasion by Google's Eric Schmidt, who praised her as "the most significant secretary of state since Dean Acheson"; Hillary reciprocated by calling Schmidt a "co-conspirator" and welcomed the participation of his company, which she said was "co-hosting" the freedom-ringing proceedings.[18]

As everyone would soon learn with the help of a National Security Agency contractor named Edward Snowden, to understand the Internet in terms of this set-piece battle of free speech versus censorship was to miss the point entirely. There's something else the Internet makes it easy for governments to do—something called "mass surveillance," and, we later learned, the very government Hillary Clinton served was the one doing it. Not some despot in Damascus. Not some terrorist in Tripoli. Her government.

Her government didn't care what you posted in the chat room or whether you talked on your phone all day long—they just wanted to watch and listen as you did. They recorded people's calls. They read people's email. They spied on the president of Mexico. They spied on French business leaders. They listened to the phone calls of some thirty-five world leaders. They hacked the cellphones of entire nations. They spied on low-level foreign diplomats in order to swindle them at the bargaining table.

And Hillary would be spied upon in turn. Her and her colleagues' emails would all be made public, either by foreign hackers or by WikiLeaks or by the State Department itself, which rudely published the correspondence Hillary tried to keep private with a homemade server. As Hillary's presidential ambitions shrank under this exposure, it sometimes seemed as if history itself was trying to make her understand that smartphones and social media weren't merely devices of liberation. That access to the Internet was not all one needed to bring a country from a backwater to American-style prosperity.

Take the case of Western intervention in Libya, which her State Department once regarded as something of a triumph. According to a 2011 State Department press release, the Libya intervention showed how we could achieve "post-conflict stabilization using information networks":

> A leadership team at the ministry formed a plan called "e-Libya" to increase Internet access in the country and leverage this information network as a tool to grow new businesses, deliver government services, improve education, and interconnect Libyan society. Since the Qaddafi regime denied Internet access to more than 90% of Libyans, the potential for positive social, political, and economic change through access to information networks is considerable. The State Depart-

> ment led a delegation of experts to Tripoli to provide concrete expertise in network architecture, law and policy, e-commerce, and e-government for the e-Libya plan. It may become a model for "digital development" through technical knowledge exchange and partnerships across the public and private sectors.[19]

And then: Libya sank into civil war, with armed factions, outrageous brutality, and fleeing refugees. Making a stand for Internet Freedom sounded like a noble goal back in 2011—a cheap way to solve Libya's problems, too—but in retrospect it was hardly sufficient to quell the more earthly forces that roiled that unhappy land.

"THE HILLARY DOCTRINE"

The other great diplomatic initiative during Hillary Clinton's years as secretary of state was to recast the United States as the world's defender of women and girls. This was the so-called Hillary Doctrine—a virtue-quest of the most highly principled kind.[20] The one superpower was no longer to be an overbearing hegemon or a bringer of global financial crisis.

The secretary described the elements of the Hillary Doctrine in 2010 at a TED conference, that great agora of the liberal class. "I have made clear that the rights and the roles of women and girls will be a central tenet of American foreign policy," she said, "because where girls and women flourish, our values are also reflected."* It is, Clinton continued, "in the vital

---

* For what it's worth, two of the most feminist countries in history, at least formally, were our archenemies, the Soviet Union and communist Cuba.

interests of the United States of America" to care about women and girls. Here was her reasoning: "Give women equal rights, and entire nations are more stable and secure. Deny women equal rights, and the instability of nations is almost certain." Here was her conclusion: "the subjugation of women is therefore a threat to the common security of our world and to the national security of our country."[21]

I was a little bit alarmed when I heard Secretary Clinton speak these phrases in her deliberate way. Ordinarily, the words "vital interest" and "national security," when combined like this, suggest strong stuff: that the U.S. has a right to freeze assets, organize embargoes, and maybe even launch airstrikes—in this case, I suppose, against countries that score poorly on the gender-equality scale.

Not to worry. Like so many of the administration's high-minded initiatives, this one turned out to be pretty mundane: the Hillary Doctrine was concerned largely with innovation, with foundations and private companies who would partner with us to do things like "improve maternal and child health," "close the global gender gap in cellular phone ownership," "persuade men and boys to value their sisters and their daughters," and "make sure that every girl in the world has a chance to live up to her own dreams and aspirations."[22]

Above all, the Hillary Doctrine was about entrepreneurs. It was women-in-business whose "potential" Hillary Clinton wished to "unleash"; it was their "dreams and innovations" that she longed to see turned into "successful businesses that generate income for themselves and their families."[23]

Let us note in passing that, although the Hillary Doctrine sounded idealistic, it actually represented no great change in U.S. foreign policy. Its most obvious application was as a justification for our endless wars in the Middle East, which had commenced as a response to the terrorism of 9/11 and were now mutating into an armed campaign against sexism. Indeed, the principals of the Bush administration themselves sometimes cast their war with radical Islam as a feminist crusade, and the Hillary Doctrine merely picked up where the Bush Doctrine left off.[24]

But let's not be too quick to brush the whole thing off as empty propaganda. Among other things, the Hillary Doctrine helps us understand what Hillary really thinks about the all-important issue of income inequality. Women entrepreneurs as the solution for economic backwardness is not a new idea, after all. It comes directly from the microfinance movement, the poverty-fighting strategy that has been pushed by the World Bank since the 1990s, and Hillary's idea brings with it an entire economic philosophy. For starters, it is closely connected with the World Bank's larger project of "structural adjustment," in which countries were required to reform their economies in the familiar market-friendly ways—privatizing, deregulating, and downsizing—and, on the bright side, Western organizations would help those countries' poor people with microloans.

It is hard to overstate the attraction of microlending to the liberal class, or at least to that part of it working in the foreign-aid sector. Microlending, such people came to believe, was the magic elixir for the disease of poverty, the financial innovation that would save the third world. Foundations embraced it. Thousands of careers were built on it. Billions of dollars were spent advancing it. The United Nations declared 2005 the "International Year of Microcredit." Muhammad Yunus, the Bangladeshi economist and Clinton friend who popularized microlending, won a Nobel Prize in 2006. Three years later, Barack Obama gave Yunus the Presidential Medal of Freedom.

It was all so simple. While national leaders busied themselves with the macro-matters of privatizing and deregulating, microlending would bring the science of markets down to the individual. Merely by providing impoverished individuals with a tiny loan of fifty or a hundred dollars, it was thought, you could put them on the road to entrepreneurial self-sufficiency, you could make entire countries prosper, you could bring about economic development itself.

What was most attractive about microlending was what it was not, what it made unnecessary: any sort of collective action by poor people, coming together in governments or unions. The international development community now knew that such institutions had no real role in human prosperity. Instead, we were to understand poverty in the familiar terms of entrepreneurship and individual merit, as though the hard work of millions of single, unconnected people, plus cellphones, bank accounts, and a little capital, were what was required to remedy the third world's vast problems. Millions of people would sell one another baskets they had made or coal they had dug out of the trash heap, and suddenly they were entrepreneurs, on their way to the top. The key to development was not doing something to limit the grasp of Western banks, in other words; it was *extending Western banking methods to encompass every last individual on earth.*[25]

Microlending is a perfect expression of Clintonism, bringing together wealthy financial interests with rhetoric that sounds outrageously idealistic. Microlending permits all manner of networking, virtue-seeking, and profit-taking among the lenders while doing nothing to change actual power relations—the ultimate win-win.

Bill Clinton's administration made microlending a proud point of emphasis in U.S. foreign policy, and Hillary has been a microlending enthusiast since her first days on the national stage. She promoted it as a form of female empowerment in a famous 1995 speech she made in Beijing and she supported microlending efforts wherever the first family traveled in the 1990s—there's an exhibit on the subject at the Clinton Presidential Library that shows Hillary giving a speech in the Gaza Strip in front of a sign that reads, "Women's Empowerment Through Micro Lending." In 1997 she cohosted a global Microcredit Summit in Washington, D.C., replete with the usual third-world delegations. Hillary's own remarks on that occasion were unremarkable, but those of the president of the Citicorp Foundation were well worth remembering. Here is what he said to the assembled saviors of the third world:

> Everyone in this room is a banker, because everyone here is banking on self-employment to help alleviate poverty around the world.

At the closing session of the summit, bankers joined national leaders singing "We Shall Overcome."[26]

In the decade that followed, the theology of microlending developed a number of doctrinal refinements: the idea that women were better borrowers and better entrepreneurs than men; the belief that poor people needed mentorship and "financial inclusion" in addition to loans; the suggestion that they had to be hooked up to a bank via the Internet; the discovery that it was morally OK to run microlending banks as private, profit-making enterprises—many of the arguments that I had heard at the No Ceilings conference, expressed in the unforgettable tones of international female solidarity.

These ideas were the core of the Hillary Doctrine. Hillary's ambassador-at-large for global women's issues, Melanne Verveer, declared in 2011 that "financial inclusion is a top priority for the U.S. government" and announced her terrible chagrin that

"3 billion people in the world remain unbanked; the majority of them are women." Hillary's undersecretary for democracy and global affairs, Maria Otero, came to State from one of the biggest American microlending institutions; in her official U.S. government capacity, she expressed her joy at how microfinance had evolved "from subsidized microloans to a focus on self-sufficiency, to an emphasis on savings, to a full suite of financial products delivered by commercial regulated banks" and how all this had "affirmed the capacity of the poor to become economic actors in their own right." Hillary herself proudly recalls in her memoirs how the State Department rebuilt Afghanistan by handing out "more than 100,000 small personal loans" to the women of that country.[27]

These are fine, sterling sentiments, but they suffer from one big problem: *microlending doesn't work.* As strategies for ending poverty go, microlending appears to be among the worst that has ever been tried, just one step up from doing nothing to help the poor at all. In a carefully researched 2010 book called *Why Doesn't Microfinance Work?*, the development consultant Milford Bateman debunks virtually every aspect of the microlending gospel. It doesn't empower women, Bateman writes; it makes them into debtors. It encourages people to take up small, futile enterprises that have no chance of growing or employing others. Sometimes microborrowers don't even start businesses at all; they just spend the loan on whatever. Even worse: the expert studies that originally sparked the microlending boom turn out, upon reexamination, to have been badly flawed.

Nearly every country where microlending has been an important development strategy for the last few decades, Bateman writes, is now a disaster zone of indebtedness and economic backwardness. When the author tells us that

> the increasing dominance of the microfinance model in developing countries is causally associated with their progressive deindustrialization and infantilization

he is being polite. The terrible implication of the facts he has uncovered is that what microlending achieves is the *opposite* of development. Even Communism, with its Five Year Plans, worked better than this strategy does, as Bateman shows in a tragic look at microloan-saturated Bosnia.[28]

There's a second reason the liberal class loves microfinance, and it's extremely simple: microlending is profitable. Lending to the poor, as every subprime mortgage originator knows, can be a lucrative business. Mixed with international feminist self-righteousness, it is also a bulletproof business, immune to criticism. The million-dollar paydays it has brought certain microlenders are the wages of virtue. This combination is the real reason the international goodness community believes that empowering poor women by lending to them at usurious interest rates is a fine thing all around.[29]

GLOBALIZED COMPASSION MARKETS

The only entrepreneur who really matters here—Hillary herself—did extremely well by doing so much good. Companies needing a stiff shot of whitewash fell over one another to enlist in her State Department's crusade to build "solutions for good."[30] The investment bank Goldman Sachs "partnered" with the State Department in 2011 to give out business school scholarships to women entrepreneurs from Latin America. The following year, Clinton's old friends at the low-wage retailer Wal-Mart announced a $1.5 million gift to State's Women Entrepreneurship in the Americas program ("the effort will support the dreams of up to 55,000 potential women entrepreneurs," the company boasted).[31] ExxonMobil was on board, too, helping State to register women-owned businesses in Mexico.

The figure of the female third-world entrepreneur, rescued from her "unbanked" state by Wall Street–backed organizations, mentored by her friends in the American professional class, expressing herself through social media—to this day it remains among the most cherished daydreams in the land of money. Everyone is infatuated with her—the foundations, the State Department, the corporations. Everyone wants to have his picture taken with her. Everyone wants to partner with everyone else to advance her interests and loan her money.

The professionals' fantasies blend seamlessly one into another. The ideas promoted by the Goldman Sachs "10,000 Women project," for example, are not really different from those of Hillary's own Vital Voices Global Partnership or Coca-Cola's "#5by20" initiative or even the conscientious statements you find in State Department press releases. People move from one node of this right-thinking world to another and no one really notices, because the relocation signifies no meaningful change. They give one another grants and prizes and named chairs; they extol one another's ideas and books; they appear together with their banker pals on panel discussions in Bali or maybe Davos; and they all come together to fix Haiti, and then to fix Haiti again, and then to fix Haiti yet again.

Hillary herself eventually moved from State to the Clinton Foundation, where she presided over a dizzying program of awards for the usual people, grants for some genuinely good causes, and the organizing of great spectacles of virtue like the one I attended in New York, a costly praise-o-rama featuring many of the very same people who worked for her in government.

What I concluded from observing all this is that there is a global commerce in compassion, an international virtue-circuit featuring people of unquestionable moral achievement, like Bono, Malala, Sting, Yunus, Angelina Jolie, and Bishop Tutu; figures who travel the world, collecting and radiating goodness. They come into contact with the other participants in this market: the politicians and billionaires and bankers who warm themselves at the incandescent virtue of the world-traveling moral superstars.[32]

What drives this market are the buyers. Like Wal-Mart partnering with the State Department, or Goldman Sachs paying two hundred grand for a single speech, what these virtue-consumers are doing is purchasing liberalism offsets, an ideological version of the carbon offsets that are sometimes bought by polluters in order to compensate for the smog they churn out.

At the apex of all this idealism stands the Clinton Foundation, a veritable market-maker in the world's vast, swirling virtue-trade. The former president who stands at its head is "the world's leading philanthropic dealmaker," according to a book on the subject.[33] Under his watchful eye all the concerned parties are brought together: the moral superstars, the billionaires, and of course the professionals, who organize, intone, and advise. Virtue changes hands. Good causes are funded. Compassion is radiated and absorbed.

This is modern liberalism in action: an unregulated virtue-exchange in which representatives of one class of humanity ritually forgive the sins of another class, all of it convened and facilitated by a vast army of well-graduated American professionals, their reassuring expertise propped up by bogus social science, while the unfortunate objects of their high and noble compassion sink slowly back into a preindustrial state.

WHAT'S MISSING FROM THIS PICTURE?

One of the motifs of that Clinton Foundation event I attended the day after International Women's Day in 2015 was the phrase "Not There," a reference to the women who aren't present in the councils of state or the senior management of powerful corporations. The foundation raised awareness of this problem by producing visuals in which fashion models disappeared from the covers of popular magazines like *Vogue*, *Glamour*, *SELF*, and *Allure*. According to a *New York Times* story on the subject, the Clinton people had gone to a hip advertising agency to develop this concept, so that we would all understand that women were missing from the high-ranking places where they deserved to be.

There was an even grander act of erasure going on here, but no clever adman will ever be hired to play it up. International Women's Day, I discovered when I looked it up, began as a socialist holiday, a sort of second Labor Day on which you were supposed to commemorate the efforts of female workers and the sacrifices of female strikers. It is a vestige of an old form of feminism that didn't especially focus on the problems experienced by women trying to be corporate officers or the views of some mega-billionaire's wife.

However, one of the things we were there in New York to consider was how unjust it was that women were underrepresented in the C-suites of the Fortune 500—and, by implication, how lamentable it was that the United States had not yet elected a woman president.

There was no consideration—I mean, zero—of the situation of women who work on the shop floors of the Fortune 500—for Wal-Mart or Amazon or any of the countless low-wage employers who make that list sparkle. Working-class American women were simply . . . not there. In this festival of inclusiveness and sweet affirmation, *their* problems were not considered, *their* voices were not heard.

Now, Hillary Clinton is not a callous or haughty woman. She had much to recommend her for the nation's highest office—for one thing, her knowledge of Washington; for another, the Republican vendetta against her, which was so vindictive and so unfair that I myself voted for her just to show what I thought of it. A third: her completely average Midwestern suburban upbringing, an appealing political story that is the opposite of her technocratic image. And she has, after all, made a great effort in the course of the last year to impress voters with her feelings for working people.

But it's hard, given her record, not to feel that this was only under pressure from the Bernie Sanders movement. Absent such political force, Hillary tends to gravitate back to a version of feminism that is a straight synonym of "meritocracy," that is concerned almost exclusively with the struggle of professional women to rise as high as their talents will take them. No ceilings!

As I sat there in the Best Buy theater, however, I kept thinking about the infinitely greater problem of *no floors*. On the train to New York that morning I had been reading a book by Peter Edelman, one of the country's leading experts on welfare and a former friend of the Clintons. Edelman's aim was to document the effect that the Clintons' welfare reform measure had on poor people—specifically on poor women, because that's who used to receive welfare payments in the days before the program was terminated.

Edelman was not a fan of the old, pre-1996 welfare system, because it did nothing to prepare women for employment or to solve the problem of daycare. But under the old system, at least our society had a legal obligation to do something for these people, the weakest and most vulnerable among us. Today, thanks to Hillary and her husband, that obligation has been cancelled and we do almost nothing. The result, Edelman maintains, has been exactly what you'd expect: extreme poverty has increased dramatically in this country since Bill Clinton signed welfare reform in 1996.

For poor and working-class American women, the floor was pulled up and hauled off to the landfill some twenty years ago. There is no State Department somewhere to pay for their cellphones or pick up their daycare expenses. And one of the people who helped to work this deed was the very woman I watched present herself as the champion of the world's downtrodden femininity.

Sitting there in gilded Manhattan, I thought of all the abandoned factories and postindustrial desolation that surround this city, and I mused on how, in such places, the old Democratic Party was receding into terminal insignificance. It had virtually nothing to say to the people who inhabit that land of waste and futility.

But for the faithful liberals at the Clinton Foundation gathering in New York, none of that mattered. The party's deficit in relevance to average citizens was more than made up by its massive surplus in moral virtue. Here, inside the theater, the big foundations and the great fashion magazines were staging a pageant of goodness unquestionable, and the liberal class was swimming happily in its home element.

They knew which things were necessary to make up a liberal movement, and all of the ingredients were present: well-meaning billionaires; grant makers and grant recipients; Hollywood stars who talked about social media; female entrepreneurs from the third world; and, of course, a trucked-in audience of hundreds who clapped and cheered enthusiastically every time one of their well-graduated leaders wandered across the screen of the Jumbotron. The performance of liberalism was so realistic one could almost believe it lived.

CONCLUSION

Trampling Out the Vineyard

Were you to draw a Venn diagram of the three groups whose interaction I have tried to describe in this book—Democrats, meritocrats, and plutocrats—the space where they intersect would be an island seven miles off the coast of Massachusetts called Martha's Vineyard.

A little bit smaller in area than Staten Island but many times greater in stately magnificence, Martha's Vineyard is a resort whose population swells each summer as the wealthy return to their vacation villas. It is a place of yachts and celebrities and fussy shrubbery; of waterfront mansions and Ivy League professors and closed-off beaches. It is also a place of moral worthiness, as we understand it circa 2016. The people relaxing on the Vineyard's rarefied sand are not lazy toffs like the billionaires of old; in fact, according to the *Washington Post*, they have "far higher IQs than the average beachgoer." It is an island that deserves what it has. Some of its well-scrubbed little towns are adorned in Victorian curlicues, some in the severe tones of the Classical Revival, but whatever their ornament might be they are always clad in the unmistakable livery of righteous success.[1]

It is ever so liberal. This is Massachusetts, after all, and the markers of lifestyle enlightenment are all around you: Foods that are organic. Clothing that is tasteful. A conspicuous absence of cigarette butts.

Here it is not enough to have a surgically precise garden of roses and topiary in the three-foot strip between your carefully whitewashed house and the picket fence out front; the garden must also be accessorized with a sign letting passersby know that "this is a chemical-free Vineyard lawn, safe for children, pets, and ponds."

It is ever so privileged, ever so private. This is not Newport or Fifth Avenue, where the rich used to display their good taste to the world; the Martha's Vineyard mansions that you read about in the newspapers are for the most part hidden away behind massive hedges and long, winding driveways. Even the beaches of the rich are kept separate from the general public—they are private right down to the low-tide line and often accessible only through locked gates, a gracious peculiarity of Massachusetts law that is found almost nowhere else in America.[2]

Over the last few decades, this island has become the standard vacation destination for high-ranking Democratic officials. Bill Clinton started the trend in 1993 and then proceeded to return to Martha's Vineyard every year of his presidency except two—after presidential puppeteer Dick Morris took a poll and convinced Bill it would be more in keeping with the mood of the country if the first family visited a National Park instead.

Barack Obama, the next Democrat to occupy the White House, mimicked Clinton in policy decisions and personnel choices, and so it made sense to do exactly as his predecessor had done in vacation destinations. Obama, too, spent all his presidential holidays on Martha's Vineyard with one exception—the year he ran for reelection and needed to burnish his populist image. When you research the place, you keep bumping into cozy details like the following: the Martha's Vineyard estate where Obama stayed in the summer of 2013 belonged to one David Schulte, a corporate investment adviser and Clinton intimate who met Bill at Oxford and Hillary at Yale, where Schulte was editor of the *Yale Law Journal*.[3]

People on Martha's Vineyard sometimes say that politicians choose to vacation among them because the residents here are so blasé about celebrity that it's no big deal, a president can just ride his bike down the street and no one cares. It's a nice thought, but I suspect the real reasons Democratic politicians like to come here are even simpler. First of all, there's security. Martha's Vineyard is an island; it is remote by definition and difficult to travel to. People in many parts of the country have never even heard of it.

Then there's the money. What has sanctified the name of Martha's Vineyard among Democratic politicians are the countless deeds of fund-raising heroism that have graced the island's manicured golf courses, its quaint hotels, and its architecturally celebrated interiors. During the summer season, when the island's billionaires have returned like swallows to the fabulous secluded coastal estates they own, there are fundraisers every night of the week. Often these are thrown for the benefit of worthy charitable causes, not politicians, but of course it is the political fundraisers that make the headlines.

Political fund-raisers for Democrats, that is. In terms of partisanship, everyone is pretty much on the same page here. The only moment in recent years to cause the billionaires of Martha's Vineyard to feel pangs of political unease was 2007, when both Hillary Clinton and Barack Obama were hitting the sweet spot of the liberal class. Both politicians showed up here to raise money, sometimes within a few days of each other. Who would line up with whom? Tensions ran high. Tycoon turned against tycoon. On Martha's Vineyard, declared the *New York Times*, the presidential race "is dividing old loyalties, testing longtime friendships and causing a few awkward moments at the island's many dinner parties." The struggle between the two Democrats made situations fraught at resort communities across the country, the paper allowed. "But perhaps nowhere is the intensity as great as on the Vineyard because of its history, the pedigree of its residents and those residents' proximity to power."[4]

In the summer of 2015, all that fratricidal stuff was over. The Obamas and the Clintons were again sharing the island, but the mood was happy. This time, Hillary Clinton's fund-raising operations could proceed without any real competition. Both first families went peacefully to Vernon Jordan's birthday party, an important annual event in the Democratic calendar. Bill and Barack even played a round of golf together. And Hillary was the beneficiary of a fundraiser cosponsored by her admirer, Lady Lynn Forester de Rothschild, an honest-to-god member of Europe's most famous family of Gilded Age banker-aristocrats.[5]

THE LAND THAT LIBERALS FORGOT

Back in 1975, when Martha's Vineyard was in the course of being gentrified from a working-class fishing community to what it is today, Tom Wolfe published a humorous story in which he told how "Media & Lit. people" from New York had started vacationing on that island, and how they were initially shunned by the flamboyantly preppy "Boston people" who then dominated the resort's summer scene. But then the two groups start to mingle, and a sort of revelation comes. At a cocktail party one day in the mid-1970s, Wolfe's narrator, an unnamed New York author, sees "a glimmer of the future":

> something he could barely make out . . . a vision in which America's best minds, her intellectuals, found a common ground, a natural unity, with the enlightened segments of her old aristocracy, her old money . . . the two groups bound together by . . . but by what? . . . he could almost see it, but not quite . . . it was *presque vu* . . . it was somehow a matter of taste . . . of sensibility . . . of grace, natural grace.[6]

Today the melding of money with the literary sensibility is, in certain circles, an accomplished fact, and sometimes the perversity of the thing is capable of slapping you right in the face. I was reminded of this as I strolled through one of the polished, stately towns on Martha's Vineyard and came across a shop selling reproductions of old T-shirts and sports memorabilia and the like. On the outside wall of the shop hung a poem by Charles Bukowski, because of course nothing goes better with tasteful clothing than transgressive poetry. It's about the horror of blue-collar life, about how dehumanizing it is to do the kind of work that no one who passes by here ever does anymore:

I think of the men
I've known in
factories
with no way to
get out—
choking while living
choking while laughing

When I think of the men I've known in factories, I think of those locked-out workers I met in Decatur, Illinois, in the early days of the Clinton administration. What concerned them was not so much the existential frustration of blue-collar work as it was the fraying of the middle-class promise. Although they were "out," they weren't particularly interested in staying out; they would have been happy to go back in provided their jobs were safe and paid well. They wanted to live what we used to think of as ordinary lives.

In a scholarly paper about social class published in 1946, the sociologist C. Wright Mills found that "Big Business and Executives" in Decatur earned a little more than two times as much as the town's "Wage Workers" did.[7]

In 2014, the CEO of Archer Daniels Midland, a company that dominates Decatur today, earned an estimated 261 times as much as did average wage workers. The CEO of Caterpillar, the focus of one of the Decatur "war zone" strikes I described in Chapter Three, made 486 times as much.[8] Caterpillar's share price, meanwhile, is roughly ten times what it was at the time of the strike.

Other changes to sweep that town since the war zone days of the 1990s are just as familiar, just as awful. For one thing, Decatur's population has shrunk by about 12 percent since back then. Despite this outflow of people, as of early 2015 the place still had the highest unemployment rate in the state of Illinois. As a few minutes of Internet clicking will tell you, Decatur's own citizens now rank their town extremely low on certain quality-of-life metrics; in a photographic guide to Decatur meant to promote tourism, the photographer recounts being threatened in a park while taking pictures.[9]

The two-class system that those men-in-factories spoke of during the strikes has pretty much come to pass. I mean this not only in the sense that Wall Street traders are very rich, but in the highly specific way that the two-tiered system the Caterpillar workers were protesting has been installed in workplaces across the country; as a result, younger workers will never catch up to the pay earned by their seniors no matter how many years they log on the job.

In 2015 I went back to Decatur to catch up with veterans of the war zone like Larry Solomon, who had been the leader of the local United Auto Workers union at the Caterpillar plant. He went back in after the strike ended but retired in 1998. When I met Solomon in his tidy suburban home, he talked in detail about the many times he got crossways with management in days long past; about all the grievances he filed for his coworkers over the years and all the puffed-up company officials he recalls facing down.

Think about that for a moment: a blue-collar worker who has retired fairly comfortably, despite having spent years confronting his employer on picket lines and in grievance hearings. How is such a thing possible? I know we're all supposed to show nothing but love for the job creators nowadays, but listening to Solomon, it occurred to me that maybe his semi-adversarial attitude worked better. Maybe it was that attitude, repeated in workplace after workplace across the country, that made possible the middle-class prosperity that once marked us as a nation.

"We were promised, all during the time we worked at Caterpillar, that when you retire, you're going to have a pension and full benefits at no cost to you," Solomon recalled. He told about a round of contract negotiations he and his colleagues attended in the 1960s during which a management official complained, "We already take care of you from the cradle to the grave. What more could you want?"

Today, that old social contract is gone—or, at least, the part of it that ensured health care and retirement for blue-collar workers. Now, as Solomon sees it, companies can say, "We want your life, and when your work life is over, then good-bye. We thank you for your life, but we're not responsible for you after we turn you out."

Mike Griffin had been another outspoken union activist, in his case during the lockout at Tate & Lyle. We talked about the situation that faces the younger generation in Decatur, people for whom the basic components of middle-class life are growing farther and farther out of reach. Though they might not always get it politically, Griffin said, those workers can most definitely see how screwed they are. "One of the things that they do understand is that they got shit jobs with shit wages and no benefits and no health insurance," he told me.

> And they understand that they're working two and three jobs just to get by, and a lot of them can't own anything, and they understand seeing mom and dad forced into retirement or forced out of their job, now they're working at Hardee's or McDonald's to make ends meet so they can retire in poverty. People understand that. They see that.

YOU! *HYPOCRITE LECTEUR!*

This book has been a catalogue of the many ways the Democratic Party has failed to tackle income inequality, even though that is the leading social issue of the times, and its many failures to get tough with the financial industry, even though Wall Street was the leading culprit in the global downturn and the slump-that-never-ends. The larger message is that this is what it looks like when a leftish party loses its interest in working people, the traditional number one constituency for left parties the world over.

But we should also acknowledge the views of the people for whom the Democrats are all you could ask for in a political party. I am thinking here of the summertime residents on Martha's Vineyard—the sorts of people to whom the politicians listen with patience and understanding. No one treats this group as though they have "nowhere else to go"; on the contrary, for them, the political process works wonderfully. It is responsive to their concerns, its representatives are respectful, and the party as a whole treats them with a gratifying deference.

For them, the Democrats deliver in all the conventional ways: generous subsidies for the right kinds of businesses, a favorable regulatory climate, and legal protection for their innovations. Hillary Clinton's State Department basically declared access to certain Silicon Valley servers to be a human right.

Then there are the psychic deliverables—the flattery, for starters. To members of the liberal class, the Democratic Party offers constant reminders that the technocratic order whose upper ranks they inhabit is rational and fair—that whether they work in software or derivative securities they are a deserving elite; creative, tolerant, enlightened. Though it is less tangible, the moral absolution in which Democrats deal is just as important. It seems to put their favorite constituents on the right side of every question, the right side of progress itself. It allows them to understand the war of our two parties as a kind of cosmic struggle between good and evil—a struggle in which they are on the side of light and justice, of course.

For people in the group I have been describing, there's nothing dysfunctional or disappointing about Democratic politics; it feels exactly right. And what is rightest and most inspiring about it is the Democrats' prime directive: to defeat the Republicans, that unthinkable brutish Other. There are no complexities to make this mission morally difficult; to the liberal class, it is simple. The Democratic Party is all that stands between the Oval Office and whomever the radicalized GOP ultimately chooses to nominate for the presidency. Compared to that sacred duty, all other issues fade into insignificance.

Let me acknowledge that I sometimes feel this way, too. I think it is a terrible thing when Republicans periodically capture the nation's commanding heights.

But even when it comes to containing the Republicans—the area where the Democratic Party's mission is so clear and straightforward—it has not been a great success. Despite their highly convincing righteousness, despite their oft-touted demographic edge, and even despite a historic breakdown of the GOP's free-market ideology, the Democrats have been unable to suppress the Republican challenge. The radicalized Republican Party seems to be conquering the nation, one state legislature at a time. What I saw in Kansas eleven years ago is now everywhere.

Even if Democrats do succeed, it won't save us. While there are many great Democrats and many exceptions to the trends I have described in this book, by and large the story has been a disappointing one. We have surveyed this party's thoughts and deeds from the Seventies to the present, we have watched them abandon whole classes and regions and industries, and we know now what the results have been. Their leadership faction has no intention of doing what the situation requires.

It is time to face the obvious: that the direction the Democrats have chosen to follow for the last few decades has been a failure for both the nation and for their own partisan health. "Failure" is admittedly a harsh word, but what else are we to call it when the left party in a system chooses to confront an epic economic breakdown by talking hopefully about entrepreneurship and innovation? When the party of professionals repeatedly falls for bad, self-serving ideas like bank deregulation, the "creative class," and empowerment through bank loans? When the party of the common man basically allows aristocracy to return?

Now, all political parties are alliances of groups with disparate interests, but the contradictions in the Democratic Party coalition seem unusually sharp. The Democrats posture as the "party of the people" even as they dedicate themselves ever more resolutely to serving and glorifying the professional class. Worse: they combine self-righteousness and class privilege in a way that Americans find stomach-turning. And every two years, they simply assume that being non-Republican is sufficient to rally the voters of the nation to their standard. This cannot go on.

Yet it will go on, because the most direct solutions to the problem are off the table for the moment. The Democrats have no interest in reforming themselves in a more egalitarian way. There is little the rest of us can do, given the current legal arrangements of this country, to build a vital third-party movement or to revive organized labor, the one social movement that is committed by its nature to pushing back against the inequality trend.

What we *can* do is strip away the Democrats' precious sense of their own moral probity—to make liberals live without the comforting knowledge that righteousness is always on their side. It is that sensibility, after all, that prevents so many good-hearted rank-and-file Democrats from understanding how starkly and how deliberately their political leaders contradict their values. Once that contradiction has been made manifest—once that smooth, seamless sense of liberal virtue has been cracked, anything becomes possible. The course of the party and the course of the country can both be changed, but only after we understand that the problem is us.

AFTERWORD TO THE 2017 EDITION

The Year They Found Somewhere Else to Go

And then came the deluge. The right-wing flood that overswept the Democrats in 2016 was a surprise to everyone, but what made it possible was the long-term Democratic strategy I have described in the pages of this book.

The Washington political world anticipated another boring presidential battle fought out along the same lines as always: A nicely polished candidate would be chosen by the Republican Party's billionaire donors, and he would advance with trumpets blaring over the extremely familiar terrain of the culture wars. As the Democrats prepared to meet the anticipated Republican foe, they felt that they, too, could do what they always do: offer bromides on the economy and encouraging words to the various groups that made up their coalition. They would talk about innovation and education; they would demonstrate how responsible they were to the swing voters who inhabited the political "center," and ultimately demographics would deliver the victory. The coalition of the ascendant would ascend a little more.

It was a ritual, in other words, and Democrats approached it almost mechanically. Hillary Clinton was the consensus choice of their leadership faction, largely because it was her turn and in spite of the scandals and historical baggage that would eventually weigh her down. No prominent Democrat stood against her, thanks largely to the efforts of President Obama, who clearly regarded her as his hand-picked successor.

The process by which Clinton was chosen looked a lot like dynastic succession, but there was also a good deal of liberal idealism mixed in. She was a perfect embodiment of the Democrats' white-collar ideology, and as the election unfolded voters were often reminded of what made her so special. Hillary was a brilliant and highly accomplished professional, we were told; according to President Obama, she was the most qualified person ever to stand for the nation's highest office. On the question of actual political issues, her one overarching cause during the campaign was opposing discrimination, the unfair "barriers" that kept the talented from rising.

This was her issue, and it was also the object of her personal crusade: shattering the "glass ceiling" of the presidency. But there were obstacles to the Clinton coronation. The independent Senator Bernie Sanders, a self-described democratic socialist from Vermont, raised an unlikely challenge during the Democratic primaries. Widely regarded as a marginal figure in Washington, the 74-year-old Sanders nevertheless sparked the imagination of a generation of young voters with decidedly old-fashioned proposals like single-payer health insurance, a regulatory war on big banks, and free college tuition at state universities. With massive stadium rallies and a string of surprising wins over Clinton, the Sanders phenomenon should have confirmed that 2016 was to be a year for outsiders; a year of outrage.

The liberal establishment didn't listen, however. They didn't want to listen. There was just something about the Vermonter that triggered their contempt. Like the "prairie populist" who challenged the Bill Clinton character in *Primary Colors* (see

Chapter Three), Sanders was a living symbol of what the Democrats used to stand for, and party leaders didn't seem to appreciate being reminded of how far they had strayed. Elected Democratic officials lined up almost unanimously against Sanders. The President made it clear he stood with Clinton. Even the Democratic National Committee, supposedly a neutral party during the primaries, was later discovered to have consistently taken the side of the Clinton campaign.

The prestige press, meanwhile, seemed to despise the avuncular senator. Editorials and opinion pieces in the *Washington Post*, to choose one important organ, ran about five to one against him. "Nominating Sanders Would Be Insane," a typical op-ed headline announced in January of 2016; "Mr. Sanders' Attack on Reality," was how the paper expressed its editorial position in February. Even more typical of the journalistic climate was the headline that the *New York Times* chose to affix to a news story when Clinton finally prevailed in June: "Hillary Clinton Made History, But Bernie Sanders Stubbornly Ignored It."

In the Republican primaries, meanwhile, the insurgent candidate came out on top. Donald Trump, the real-estate billionaire and reality TV star, defeated a host of more established politicians to make himself the nominee. He did it by downplaying certain elements of the Republican approach—family values and free trade—and bringing to the surface the class-based appeal that had long been a subtle element of the formula. Like Sanders, Trump aimed to connect not with party hierarchs but with ordinary voters. And with his blunt way of talking and his massive stadium rallies, Trump proceeded to stoke the frustrations of working-class Republicans into the greatest fake-populist rising the country has ever seen.

To call this billionaire man-of-the-people a "demagogue" would not be inaccurate. Obviously there was some kind of deception at work when the traditional party of business inflamed the passions of millions of working people. The difficulty lay in identifying the exact species of demagoguery Trump practiced. What did this man stand for? Why were ordinary people rallying to him in such alarming numbers? The mainstream press thought they knew the answer: Trump represented racist bigotry, pure and simple, a latter-day outbreak of Ku Kluxery, with its hateful goals only barely concealed.

Trump himself sometimes furnished excellent evidence for this finding. The man campaigned as a sort of insult clown, going systematically down the list of American ethnic groups and offending them each in turn. He promised to deport millions of undocumented immigrants and to bar Muslims from entering the United States. He expressed admiration for various foreign strongmen and dictators and drew the enthusiastic endorsement of leading racists of every persuasion, a gorgeous mosaic of haters, each of them quivering excitedly at the prospect of a real, honest-to-god bigot in the White House.

For liberals, Trump was the embodiment of all they feared and hated about Republicans—the ideal monster, as perfectly nightmarish as if he had been assembled from spare parts in the Fox News laboratory. Naturally, they projected their distaste for him onto his followers. And in so doing, they persistently overlooked what was driving his uprising. Stories marveling at the stupidity of Trump voters were published nearly every day during the campaign. Articles accusing Trump's followers of being bigots appeared by the hundreds, if not the thousands. Every liberal with a newspaper column could see what was going on: Trump's followers' passions are nothing more than the ignorant blurtings of the white American id, driven to madness by the presence of a black man in the White House.

But intolerance was only part of the story. If you listened to

Trump's speeches, you noticed a peculiar thing. In addition to his insults and his boasting, he also spoke about an entirely legitimate issue. Donald Trump was a bigot, yes, and this was inexcusable, but he also talked about trade: the destructive free-trade deals our leaders have made, the many companies that have moved their production facilities to other lands, the phone calls he would make to those companies' CEOs in order to threaten them with steep tariffs unless they move back to the U.S.

At a rally in March 2016, for example, Trump called the Trans-Pacific Partnership, President Obama's great, final bid for bipartisan consensus, "a horrible deal for our country." In fact, Trump continued, "every single deal we do is bad." Why? Remarkably, given that he is a businessman who has donated generously to politicians, Trump suggested that it was because businessmen donate generously to politicians. And so, Trump asserted, when our leaders make trade deals that harm average Americans, "they're not stupid, they know it's bad, but they do it because they get essentially paid a fortune in campaign contributions and probably other things honestly that we don't know about."

Trump embellished this vision with other perfectly legitimate populist ideas: Under his leadership, he said, the government would "start competitive bidding in the drug industry." He extended the critique to the military-industrial complex, describing how the government is forced to buy lousy but expensive airplanes thanks to the power of industry lobbyists.

Eventually Trump would come around to his curious selling proposition: Because he is personally so wealthy, he is supposedly unaffected by lobbyists and corporate donors. And because he is free from the corrupting power of modern campaign finance, the famous dealmaker Donald Trump could make deals on our behalf that were "good" instead of "bad."

Of course, the chance that Trump will actually do such things as president is very small. Every indicator suggests that his administration will do the opposite: deliver favors for his fellow business leaders that are even more generous than those of his Republican predecessors. Besides, as many pointed out during the campaign, he was a hypocrite on the trade issue as well as so many other things, having his name-brand shirts and ties made overseas. But what mattered in 2016 was that Trump was giving voice to people's economic frustration.

COMPLACENCY

An indelible image from 2016: an amateur video going around on the Internet that showed a room full of workers at a Carrier air conditioning plant in Indiana being told by an officer of the company that the factory is being moved to Monterrey, Mexico, and that they're all going to lose their jobs.

As I watched the famous footage, I thought of all the arguments over trade that we've had in this country since the Bill Clinton days, all the sweet words from our economists about the scientifically proven benevolence of free trade, all the ways in which our newspapers mock people who say that treaties like NAFTA allow companies to move jobs to Mexico. Well, here is a video of a company moving its jobs to Mexico, courtesy of NAFTA. This is what it looks like. The Carrier executive talks in that familiar and highly professional HR language about the need to "stay competitive" and "the extremely price-sensitive marketplace." A worker shouts, "Fuck you!" at the executive. The executive asks people to please be quiet so he can "share" his "information." His information about all of them losing their jobs.

It was raw class conflict, and Donald Trump was right on

top of it. He referred to that video constantly on the campaign trail, regaling audiences with accounts of the revenge he would exact upon Carrier unless they left the jobs in Indiana. (Trump would partially make good on his promise after being elected.)

Trump's rejection of free trade was remarkable for a Republican, as was his incredible plan to make the GOP into a "workers' party." But conservative Republicans were not the only ones who should have been alarmed: This represented a profound threat to the Democrats as well. After all, NAFTA was the classic they-have-nowhere-else-to-go betrayal by the Democrats. The Clinton name was associated permanently with that betrayal, and Hillary herself was implicated personally as well, thanks to her service in the free-trade Obama administration. Centrism of the Clinton variety worked when Republicans were reliably to the right of the Democrats on trade matters, but change that essential element of the political framework and the whole structure would start to shake.

The Democrats might have understood better had they spoken to labor leaders like Tom Lewandowski, then the president of the Northeast Indiana Central Labor Council in Fort Wayne, Indiana. "These people aren't racist, not any more than anybody else is," he told me when I asked him about working-class Trump supporters in March. "When Trump talks about trade, we think about the Clinton administration, first with NAFTA and then with PNTR China, and here in Northeast Indiana, we hemorrhaged jobs."

> . . . And here's Trump talking about trade, in a ham-handed way, but at least he's representing emotionally. We've had all the political establishment standing behind every trade deal, and we endorsed some of these people, and then we've had to fight them to get them to represent us.

What our consensus politics have done to working people is obvious to anyone outside the prosperous enclaves on the two coasts. Ill-considered trade deals and generous bank bailouts and guaranteed profits for insurance companies but no recovery for average people, ever—these things have taken their toll. As Trump himself liked to say at his campaign rallies, "we have rebuilt China and yet our country is falling apart. Our infrastructure is falling apart. . . . Our airports are, like, Third World."

For all Trump's nativism and bluster, the 2016 campaign was very much concerned with the One Big Grievance of our time: The economic system is "rigged" against working-class people, to use the word of the year. It is true that Trump's solutions, when he bothered to identify them, were unlikely to succeed. But the fact remains: Eight years after the crash of 2008, the country was still incandescent with rage, and "Make America Great Again" was as obvious a slogan as they come.

To listen to the leading figures of the Democratic Party establishment, however, you would never have guessed this. Outrage has always been a difficult emotion for our modern Democrats, and this time around it was especially hard, since one of their own was occupying the White House. Instead, cool contentment was the governing sentiment here, and for 2016 the Dems planned a campaign of what one might call militant complacency. The least inspiring presidential candidate in many years, Hillary Clinton was famous for her intimate friendship with Wall Street bankers. At one point she actually scolded Bernie Sanders for wanting to get tough with the financial industry because such a policy, by itself, would not also end racism and sexism—a new low in self-serving sophistry. The Democrats' unofficial slogan, "America is already great," sounded like the kind of thing you'd see inscribed in a country club logo somewhere.

And yet it was under the banner of economic complacency that the liberals prepared themselves for what they claimed to be the most important electoral battle of our lifetimes. President Obama attacked public cynicism in his final State of the Union speech, criticizing those who believe "the system is rigged" for their groundless pessimism. In March, he voiced what would become the quasi-official Democratic theme: "America's pretty darn great right now." In May, *New York Times* columnist Charles Blow scolded those who believe that "life in America has gotten worse . . . compared with 50 years ago," suggesting that such a pessimistic view betrayed an "implicit, or even explicit, critique" of the achievements of the Obama Administration—a critique he felt to be obviously impermissible. It was not to be thought.

"The system isn't rigged" became a sort of rallying cry among the liberal class, useful for slapping down both Sanders and Trump. On some occasions, liberals would simply deny that white working-class people were actually being drawn to the Republicans. On others, they would demand that Democratic leaders confront disgruntled working people and inform them that "to have a lifelong job, you need to be a lifelong learner, constantly raising your game." And just four days before the election, the headline on a *New York Times* editorial assailed "Donald Trump's Denial of Economic Reality."[1] Times were great in America. Couldn't this stupid billionaire see it?

INTERLUDE

Here is a glimpse of what it all looked like in the early summer of 2016, before the great shocks started to mount—the Brexit vote, the shooting of numerous police officers in Dallas, the notorious *Access Hollywood* tape, the hacked Democratic emails, and the FBI disclosures.

For now, all was serene in America. The threat posed by Senator Bernie Sanders had been suppressed. The Republicans had chosen the preposterous windbag Trump to lead them; the consensus was that he would be easy to defeat. The leadership faction of the country's professional class had once again got its way.

In June President Barack Obama did an interview with *Businessweek* in which he was congratulated for his stewardship of the economy and asked "what industries" he might choose to join upon his retirement from the White House. The president replied as follows: "But what I will say is that—just to bring things full circle about innovation—the conversations I have with Silicon Valley and with venture capital pull together my interests in science and organization in a way I find really satisfying."

Venture capital! The man Americans elected in 2008 to get tough with high finance and stop the revolving door was now, in 2016, considering taking his own walk through that revolving door and getting a job in high finance.

Nine days later, Obama was in California addressing an audience at Stanford University, the preeminent educational institution of Silicon Valley. The occasion of the president's remarks was the annual Global Entrepreneurship Summit, and the substance of his remarks was straight globaloney, flavored with a whiff of vintage dot-com ebullience. Obama marveled at all the smart young creative people who start tech businesses. He deplored bigotry as an impediment that sometimes keeps these smart creative people from succeeding. He demanded that more power be given to the smart young creatives who are transforming the world. Keywords included "innovation," "interconnection," and of course "Zuckerberg," as in the name of the Facebook CEO, who appeared with Obama on so many occasions and whose successful company was often used as shorthand by Democrats to signify everything wonderful about our era.

Everyone was down with the international entrepreneuriat. Less than a week after Obama's salute to them at Stanford, Hillary Clinton paid her own visit to an innovative co-working space in Denver and rolled out a plan for rewarding this very same cohort of clear-eyed, tech-respecting citizens. "Today's dynamic and competitive global economy demands an ambitious national commitment to technology, innovation and entrepreneurship," declared the "briefing" her campaign released on that occasion; to make that commitment, Clinton proposed deferring the student loans of young people who start businesses... because the promise of tech riches wasn't incentive enough, I suppose.

It felt so right, this Democratic infatuation with the triumphant young global professional. So right, and for a certain class of successful Americans, so very, very obvious. What you do with winners is you celebrate them. Winners need to win. Winners need to have their loan payments deferred, to have venture capital directed their way by a former president. That all these gestures might actually represent self-serving behavior by an insular elite does not appear to have crossed our leaders' minds in those sunny days of June 2016.

EMPTY CLEVELAND

The Republican National Convention came in July and was held in Cleveland, Ohio. Under ordinary circumstances, Cleveland would be just about the worst possible place to hold a Republican gathering. Not only is this blue-collar town a traditional stronghold of the Democrats, but virtually every prospect you see, every corner you turn, somehow reminds you of the ways in which Republican economic policies have rained down ruin and destruction on working people for the better part of the last four decades. White flight to the suburbs has depopulated Cleveland's inner city while industrial flight to Mexico and the South has decimated the region's manufacturing jobs. Today Cleveland is less than half the size it was in the Fifties. One of the country's five largest cities in 1920, it now ranks forty-eighth. The only fields in which Cleveland serves today as a leader, as an urban exemplar, are foreclosure and empty housing.

To prepare for the Republican gathering, I took a tour of the once-industrial east side of the city, gazing over its landscape of crumbling factory buildings and old apartment houses now colonized by vines. I passed a vast abandoned factory marked with the words, "National Acme." A former General Electric facility. A still-operating General Electric facility. The site of the old Fisher Body plant, famous for a 1936 strike, its buildings replaced now with the severe-looking dormitories of the Cleveland Jobs Corps Center, a facility for disadvantaged youth. And everywhere I went in this vast quadrant I saw vacant lots. Empty street corners. Missing houses. Land returned to the wildlife and the scrub trees.

Even the properly functioning quarters of the city seemed half-empty. The Hungarian restaurant where my colleague and I ate a late lunch one day: all to ourselves. The shopping mall where we bought clothes: nobody at the register. The old-fashioned hamburger stand with the electric train running around the dining room: almost empty. Even downtown Cleveland, where we pulled up after a five-hour drive: Just put the car wherever you want. Nobody cares.

In most years, to hold a convention of the Republican Party in such a place would be like mounting the ruins of a collapsed highway bridge to demand that maintenance for highway bridges be terminated at once. But 2016 brought a different sort of Republican: Donald Trump and his angry populist circus. If ever there was a landscape that had been ruined by the conventional politics of the last few decades, by the decline of manufacturing and by terrible trade deals, this was it. If ever there was an American landscape that needed to be made great again, it was Cleveland, Ohio.

In one single area that I saw did Cleveland achieve an approximation of urban density. This was East Fourth Street, a popular restaurant district in the city's downtown. For that one week in July, it had been made into a kind of intake chute to the city's arena, a crowded and slowly churning political carnival, jammed at all hours with sidewalk vendors, delegates, journalists, protesters, and amused spectators.

As you proceeded through the slow churn, you passed restaurants that had been rented out by news organizations. Protesters with straightforward slogans; protesters with long-winded didactic ones. People selling Trump bobble heads. A man wearing a red Trump hat and a pistol, leaning quietly against the railing of a sidewalk café. And everywhere you looked, antisocial impulses expressed in terms of mild vulgarity. There were T-shirts that showed a cartoon Trump flipping the bird to this person and that. T-shirts inviting you to contemplate the different ways Hillary Clinton and Monica Lewinsky could be said to suck. T-shirts reading, "Donald Fuckin' Trump." T-shirts showing a human scrotum painted up like the stars and stripes.

As you advanced toward the arena, the police presence became thicker and thicker and the scenery came to look more and more like the Green Zone in Baghdad. Soon you were walking not down a city street but between two lines of police standing shoulder to shoulder, then in a narrow chute between steel mesh walls. Credentials were checked, checked again, checked a third and fourth and fifth and sixth time.

The Republican convention itself, except for the final night, was not particularly well attended. Virtually none of the GOP's former leaders were in attendance: No Mitt Romney, no John McCain, no representatives of the Bush family. Production values were poor. Featured speakers were often obscure: minor celebrities or unknown businesspeople. Many of them had clearly not bothered to rehearse their remarks before delivering them.

The few Republican officials who did make an appearance were among the lamest public speakers I have ever sat and listened to. Speaker of the House Paul Ryan took care to do no more than was technically required of him by the party's rules. Mitch McConnell, the strikingly boring senator from Kentucky, was actually booed by the audience as he boasted lamely about his achievements in Congress. New Jersey governor Chris Christie gave a keynote speech enumerating Hillary Clinton's foreign policy screw-ups, not seeming to notice that in so doing he was flatly contradicting Donald Trump's own foreign policy positions.

There was plenty of the usual emotional manipulation. Delegates would be asked to admire some act of patriotic derring-do and then to grow outraged over some act of crime or treason. Up the mood would mechanically go, and then down: America—the greatest! America—horrifically betrayed! America—we must save her! There were heroic former soldiers, bearing noble words and tales of adventure. There were tragic victims, grieving relatives of people killed by illegal immigrants. There was a ritual deploring of crime in the streets. We learned that America was brave, that America was victimized, that America's leaders perversely refused even to "call the enemy by his rightful name."

Then there was the chant that would break out whenever people got enthusiastic: "Lock her up!" "Her" meaning Hillary Clinton, who was painted here with the exact opposite of the saintly goodness she preferred. Instead of the high-minded professional who fought for women and children, this Hillary was a criminal; instead of the holy warrior I saw at that Clinton Foundation gathering in New York, this Hillary was a jailbird who deserved a cell in Leavenworth. The glee and even hilarity with which the Trump delegates inverted Hillary's saintly image was remarkable: The delegates among whom I was sitting when the "Lock Her Up" chants first began were actually eating popcorn. Eventually a kindly old lady behind me asked my permission to steady herself on my shoulder as she got up and sat down. Then, just a few minutes later, I heard her frail voice raised in excitement: "Lock! Her! Up!"

When the smarmy, moralizing Senator Ted Cruz took the stage, however, things did not go as planned. Cruz delivered the kind of empty bloviating that ordinarily makes right-wingers purr. But after twenty minutes of applesauce, the audience noticed something: Cruz had not endorsed Trump, his bitter rival from the primary elections. As Cruz prepared to conclude, the delegates erupted, shouting "En! Dorse! Trump!" A man standing near me rolled his placard into a megaphone and screamed at the podium. The dealer in traditional right-wing platitudes was booed off the stage.

This was not Ted Cruz's Republican Party. Sitting in the audience, his wife was actually taunted with cries of "Goldman Sachs," the investment bank where she was employed. Even the culture wars, that staple of American reaction, were on hiatus in Cleveland. In the convention's most telling moment, an openly gay speaker condemned the culture wars for being a trick and a diversion and was applauded for saying so. No one here moaned about the horror of entitlement spending. Free trade, that pillar of the Republican faith, was completely gone.

Finally Donald Trump, whom one speaker called "America's blue-collar billionaire," stepped forward to cast himself as the protector of working-class America. And in comparison to everything else that had transpired over the course of the week, the man actually sounded . . . almost reasonable.

Of course, much of what Trump tried to sell the nation that night was a grossly exaggerated vision of terrorism and crime-in-the-streets. But the underlying fear to which Trump appealed was real. The American middle class really was disintegrating, and a part of the blame really did lie with lousy trade deals and a weirdly indifferent Democratic administration in Washington. For much of the country, it was true that the economy no longer worked, and it was also true that democracy often seemed like a theatrical performance in which only the powerful were served. Trump summoned this all-American cynicism in remarkably direct terms. "Big business, elite media, and major donors are lining up behind the campaign of my opponent because they know she will keep our rigged system in place," he said. "They are throwing money at her because they have total control over every single thing she does. She is their puppet, and they pull the strings."

The Republican also pledged himself to the working-class voters left behind by the current recovery. "I have visited the laid-off factory workers, and the communities crushed by our horrible and unfair trade deals," Trump announced at the apogee of his rhetoric, in an unmistakable echo of liberal hero Franklin Roosevelt. "These are the forgotten men and women of our country. People who work hard but no longer have a voice. I am your voice."

There was brilliance in the billionaire's bluster. By denouncing free trade and the culture wars, he was dynamiting the consensus orthodoxy that had dominated Washington for many years. This orthodoxy had, among other things, made possible endless sell-outs of working people by Democrats, who could savor their Tom Friedman columns and celebrate globalization's winners and still count on the votes of the angry working class because such people had "nowhere else to go." Clintonism would only work, however, as long as Republicans did their part and adhered to free-market orthodoxy. Take that consensus away and leave the Democrats as the only party of globalization, and they would immediately be exposed to a working-class revolt within their ranks.

Trump was openly calling for just such a revolt. He was explicitly casting himself as a protector of blue-collar workers. And working-class people, or the white ones, anyway, were flocking to his rallies. Polls taken shortly after the convention showed the political novice Trump actually catching up with the ultimate insider Hillary Clinton. Would Democrats notice that the political equation had changed?

VIRTUOUS PHILADELPHIA

The official slogan of the Democratic convention in Philadelphia was "stronger together," a jab at Trumpian divisiveness. But the real theme of the gathering was moral goodness, the same quality I saw enacted at the Best Buy Theater in New York back in 2015. Hillary's 2016 campaign was to be the greatest virtue quest of all time.

Virtue strident and highly rectified; *virtue* that was proud and in-your-face; *virtue* that was so stratospherically saintly that under no conditions could you hope to surpass it. These were *better people* on the stage of Philadelphia's Wells Fargo Center, miles better than Donald Trump's foul-mouthed Republicans.

Moral goodness geysered forth from the stage in an inexhaustible stream. Delegates heard about people succeeding despite disabilities or terrorism or horrible injuries or difficult medical conditions. People who had been hugged by President Obama and who wished "every American could hug President Obama." People who had been in Iraq and who believed in Hillary's powers of leadership.

Tears could be seen coursing down noble faces again and again. A video telling the story of a formerly undocumented person showed her trying to hold back tears three separate times. In another convention video, we watched a small girl cry because she was worried her parents would be deported. When Hillary Clinton then took the frightened child on her lap and promised to protect her, it triggered still more tears, this time from the grownups sitting next to the virtuous and protective Clinton.

There was a necessary and healthful aspect to all this. Trump richly deserved to be called out for his bigotry and sexism. Many voters would eventually back Hillary purely to show their disgust with Republican racism. But it is not easy to turn a political convention into a Sunday school. And what I saw in Philadelphia was a hollow performance. The virtue quest kept being defeated by the ugly facts on the ground. The lavish investment-bank parties about which attendees kept hearing, for example. Or the special deal that the party of organized labor struck with Uber to ferry delegates back and forth from the convention center.

Each of these contradictions exposed the larger problem the Democratic Party faced in 2016: It's hard for a group to make a stand against the powerful when the powerful are celebrated members of that very group. Countless delegates at the convention, for example, could be seen waving signs opposing the Trans-Pacific Partnership trade agreement and chanting "No TPP!" On day three of the convention, however, many of these same delegates cheered lustily for Barack Obama, who was working hard to make the TPP the final great achievement of his administration.

On another occasion, former presidential candidate Howard Dean told the Democrats that "We need a president who will ensure that the wealthiest among us play by the same rules as hard working, middle-class Americans"—worthy words, and very much in keeping with 2016's spirit of revolt. But only a short time before, the convention had welcomed former Attorney General Eric Holder, whose name is synonymous with the government's failure to hold wealthy bankers responsible for anything.

In the convention's keynote address, Elizabeth Warren, the senator from Massachusetts, recounted the various challenges besetting working-class citizens and then reminded delegates that "The stock market is breaking records. Corporate profits are at all-time highs. CEOs make tens of millions of dollars. There's lots of wealth in America, but it isn't trickling down to hard-working families like yours. Does anyone here have a problem with that?"

Anyone here? These things were taking place under the Democratic administration of Barack Obama. The failure of the wealth to trickle down was directly attributable to policy choices made by Obama and his Democratic predecessor, Bill Clinton, both of whom would be apotheosized in the days that followed.

In short, Democratic aspirants would have trouble enunciating an attractive economic message in 2016 because it was immediately contradicted by the deeds or failures of an actual existing Democratic administration. That left them to try to make the sale to voters on righteousness alone.

At the culmination of the Democrats' weeklong pageant of excellence and high moral achievement came Hillary Clinton herself, a vision of virtue dressed all in white, proclaiming unto us a series of thrilling banalities. The nation was facing a grave challenge, she announced, a veritable "moment of reckoning." The name of the threat was Donald Trump, a man, Clinton accused, who "wants to divide us—from the rest of the world, and from each other."

Clinton also assured us that she was a person who focused on details, who knew how to deliver real-world, "step-by-step" solutions to real problems. Then, turning to the frustrated working-class Americans who would ultimately decide the election, she promised "more good jobs with rising wages" and outlined exactly how she would make step-by-step, real-world progress on their problems:

> I believe America thrives when the middle class thrives. I believe our economy isn't working the way it should because our democracy isn't working the way it should.
>
> That's why we need to appoint Supreme Court justices who will get money out of politics and expand voting rights, not restrict them.

If the assembled Democrats noticed the disconnect between problem and solution in this oratorical maneuver, they didn't show it. Perhaps, like Hillary Clinton, they thought that the real divide between the two parties in 2016 was more about moral goodness than about proposing a program that made sense for ordinary people. "We will stand up against mean and divisive rhetoric wherever it comes from," candidate Clinton pronounced, alluding to Trump's many cruel and racist remarks. "[I]n the end," she said in conclusion, "it comes down to what Donald Trump doesn't get: America is great—because America is good."

When I think of the Democrats' convention, however, the image that always comes back to me is not one of transcendent goodness, but one of bewildering professional-class nonsense. I am walking across the vast Sahara of the Philadelphia convention center's parking lot in the hundred-degree summer heat—in heat so intense, so magnified by the asphalt that it is difficult to think. There were guards and a security fence to keep us all in line as we walked, of course, but on the other side of the enclosure, some well-connected someone had parked a school bus and as the sweating masses trudged by, this person stood there lecturing us through a bullhorn about the importance of innovation.

THE CAMPAIGN OF NATIONAL UNITY AND HOW IT FAILED

Then came the momentous upset. Nearly every poll, from the most scientific to the most amateurish, showed Hillary Clinton winning. Nearly every serious newspaper endorsed her, nearly every celebrity took her side. She reached out to Republicans. She chose a moderate for a running mate. She outspent Trump nearly two to one. She had the enthusiastic backing of Wall Street and Silicon Valley, of Republicans like Colin Powell and Hank Paulson. She ran a campaign of national unity—a great coming-together of the accomplished and the respectable—and it flopped. Donald Trump, a man who knew little about governing, who fractured his own party and who needlessly insulted millions of voters, rallied enough support in Ohio,

Pennsylvania, and Michigan to beat her soundly in the electoral college.

The blunders and scandals with which the campaign ended are worth remembering, of course: Hillary's complete failure to visit the formerly liberal state of Wisconsin, which she proceeded to lose; the hacking of various Democratic officials' email accounts; the FBI's apparent revival of its investigation of her shortly before election day; and the big increases in Obamacare premiums, which came (as if sent by Trump himself) just before the contest came to an end.

But it's pointless to evade the obvious: This was a catastrophic failure for the professional-class ideology. Hillary ran as the résumé candidate, as a hyper-competent expert who knew how everything worked and who was brought to us by the very latest in micro-targeting and big data. And yet she couldn't defeat the most unqualified candidate of all time. Her campaign strategy of flattering well-educated Republicans in the suburbs while scolding the uneducated "deplorables" who were drawn to her opponent made her a caricature of what people dislike about professionals.

Of course, Hillary's campaign was persuasive to some. Journalists at prestigious media outlets seemed to regard her campaign as a crusade, and they signed up with unprecedented enthusiasm. Her strategy of outreach to the highly educated worked so well in affluent areas and college towns that she actually bested her predecessor Barack Obama in places like the creamy suburbs of Darien, Connecticut, and Wellesley, Massachusetts.[2] And, of course, she raised and spent almost twice as much as Donald Trump did.

But it was the more thickly populated working-class precincts of the northern Midwest that did her in. County after deindustrialized county in this region abandoned their traditional political allegiance and embraced the tough-talking rich guy. Nationally, Hillary lost among white men who had not been to college by 48 points and by 27 points among non-college white women—this latter a group that Democrats had assumed would be thrilled by the prospect of a female president and appalled by Trump's crude sexism. Working-class voters of other races stuck with her but not with the enthusiasm or the numbers they had given to Barack Obama. Shortly after the election, a *New York Times* reporter visited a black neighborhood in Milwaukee, Wisconsin—one of the industrial states Hillary lost—and discovered that voters there simply didn't care about the Democratic nominee. Once upon a time, Barack Obama had been a hero to them, but as a shopkeeper put it, "then eight years happened."[3]

We will never know precisely what issues sank Hillary Clinton, but trade certainly bulked large among them. According to 2016 exit polls, those who were skeptical about free trade—and there were more of them than there were trade optimists—went for Donald Trump by 32 points.[4] What makes this result so poignant, of course, is that trade was where it all began for the Clintons: This was the issue, during the NAFTA debate of 1993, where white-collar liberalism defined itself. Trade was the spot where the smart young liberals who knew how to run an economy first stuck the knife into organized labor. Over the years, trade became the space where liberal columnists and prize-winning economists would get together to celebrate the way their enlightened worldview coincided with their amazing prosperity. And now trade has become the junkyard where it all came apart, where blue-collar America finally got even with the Clinton dynasty.

I ended the original edition of this book by exhorting my fellow white-collar liberals to look in the mirror. We are in some ways responsible, I wanted them to understand, for what has befallen average Americans, and Democrats need to change course for reasons of the country's well-being as well as for what I called "their own partisan health."

It is not hard to imagine what such a rebuilding project will look like. Democrats will need to remember who they are. They will have to rededicate themselves to the economic well-being of ordinary citizens. They must publicly attack concentration of wealth and economic power whether it happens in Silicon Valley or in farm country. They must rediscover that higher education, like health care, is a free people's right, not a privilege. They will need to turn away from fatuous (if convenient) theories about how smartphones liberate us all. They will have to shake off their fuzzy-minded admiration for Wall Street. Think twice about trade agreements. Defend the right of workers to organize. Start enforcing antitrust laws again, and tell the public why they are doing all of these things in no uncertain terms.

But even after the debacle of 2016, liberals show little taste for the self-examination that is required of them. On the contrary: They have just run a campaign that embodied everything objectionable about the professional-class outlook, and in the aftermath of its failure, they have insisted on blaming everyone but themselves. As I write this, Democratic insiders can be heard blaming Bernie Sanders for Hillary Clinton's loss. Or blaming the sexism of the public. Or blaming "fake news." Or blaming real news. Or blaming Russia. Or blaming the FBI. I have even heard some declare that any effort to win over working-class voters is a tacit capitulation to racism. Better to lose future elections than to compete for the votes of those who spurned their beloved Hillary.

Donald Trump, for his part, will make an almost perfect epitaph for the era of professional-class liberalism. He is the opposite of what it respects. Barack Obama left office by publishing scholarly articles in *Science* and *Harvard Law Review*. Trump, by contrast, lacks government experience completely, holds expertise in contempt, and is noticeably indifferent to facts—each a striking repudiation of the professional ideology. For Washington bipartisanship he gives nary a damn. He is a human middle finger to the respect for process, for consensus, and for stately contemplation that made up Barack Obama's vision of the presidency.

So we bounce on, from government by one group of affluent people to government by a different group of affluent people. Consensus-minded centrism yields to authoritarianism, which will self-destruct in time and allow the consensus-minded another chance, which they will inevitably fumble, and so on. When will it all end? When the People finally come back for their Party.

NOTES

INTRODUCTION

1. See figure 3 in the paper by Andrew Figura and David Ratner, "The Labor Share of Income and Equilibrium Unemployment," *FEDS Notes*, June 8, 2015.
2. The poll was taken by the Public Religion Research Institute, dated July 21–August 15, 2014. Seventy-two percent of the people polled said the economy was "still in a recession." The Dow hit 17,000 in July and August of 2014.
3. These are Piketty-Saez numbers as analyzed by the economist Josh Bivens of the Economic Policy Institute. Josh Bivens, "Taking Redistribution and Growth Seriously," EPI Briefing Paper (forthcoming), Table 1, p. 45. The economist Emmanuel Saez estimates that the "the top 1% captured 91% of the income gains in the first three years of the recovery" and that the "pre-tax income share" of the top 10 percent hit 50.6 percent in 2012, the highest share since the income tax began. See "Striking It Richer: The Evolution of Top Incomes in the United States (Updated with 2013 Preliminary Estimates)," a paper dated January 25, 2015, and available on the website of the Econometrics Laboratory of the University of California at Berkeley.
4. See Philip Longman, "Wealth and Generations," *Washington Monthly*, June/July 2015.
5. Sarah Anderson, "Off the Deep End: The Wall Street Bonus Pool

and Low-Wage Workers," Institute for Policy Studies, March 11, 2015.

6. *The Center Holds* is the title of Jonathan Alter's second chronicle of the Obama years. Alter, *The Center Holds: Obama and His Enemies* (Simon & Schuster, 2013).
7. Ron Brownstein of the *National Journal.* This is how he described the "coalition of the ascendant" on MSNBC on November 6, 2008, two days after Obama was elected president.
8. Suskind, *Confidence Men: Wall Street, Washington, and the Education of a President* (Harper, 2011), p. 235.

1: THEORY OF THE LIBERAL CLASS

1. Benton is quoted this way in Arthur Schlesinger Jr.'s *The Age of Jackson* (Little Brown, 1953), p. 125.
2. Brooks Jackson, *Honest Graft: Big Money and the American Political Process* (Knopf, 1988), p. 35. Jackson describes the House of Representatives this way not merely because of labor's clout but because it didn't require much money to be elected to Congress in those days and also because, once elected, incumbents tended to be reelected for years.
3. This is part of the opening sentence of Lasch's 1965 book, *The New Radicalism in America 1889–1963* (W. W. Norton).
4. Charles Derber, William A. Schwartz, and Yale Magrass, *Power in the Highest Degree: Professionals and the Rise of a New Mandarin Order* (Oxford, 1990), p. 4.
5. Illich, *Disabling Professions* (Marion Boyars, 1977), p. 17.
6. Derber et al., *Power in the Highest Degree*, pp. 16–17. On jargon and mystification, see pp. 92–94. "To maintain scarcity [as professions do] implies a tendency to monopoly," writes the sociologist Magali Larson: "monopoly of expertise in the market, monopoly of status in a system of stratification." Larson, *The Rise of Professionalism: A Sociological Analysis* (University of California Press, 1977), p. xvii.
7. On "social trustee professionalism," see Steven Brint, *In an Age of Experts: The Changing Roles of Professionals in Politics and Public Life* (Princeton, 1996), chapter 2.
8. Frank Fischer, *Technocracy and the Politics of Expertise* (Sage Publications, 1990), p. 104.

9. Fischer describes technocratic views as follows: "Few technocrats openly argue that democracy per se is wrongheaded; rather, they merely contend that it must be dramatically redefined in hierarchical, elitist terms. Democracy, as traditionally understood, is believed to be simply incompatible with the realities of a complex postindustrial society." *Technocracy*, p. 35.
10. The nineteenth-century anarchist Mikhail Bakunin warns against "the reign of scientific intelligence, the most aristocratic, despotic, arrogant and elitist of all regimes. There will be a new class, a new hierarchy of real and counterfeit scientists and scholars, and the world will be divided into a minority ruling in the name of knowledge, and an immense ignorant majority. And then, woe unto the mass of ignorant ones." The passage is famously quoted in one of Noam Chomsky's best-known essays, "Intellectuals and the State" (1977).
11. Larson, *The Rise of Professionalism*, p. 134. On the medical profession in the Age of Jackson, see Paul Starr, *The Social Transformation of American Medicine: The Rise of a Sovereign Profession and the Making of a Vast Industry* (Basic Books, 1982), chapter 1. "Mystification and concealment" are lines Starr quotes from an indignant newspaper editorial of 1833.
12. I describe it more thoroughly in *What's the Matter with Kansas?*, p. 83.
13. I am following here the account of "Professionals Versus Democracy" furnished by political scientist Albert W. Dzur in *Democratic Professionalism: Citizen Participation and the Reconstruction of Professional Ethics, Identity, and Practice* (Penn State Press, 2008). The classic account of the technocracy's failure in the Vietnam War is, of course, David Halberstam's *The Best and the Brightest*.
14. Manza and Brooks, *Social Cleavages and Political Change* (Oxford, 1999), pp. 5, 213.
15. Hedges, *The Death of the Liberal Class* (Nation Books, 2011).
16. Hayes, *Twilight of the Elites: America After Meritocracy* (Crown, 2012), p. 48.
17. Brint, "The Political Attitudes of Professionals," *Annual Review of Sociology*, vol. 11 (1985), p. 400. Brint repeats many of these findings in *In An Age of Experts*:

    No more than 40 percent strongly favor current or higher levels of spending on government social-reform programs,

> and no more than 20 percent indicate significant interest in reducing income inequalities between rich and poor. They trust business far more than labor, and government is often considered more a problem than a solution facing the country. [p. 86]

Brint concludes his 1985 survey as follows: "When economic issues are central, most members [of the professional/"new class"] will ally as junior partners to the higher bourgeoisie." p. 410.

18. Larson, *The Rise of Professionalism*, pp. xvii, 236.
19. Derber et al., *Power in the Highest Degree*, p. 174.
20. Alter, *The Promise: President Obama, Year One* (Simon & Schuster, 2010), p. 64.
21. This idea is explained by Jeff Schmidt in *Disciplined Minds: A Critical Look at Salaried Professionals and the Soul-Battering System That Shapes Their Lives* (Rowman & Littlefield, 2000), p. 208.
22. "The narcissistic individualism of professionals, each chasing a private career in a library or laboratory cubicle, impedes professional class solidarity." Derber, p. 182. Nearly every book I read about professionals included some account of their hostility to blue-collar workers and organized labor. Cf. Larson, p. x; Derber, p. 188; or the classic, Barbara Ehrenreich's *Fear of Falling: The Inner Life of the Middle Class* (Pantheon, 1989), chapter 3.
23. A helpful index to the Hamilton Project's many papers on higher ed and inequality can be found here: http://www.hamiltonproject.org/papers/hamilton_project_work_on_higher_education_policy_proposals_to_promote_/
24. Knapp, "Middle Class Is Moving Forward, Not Backward," *Washington Post*, January 15, 2012.
25. Duncan, quoted in Paul Tough, "What Does Obama Really Believe In," *New York Times Magazine*, August 15, 2012.
26. Bernanke, "Remarks on Class Day, 2008," at Harvard University, http://www.federalreserve.gov/newsevents/speech/bernanke20080604a.htm. I count Bernanke as an honorary member of the liberal class thanks to his service as Barack Obama's Fed Chairman.
27. Friedman, "My Secretary of State," *New York Times*, November 27, 2012. For more examples of this kind of talk, see Hayes, *Twilight of the Elites*, pp. 48–49.

28. William R. Emmons, Bryan J. Noeth, "Why Didn't Higher Education Protect Hispanic and Black Wealth?," *In the Balance* (a publication of the Federal Reserve Bank of St. Louis) #12, 2015.
29. Freidson, as quoted in Larson, *The Rise of Professionalism*, p. xii.
30. Galbraith, "How the Economists Got It Wrong," *The American Prospect*, December 19, 2001.
31. See Jeff Schmidt, *Disciplined Minds*, pp. 21–24.
32. On this subject, see Yves Smith, *ECONned* (Palgrave Macmillan, 2010).
33. Bernard Crick, *In Defence of Politics* (Penguin, 1964); Evgeny Morozov, *To Save Everything, Click Here* (Public Affairs, 2013), pp. 135–39; Dzur, *Democratic Professionalism*, p. 87.
34. Callahan acknowledges that the recent alignment of certain very rich people with the Democrats won't help to advance every single liberal issue, but it will help with many of them. "Right now, though, class warfare is a losing proposition," he writes. "Our better hope is that a creative new progressive politics can enlist the growing ranks of rich liberals in proactive efforts to reduce inequality and diminish their own prestige." Callahan, *Fortunes of Change: The Rise of the Liberal Rich and the Remaking of America* (John Wiley, 2010), p. 284.
35. According to historian Morton Keller, Obama took 51 percent of the campaign contributions of the financial industry that year. See *Obama's Time* (Oxford, 2014), p. 77.
36. Callahan, *Fortunes of Change*, pp. 36–37.

2: HOW CAPITALISM GOT ITS GROOVE BACK

1. In his *Making of the President* book for 1968, the journalist Theodore White wrote that "Labor's support and labor's money had been essential to every Democratic national campaign since 1936—but never did those who lead labor perform more effectively, more skillfully, with greater impact, than in 1968. In the near-miracle of the [Hubert] Humphrey comeback in October, no single factor was more important than the army of organized labor, roused to the greatest political exertion of its history." White, *The Making of the President 1968* (Atheneum, 1969), pp. 425–426. What moved the unions to such an effort, per White, was the alarming white-backlash campaign of George Wallace.

2. Here is how White characterized the change: "The new reforms had by 1972 given categorical representation to young people, to women, to blacks—but yielded no recognition at all, as a category, to men who work for a living." *The Making of the President 1972* (Harper Perennial, 2010), p. 38.
3. Ibid.
4. Shafer calls this a "circulation of elites, the replacement of one group of specialized political actors with another of noticeably different origins, values, and ways of pursuing politics." Specifically: "The old coalition was based in blue-collar constituencies, while the newer version was white-collar from top to bottom." Byron Shafer, *Quiet Revolution: The Struggle for the Democratic Party and the Shaping of Post-Reform Politics* (Russell Sage Foundation, 1983), pp. 7, 8, 530.
5. This is Shafer's larger point in *Quiet Revolution*: Whenever they were permitted to choose personnel or rules or testimony, the Democrats in charge of the McGovern Commission steered the process of party reform in this desired direction. The labor unions, which were underrepresented in the first place, basically boycotted the proceedings, making it that much easier for the reformers.
6. This was the period of what Barbara Ehrenreich calls "The Discovery of the Working Class," i.e., the media's erroneous "discovery" that the working class was racist and conservative and pro-war. See *Fear of Falling*, chapter 3.
7. On the McGovern campaign, see Jefferson Cowie, *Stayin' Alive: The 1970s and the Last Days of the Working Class* (The New Press, 2010). On McGovern's relative performance among "highly skilled professionals" and working-class voters, see John B. Judis and Ruy Teixeira, *The Emerging Democratic Majority* (Scribner, 2002), p. 38. On McGovern's appeal in Massachusetts, see Lily Geismer, *Don't Blame Us: Suburban Liberals and the Transformation of the Democratic Party* (Princeton, 2015).
8. Cowie, *Stayin' Alive*, pp. 235–6.
9. I am relying here on the description of Rick Perlstein, who writes of Hart's attitude toward old-school Democrats: "He held them in open contempt." See *The Invisible Bridge: The Fall of Nixon and the Rise of Reagan* (Simon & Schuster, 2014), p. 317. Upon Hart's retirement from politics after a 1987 sex scandal, E. J. Dionne wrote that Hart's significance arose from "his success in breaking . . .

the bond to the New Deal politics of the 1930's that has slowed the party in recent years." Dionne, "The Hart Legacy: He Broke Democrats' Link With Politics of New Deal," *New York Times*, May 12, 1987.

10. Miller Center, University of Virginia, "Interview with Alfred E. Kahn," December 10–11, 1981, available on the Miller Center's website.
11. I have written about this phenomenon so many times it makes me feel old just thinking about it. For a summary, see http://www.salon.com/2014/11/23/thomas_frank_phony_spin_even_fox_news_wont_buy.
12. The political scientist is Vicente Navarro. All of the quotations in this paragraph are drawn from the fourth edition of Leuchtenburg's book, *In the Shadow of FDR: From Harry Truman to Barack Obama* (Cornell, 2015, Kindle edition).
13. Manifesto: Charles Peters, "A Neoliberal's Manifesto," *Washington Monthly*, May, 1983. "The solutions of the thirties": Randall Rothenberg, *The Neo-Liberals: Creating the New American Politics* (Simon & Schuster, 1984), p. 27, italics in original; "Our hero": Charles Peters' manifesto. See also Robert M. Kaus, "The Trouble with Unions," *Harper's Magazine*, June 1983.
14. On the DLC's corporate backing, see Robert Dreyfuss, "How the DLC Does It," *The American Prospect*, December 19, 2001. Otherwise, I am following here the account of the DLC outlined by Kenneth S. Baer in *Reinventing Democrats: The Politics of Liberalism from Reagan to Clinton* (University Press of Kansas, 2000); Baer emphasizes the importance of working-class voters in the DLC's early thinking. "Forgotten Democrats" appears on p. 97. "Higher socioeconomic status Democrats" is a phrase used in the once-famous 1989 manifesto, "The Politics of Evasion," written for the group by the political scientists William Galston and Elaine Kamarck and available online at http://www.progressivepolicy.org/wp-content/uploads/2013/03/Politics_of_Evasion.pdf.
15. The DLC's 1990 manifesto (signed by its chairman, Bill Clinton) was called the New Orleans Declaration; its 1991 iteration was called the New American Choice Resolutions. Both are summarized in Baer, *Reinventing Democrats*.
16. Baer calls this the period of the DLC's "'futurist' outlook," p. 167.

Michael Rothschild, "Beyond Repair: The Politics of the Machine Age Are Hopelessly Obsolete," *The New Democrat*, July/August 1995.

17. Galston and Kamarck, "Five Realities That Will Shape 21st Century Politics," *Blueprint*, Fall 1998.
18. The story of the DLC's final, disastrous triangulation during the George W. Bush administration is told in Ronald Brownstein's *The Second Civil War: How Extreme Partisanship Has Paralyzed Washington and Polarized America* (Penguin, 2008), chapter 9.

3: THE ECONOMY, STUPID

1. Phillips, *The Politics of Rich and Poor: Wealth and the American Electorate in the Reagan Aftermath* (Random House, 1990), p. xx.
2. Donald Barlett and James Steele, *America: What Went Wrong?* (Andrews McMeel, 1992), p. xi.
3. The first two quotations are drawn from a *New York Times* article on "Clinton's Standard Campaign Speech," dated April 26, 1992. The third comes from a Clinton speech delivered in Portsmouth, New Hampshire, in January of 1992. Watch it here: http://www.c-span.org/video/?24051-1/clinton-campaign-speech.
4. On the influence of Reich's book, see Bob Woodward, *The Agenda: Inside the Clinton White House* (Simon & Schuster, 1994), p. 20.
5. Defining productivity as gross output per hour and wage growth as real hourly compensation of production workers, with data for both from the Bureau of Labor Statistics. See Susan Fleck, John Glaser, and Shawn Sprague, "The Compensation Gap: A Visual Essay," *Monthly Labor Review*, January 2011. There are, of course, other ways to define these categories.
6. The East Coast professor was Paul Lazarsfeld of Columbia University. See John Summers, "Perpetual Revelations: C. Wright Mills and Paul Lazarsfeld," *Annals of the American Academy of Political and Social Science*, November 2006.
7. Steven K. Ashby and C. J. Hawking describe the work-to-rule campaign and its effects in *Staley: The Fight for a New American Labor Movement* (University of Illinois Press, 2009), chapter 4. The results are described on p. 57.
8. My article on the struggles in Decatur, which I coauthored with David Mulcahey, was called "This Is War"; it appeared in the *Chi-*

cago Reader on January 20, 1995. A similar description of the twelve-hour rotating shift can be found in Ashby and Hawking, p. 64.

9. Don Fites, quoted in Stephen Franklin, *Three Strikes: Labor's Heartland Losses and What They Mean for Working Americans* (Guilford Press, 2001), p. 42.
10. Louis Uchitelle, "Union Leaders Fight for a Place in the President's Workplace of the Future," *New York Times*, August 8, 1993.
11. The quotation from Plankenhorn originally appeared in Frank and Mulcahey, "This Is War."
12. Martin Walker, *The President We Deserve: Bill Clinton, His Rise, Falls, and Comebacks* (Crown, 1996), p. 61. By "foreign," I believe Walker meant foreign to Britain.
13. On the Baird nomination, see Robert Kuttner's column for January 22, 1993, "Zoe Baird: Feminist Legal Titan"; I read it on the website of the *Baltimore Sun*. Page wrote about "Yuppie Crimes" in the *Chicago Tribune*, January 17, 1993.
14. Weisberg's article was entitled "Clincest: Washington's New Ruling Class"; it appeared in *The New Republic* for April 26, 1993.

4: AGENTS OF CHANGE

1. Carl Bernstein, *A Woman in Charge: The Life of Hillary Rodham Clinton* (Vintage, 2008). See p. 350, for example.
2. From Clinton's speech, "Remarks to the Seattle APEC Host Committee," delivered on November 19, 1993. Read the speech on the website of the American Presidency Project: http://www.presidency.ucsb.edu/ws/?pid=46137
3. This remark from 1995 is found in Walker, *The President We Deserve*, p. 343. In truth, this sort of reasoning was everywhere in the 1990s. See chapters 6 and 10 of my own Clinton-era book, *One Market Under God* (Doubleday, 2000), which are filled with the fashionable inevitability-speak of the era.
4. Clinton's remarks, dated December 8, 1993, are available on the website of the Miller Center at the University of Virginia. The stationery is described in John R. MacArthur's book, *The Selling of "Free Trade": NAFTA, Washington, and the Subversion of American Democracy* (Hill & Wang, 2000), p. 217.

5. MacArthur, *The Selling of "Free Trade,"* A transcript of Iacocca's commercial is on p. 223.
6. Ibid. This is MacArthur's great overarching point.
7. Johnson, "The Free Trade Accord: Workers on Free Trade: A Split Along Class Lines," *New York Times*, November 14, 1993. Faux: This is the first anecdote in his 2006 book, *The Global Class War: How America's Bipartisan Elite Lost Our Future—and What It Will Take to Win It Back* (Wiley), p. 1.
8. The letter was much discussed during the NAFTA debate. My quote from it is drawn from David Lauter, "283 Top Economists Back Trade Pact, Letter Shows," the *Los Angeles Times*, September 4, 1993.
9. See the 1997 study by Kate Bronfenbrenner, "We'll Close! Plant Closings, Plant-Closing Threats, Union Organizing and NAFTA," posted online at http://digitalcommons.ilr.cornell.edu/cgi/viewcontent.cgi?article=1018&context=cbpubs. The 2010 study is summarized by Robert Scott in "Heading South: U.S.-Mexico trade and job displacement after NAFTA," an Economic Policy Institute Briefing Paper dated May 3, 2011.
10. See the economist Mark Weisbrot's article, "NAFTA: 20 Years of Regret for Mexico," *Guardian*, January 4, 2014. See also the February 2014 report Weisbrot coauthored with Stephan Lefebvre and Joseph Sammut at the Center for Economic and Policy Research, "Did NAFTA Help Mexico? An Assessment After 20 Years."
11. One place where Friedman used the phrase "no-brainer" was in his column for April 3, 1997, "Gephardt vs. Gore." His remarks about CAFTA came on the Tim Russert Show, CNBC, July 29, 2006, transcript from Nexis.
12. See the article by Daniel Maliniak and Ryan Powers, "Is the Public Really Learning to Love Globalization?," which appeared on the *Washington Post*'s "Monkey Cage" blog for June 11, 2014.
13. Gergen's remark was reportedly made on a PBS news program. See "Another Attempt to Begin Again; Clinton Hopes to Reach Out To 'Forgotten Middle Class,'" *Washington Post*, December 15, 1994. Ann Devroy, "New Age 'Guru to the Glitterati' Advised Clintons," *Washington Post*, January 11, 1995.
14. Clinton's use of the term "counter-scheduling" is described in Jack Germond and Jules Witcover, *Mad As Hell: Revolt at the Ballot Box, 1992* (Warner Books, 1992), p. 265.

15. "Clinton planned the confrontation as a defining moment of his campaign, insisting that the future of the Democratic Party could not be left in the hands of the minority vote of the inner cities." Walker, *The President We Deserve*, p. 144.

    Centrists still call for "Sister Souljah moments" to this day: for example, in a June 16, 2010, column in *The Hill*, Clinton associate Lanny Davis suggested that Barack Obama stage "Sister Souljah"-style snubs of labor unions and progressive groups that thought Obama wasn't liberal enough.
16. "Finest hour" was the phrase used by the Democratic Leadership Council to describe Clinton's NAFTA win in December of 1993 (per Kenneth S. Baer in *Reinventing Democrats*, p. 218); the phrase was also used in editorials by the *Baltimore Sun* and various Hearst papers; Thomas Friedman characterized it as Vice President Al Gore's "finest hour" in his *New York Times* column for April 3, 1997. Bonus cliché points: He also described it as a "no-brainer" in the same column. "Boldest action" was Walker's phrase, *The President We Deserve*, p. 285.
17. Hitchens, *No One Left to Lie To: The Triangulations of William Jefferson Clinton* (Verso, 1999), p. 39.
18. On the evolution of the Democratic platform, see Marc Fisher, "Democratic Party Platform: An Uneven Progression Over the Years," *Washington Post*, September 4, 2012. "Upping the ante": The presidential aides in question were Bruce Reed and Jose Cerda III. They and Biden are quoted in Naomi Murakawa, *The First Civil Right: How Liberals Built Prison America* (Oxford, 2014, Kindle edition). Murakawa also points out that the 1994 crime bill established 116 new mandatory minimum sentences, considerably more than were established in the Reagan and Bush I administrations put together.
19. Lieberman quoted in Mark Pazniokas, "Tough Stands on Crime May Ignore Reality," *Hartford Courant*, October 20, 1994.
20. The crime bill of 1994 authorized the U.S. Sentencing Commission to relitigate the matter of the crack vs. powder cocaine disparity. The commission recommended that the disparity be minimized, and it would have been had not Congress then voted to overturn the commission's recommendations. Bill Clinton then signed the legislation instead of vetoing it. See his signing statement on that occasion, "Statement on Signing Legislation Rejecting U.S.

Sentencing Commission Recommendations," dated October 30, 1995 and available on the website of the American Presidency Project. See also Ann Devroy, "Clinton Signs Legislation Keeping Stiff Crack Policy," *Houston Chronicle*, October 31, 1995. The 88 percent figure comes from an editorial in the *Atlanta Journal and Constitution*, October 20, 1995.

21. One of the 1994 crime bill's provisions was to fund "Midnight Basketball" leagues around the country, a program that was derided so widely as typical Democratic pork-barrel spending that it came to eclipse the crime bill's more important crackdown elements. The chief derider was, of course, radio talker Rush Limbaugh. Among others, see Susan J. Douglas, *Listening In: Radio and the American Imagination* (Minnesota, 2004), p. 315.
22. Bill Clinton, "How We Ended Welfare, Together," *New York Times*, August 22, 2006.
23. From's remark occurs on p. 229 of his 2013 book, *The New Democrats and the Return to Power* (St. Martin's). The Harris quote can be found in his 2005 book, *The Survivor: Bill Clinton in the White House* (Random House, Kindle edition). The "personal cost" to which Harris refers is the resignation of Clinton's friend Peter Edelman from the administration. Other accounts I have read seem to take the same perspective: that this was Clinton's final arrival at the centrist sweet spot. See Steven M. Gillon, *The Pact: Bill Clinton, Newt Gingrich, and the Rivalry That Defined a Generation* (Oxford, 2008), p. 178, and Joe Klein, *The Natural: The Misunderstood Presidency of Bill Clinton* (Doubleday, 2002), p. 152.
24. Blumenthal, *The Clinton Wars* (Farrar, Straus and Giroux, 2003), p. 147.
25. Gillon, *The Pact*, p. 181.
26. Bob Woodward, *The Agenda: Inside the Clinton White House* (Simon & Schuster, 1994), p. 240.
27. Ibid., p. 165.
28. Stiglitz uses these words on p. 44 of *The Roaring Nineties: A New History of the World's Most Prosperous Decade* (W. W. Norton, 2004), his account of the Clinton years.

    Here is my understanding of the peculiar chain of events that Stiglitz describes: By signaling his intention to balance the budget (and then actually balancing it), Clinton encouraged long-term interest rates to drop. Meanwhile, in the aftermath of the S&L crisis, American banks were holding lots of long-term government bonds. The drop in interest rates handed the banks a windfall but made long-term bonds a less attractive investment going forward. This prompted the banks, as Stiglitz puts it, to go "back to their real business, which is lending." And this, in turn, got the economy going again. *The Roaring Nineties*, pp. 42–44.

29. On Al Gore, see Jeff Faux, "The Next Recession," *American Prospect*, August 15, 2000.
30. Thomas Friedman, "Stock Market Diplomacy; Clinton's Foreign Policy Includes a Regard for How a Move Plays in Global Trading," *New York Times*, April 6, 1994.
31. "Strong take over the weak": The banker in question was Hugh McColl of NationsBank (later Bank of America), who advocated interstate bank deregulation with these words in 1992, according to the Federal Reserve's history of the Riegle-Neal banking act, available online at http://www.federalreservehistory.org/Events/DetailView/50. Stiglitz: *The Roaring Nineties*, p. 90.
32. The memo was unearthed by Nomi Prins and is quoted in *All the Presidents' Bankers: The Hidden Alliances that Drive American Power* (Nation Books, 2014), p. 371. On the effects of the Riegle-Neal Act, see: Simon Johnson and James Kwak, *13 Bankers: The Wall Street Takeover and the Next Financial Meltdown* (Pantheon, 2010), p. 84; and the *Financial Crisis Inquiry Report* (2011), chapter 4.
33. Gross, *Bull Run*, p. 96. Rubin himself later wrote that he organized the bailout to prevent the "market-based" model imposed by NAFTA from being discredited, which is slightly less self-interested, I suppose. See Rubin's memoir (with Jacob Weisberg), *In an Uncertain World: Tough Choices from Wall Street to Washington* (Random House, 2003), p. 5.
34. Rubin testified to this effect before the House Committee on Banking in May 1995. His words are quoted in Nomi Prins, *It Takes a Pillage* (Wiley, 2009), p. 141.
35. "Infamous": See "These Gambling Activities," a retrospective on Glass-Steagall published in *The Region*, a publication of the Federal Reserve Bank of Minneapolis, March 2000, available online at https://www.minneapolisfed.org/publications/the-region/issues/3-2000. "Almost everybody agreed": See Keith Bradsher, "No New

Deal for Banking; Efforts to Drop Depression-Era Barriers Stall, Again," November 2, 1995.

36. Quoted in Stephen Labaton, "Agreement Reached on Overhaul of U.S. Financial System," *New York Times*, October 23, 1999.
37. The story was written by Joshua Cooper Ramo and ran in *Time*'s edition for February 14, 1999. The individual quoted in the comment about Rubin's Treasury Department is none other than future Treasury Secretary Tim Geithner.
38. On this subject, see "The Real Danger of 'One Big Regulator,'" my column in the *Wall Street Journal* for November 11, 2009.
39. Stiglitz, *The Roaring Nineties*, p. 180.

5: IT TAKES A DEMOCRAT

1. This is a theme I discussed at much greater length in *One Market Under God: Extreme Capitalism, Market Populism and the End of Economic Democracy* (Doubleday, 2000), chapter one. The quote comes from page 17.
2. Gillon, *The Pact*, p. xiv.
3. Ibid., p. 209.
4. Ibid., p. 213.
5. Ibid., pp. xvi, 217, 218–19.
6. See Christopher Glazek, "Raise the Crime Rate," *n+1*, Winter 2012. Glazek's finding is controversial, but the numbers he uses for his comparison are not contested. See also "More Men are Raped in the US than Women, Figures on Prison Assaults Reveal," London *Daily Mail*, October 3, 2013.
7. *The First Civil Right: How Liberals Built Prison America* (Oxford, 2014), p. 148.
8. During the eight years of Bill Clinton's presidency, the prison population grew by 673,000. This is significantly more than the second-place record holder, Ronald Reagan, and far more than what George W. Bush achieved. See Greg Krikorian, "Federal and State Prison Populations Soared Under Clinton, Report Finds," *Los Angeles Times*, February 19, 2001.
9. Michelle Alexander, *The New Jim Crow: Mass Incarceration in the Age of Colorblindness* (New Press, 2013), p. 56.
10. 1991: This line appears in Clinton's speech to the DLC convention in that year. 1995: This line is from remarks delivered at the Uni-

versity of Texas, as reported by the *Washington Post*, October 17. Clinton signed the crack/cocaine legislation on October 30. 2000: The *Rolling Stone* interview is from December 28. 2008: See DeWayne Wickham, "Clinton Admits 'Regret' on Crack Cocaine Sentencing," *USA Today*, March 4.

11. Bruce Reed, "The Work Decade," *Blueprint*, September/October 2001.
12. Hitchens, *No One Left to Lie To*, p. 65.
13. See Peter Edelman, *So Rich, So Poor* (New Press, 2012), chapter 5, and the policy brief, "Extreme Poverty in the United States, 1996 to 2011," issued by the National Poverty Center in February 2012. The food stamp program is now called Supplemental Nutrition Assistance Program; recipients are counted by the Food and Nutrition Service of the United States Department of Agriculture.
14. See the National Vital Statistics Report, "Nonmarital Childbearing in the United States, 1940–99," dated October 18, 2000, table 1. http://files.eric.ed.gov/fulltext/ED446210.pdf.
15. Wacquant, *Punishing the Poor: The Neoliberal Government of Social Insecurity* (Duke, 2009, Kindle edition).
16. On financialization, see Dylan Matthews, "The Clinton Economy, In Charts," *Washington Post*, September 5, 2012. On CEO compensation, see Alyssa Davis and Lawrence Mishel, "CEO Pay Continues to Rise as Typical Workers Are Paid Less," a paper dated June 12, 2014, on the website of the Economic Policy Institute.
17. Yergin and Stanislaw, *The Commanding Heights: The Battle Between Government and the Marketplace That Is Remaking the Modern World* (Simon & Schuster, 1998), p. 381. This book was later made into a PBS documentary with the same title.
18. Walker, *The President We Deserve*, pp. 333, 332.
19. Quoted in Gillon, *The Pact*, p. 268.
20. DeWayne Davis and Jeff Lemieux, "Closing the Income Gap," *Blueprint*, Summer 2000.

6: THE HIPSTER AND THE BANKER SHOULD BE FRIENDS

1. See Reagan's 1988 speech at Moscow State University; it is reprinted, among other places, on the website of the Miller Center at the

University of Virginia. The conservative author George Gilder, one of Reagan's favorites, wrote one of the earliest and most forceful accounts of the New Economy ideology in his 1989 book *Microcosm*.

2. The DLC's think tank was the Progressive Policy Institute; their 1999 report was called "The State New Economy Index." Other installments were issued periodically throughout the decade to come. Later on, authorship of the index was taken over by the Ewing Kauffman Foundation and the Information Technology & Innovation Foundation, a Washington think tank. The coauthor of the 2007 State New Economy Index, Daniel Correa, later became President Obama's Senior Adviser for Innovation Policy.
3. This passage can be found in Chapter 1 of *Cluetrain*; it is signed by Christopher Locke (the author of *Gonzo Marketing*) and available online at http://www.cluetrain.com/book/apocalypso.html.
4. Pritzker once chaired the board at Superior Bank of Chicago, a securitizer of subprime real estate loans that closed in 2001. See David Moberg, "3 Troubling Things to Know about Penny Pritzker," *In These Times*, May 3, 2013. According to her bio on a government website, Lee formerly worked as Head of Patents and Patent Strategy for Google. See http://www.uspto.gov/about-us/executive-biographies/michelle-k-lee.
5. Gross, *Bull Run*, p. 83.
6. Steven Gaines, Hamptons author, quoted in the *New York Observer*, August 3, 1998, quoted in turn in Gross, *Bull Run*, p. 142.
7. Gross, *Bull Run*, p. 103.
8. Matt Bai, "Wiring the Vast Left-Wing Conspiracy," *New York Times Magazine*, July 25, 2004.
9. *Fortune*. July 9, 2007. A *Financial Times* story about Mack's fundraiser appeared on July 15.
10. Svea Herbst-Bayliss, "Hedge Fund Managers Throw Weight Behind Obama," July 11.
11. Callahan, *Fortunes of Change*, p. 66.
12. *The Great Divide: Retro vs. Metro America* (PoliPoint, 2004), pp. xvii, 5, 64, 75, 91.
13. Florida, *The Rise of the Creative Class* (Basic Books), pp. xxix, 5 (italics in original), 21.
14. Florida, "How the Crash Will Reshape America," *Atlantic*, March

2009. See also Alec MacGillis, "Richard Florida, Mr. Creative Class, Is Now Mr. Rust Belt," *New Republic*, December 18, 2013.

15. "Creative Class War," *Washington Monthly*, January/February 2004.
16. Peter Culshaw, "Barack Obama: Power to the New Creatives," *Telegraph* (London), June 14, 2008.

7: HOW THE CRISIS WENT TO WASTE

1. Scholars who have studied them: Elizabeth McKenna and Hahrie Han, *Groundbreakers: How Obama's 2.2 Million Volunteers Transformed Campaigning in America* (Oxford, 2015), p. 44. Crowd sizes: See Jackie Calmes, "Obama Drawing Big Crowds, but Not Like in '08," *New York Times*, August 9, 2012.
2. Both of these examples, plucked from dozens more, are given by William Leuchtenburg in *In the Shadow of FDR*, chapter 10. Obama appeared on *60 Minutes* on November 16, 2008.
3. Weisberg, "The Brilliant Brain Trust," *Newsweek*, November 14, 2008.
4. Alter, *The Promise*, p. 64. McCaskill: Quoted in Alec MacGillis, "Obama Assembles an Ivy-Tinged League," *Washington Post*, December 7, 2008. The Nobelist was Energy Secretary Steven Chu; the Pulitzer winner was Samantha Power; the MacArthur genius was Jane Lubchenco, Obama's administrator of the National Oceanic and Atmospheric Administration. Among Obama's Rhodes Scholars were Nancy-Ann De Parle and Susan Rice.
5. Quoted in Ron Suskind, *Confidence Men: Wall Street, Washington, and the Education of a President* (Harper, 2011), pp. 196–97.
6. Summers allowed that the bonuses were "outrageous" but then said nothing could be done, according to a recap of his TV appearance in the *New York Times*: "'We are a country of law,' said Mr. Summers, one of several economic officials to hit the Sunday-morning talk show circuit. 'There are contracts. The government cannot just abrogate contracts.'" Edmund Andrews and Peter Baker, "Bonus Money at Troubled A.I.G. Draws Heavy Criticism," March 15, 2009.
7. Elizabeth Warren, *A Fighting Chance* (Metropolitan, 2014), p. 124.

8. This period of the Obama administration was painstakingly reconstructed by Ryan Lizza in the *New Yorker*, January 30, 2012.
9. The education part of the stimulus included Obama's "Race to the Top" program. For my description, I am relying upon Diane Ravitch's *Reign of Error: The Hoax of the Privatization Movement and the Danger to America's Public Schools* (Knopf, 2013), pp. 15–17.
10. On direct federal hiring, Jonathan Alter writes: Obama's "advisors rejected WPA-style direct government hiring, an idea that had fallen out of fashion in the 1970s. . . . Government jobs would have attacked unemployment immediately." This decision, Alter continues, would "haunt the administration in the months ahead." Alter, *The Promise*, p. 86. See also my own reflections on the subject, "More Government, Please!," *Harper's Magazine*, December 2011.
11. Suskind, *Confidence Men*, p. 355.
12. Alter, *The Promise*, p. 318.
13. Barofsky, *Bailout: An Inside Account of How Washington Abandoned Main Street While Rescuing Wall Street* (Free Press, 2012), pp. 156–157.
14. I wrote about this in the *Wall Street Journal* on April 22, 2009.
15. The economist is Greg Mankiw, former head of George W. Bush's Council of Economic Advisors. See his essay, "Economists Actually Agree on This: The Wisdom of Free Trade," *New York Times*, April 24, 2015. Obama's "drawbridge" remark was reported in the *Times* on May 8, 2015.
16. CFPB mission statement: See http://www.consumerfinance.gov/the-bureau/creatingthebureau.
17. Osawatomie is symbolically important because it was the home of John Brown as well as the place where Theodore Roosevelt went to announce his conversion to progressivism in 1910. Obama adviser: Balz does not give the adviser's name, but his words appear in Dan Balz, *Collision 2012: Obama vs. Romney and the Future of Elections in America* (Viking, 2013), p. 58.
18. Ibid., p. 324.
19. GDP and wage growth: I am using numbers from the Bureau of Labor Statistics accessed via the website of the St. Louis Fed; the series I used for wages is called "Nonfarm Business Sector: Real Compensation Per Hour." Private-sector labor union density: I am using numbers from the Current Population Survey, which is con-

ducted by the Bureau of Labor Statistics and the Census Department. (http://www.bls.gov/news.release/union2.nr0.htm) My source for labor share and the profit share are given in note 1 of the Introduction.

20. According to Syracuse University's Transactional Records Access Clearinghouse, which parses Justice Department data. See their report, "Federal White Collar Crime Prosecutions at 20-Year Low," http://trac.syr.edu/tracreports/crim/398.
21. Breuer's remarks were addressed to the New York City Bar Association and dated September 13, 2012. They are available on the Justice Department's website: http://www.justice.gov/opa/speech/assistant-attorney-general-lanny-breuer-speaks-new-york-city-bar-association.
22. See Jonathan Alter, *The Center Holds: Obama and His Enemies* (Simon & Schuster, 2013), p. 111.
23. Bruni, "The Man or the Moment," *New York Times*, January 6, 2015. For a longer list of pundits making similar arguments, see my essay in *Salon*, "It's Not Just Fox News," January 11, 2015. http://www.salon.com/2015/01/11/its_not_just_fox_news_how_liberal_apologists_torpedoed_change_helped_make_the_democrats_safe_for_wall_street.
24. Maron, "WTF," Episode 613, June 22, 2015. http://www.wtfpod.com/podcast/episodes/episode_613_-_president_barack_obama.
25. Peter Thiel, the venture capitalist who founded PayPal, published a famous essay called "Competition Is for Losers" (*Wall Street Journal*, September 12, 2014). "Actually, capitalism and competition are opposites," he wrote. "Capitalism is premised on the accumulation of capital, but under perfect competition, all profits get competed away." And: "Monopoly is . . . not a pathology or an exception. Monopoly is the condition of every successful business."
26. These numbers can be found on the "Division Operations" section of the Antitrust Division's website; I am using the numbers for "Sherman Act § 2 —Monopoly." http://www.justice.gov/atr/division-operations.
27. Dorgan, a populist from North Dakota, had been an early supporter of Obama. Upon hearing whom he'd named to his economic team, Dorgan said, "I don't understand how you could do this. You've picked the wrong people!" (Suskind, *Confidence Men*, p. 164).

28. This is one of the themes of Tim Geithner's memoir of his period as Treasury secretary, *Stress Test: Reflections on Financial Crises* (Crown, 2014).

8: THE DEFECTS OF A SUPERIOR MIND

1. The Massachusetts official was Jon Kingsdale, who once ran that state's insurance exchange. Both of these quotes were brought to my attention by Washington state insurance commissioner Brendan Williams, whose 2015 book, *Compromised*, is an able summary of the legislation from its beginning to its present-day problems with increasing premiums and high deductibles.
2. Gruber spoke at the Annual Health Economics Conference in 2013. The video sparked an enormous controversy and can be watched on the website of the *Washington Post:* https://www.washingtonpost.com/news/post-politics/wp/2014/11/11/obamacare-consultant-under-fire-for-stupidity-of-the-american-voter-comment/.
3. The main proponent of this viewpoint was Gabriel Kolko, author of *The Triumph of Conservatism: A Reinterpretation of American History, 1900–1916* (1963).
4. This particular passage is drawn from an email written by Bryant Hall, a lobbyist with PhRMA, in July of 2009. The emails were reprinted in many places, most notably the *Wall Street Journal* for June 13, 2012.
5. This astonishing record was compiled by Patrick Egan. See "Ashton Carter and the Astoundingly Elite Educational Credentials of Obama's Cabinet Appointees," *Washington Post*, December 5, 2014.
6. See Louise Story, "A Rich Education for Summers (After Harvard)," *New York Times*, April 5, 2009, and Joe Wiesenthal, "At D.E. Shaw, Larry Summers Worked Just One Day A Week," on the Business Insider website, dated April 6, 2009. The median household income in the U.S. was $51,939 in 2013, according to the Census Bureau's report, "Income and Poverty in the United States: 2013."
7. Barofsky, *Bailout*, p. 139.
8. Warren, *A Fighting Chance*, p. 149, italics in original.
9. Alter, *The Promise*, p. 317.

10. The deputy attorney general who made this remark, James Cole, did so in order to get the Justice Department off the hook for failing to prosecute any high-ranking financiers for the many obvious frauds of the preceding decade. See Del Quentin Wilber, "Top Justice Deputy Cole Ready to Leave Post with Holder," Bloomberg, October 16, 2014.
11. Carney's remarks were made on December 2, 2011 at a routine White House briefing; I report them as they were transcribed by Political Transcript Wire. See also my essay in *Baffler* 19 (2012), "Too Smart to Fail."
12. "Remarks by the President on Health Care and the Senate Vote on F-22 Funding," from the website of the White House, July 21, 2009. See https://www.whitehouse.gov/the-press-office/remarks-president-health-care-and-senate-vote-f-22-funding
13. Bernard Crick, *In Defence of Politics* (Penguin, 1964), p.100: "Politics is, to many social scientists, a kind of disease: society is a patient ridden with tensions and political events are the unreal, neurotic fixations by which it tries to rationalize these contradictions."
14. Iowa Democrat: Bruce Braley leveled the "law school" insult at Chuck Grassley. McChrystal: See Friedman, "What's Second Prize?," *New York Times*, June 23, 2010. Snowden: David Brooks called Snowden "the ultimate unmediated man" ("The Solitary Leaker," *New York Times*, June 11, 2013). Writing in *Politico*, Roger Simon called Snowden a "total slacker," a man with "all the qualifications to become a grocery bagger" ("Slacker Who Came in from the Cold," June 11, 2013).
15. Alter, *The Promise,* p. 338. In truth, most professions resist outside accountability; that's part of the definition of the category. What's different is that they don't resist through a union.
16. Suskind, *Confidence Men*, p. 197.
17. I describe the electoral backlash against Obama and company at length in my last book, *Pity the Billionaire*, so I hope you will excuse me if I don't belabor it here.

9: THE BLUE STATE MODEL

1. Bruni, "A Democrat to Watch in 2015," *New York Times*, December 30, 2014.

2. “Gina Raimondo for Governor: JOBS PLAN,” n.d. (2014), found online at http://www.ginaraimondo.com/sites/ginaraimondo/files/gina-raimondo-jobs-plan.pdf.
3. Emanuel’s bemoaning of middle-class decline can be found in the book he coauthored with Bruce Reed, *The Plan: Big Ideas for America* (Public Affairs, 2006), especially in the Prologue and Chapter 3. The quotations from Emanuel are taken, respectively, from his introduction to the City of Chicago’s Technology Plan and his essay for *CNN Money,* “How Chicago Saved Its Small Businesses,” December 16, 2014. http://money.cnn.com/2014/12/12/smallbusiness/chicago-rahm-emanuel-innovation.
4. Cuomo’s book is available online at http://andrewcuomo.com/wp-content/uploads/sites/44/2014/10/Moving-the-New-NY-Forward-by-Andrew-M-Cuomo.pdf. Unfortunately, the Startup NY program has cost the state government many millions but has “created fewer than 100 jobs,” according to Susanne Craig and Jesse McKinley: “Jobs Effort That Cuomo Vowed Would Fire Up Economy is Slow to Take Hold,” *New York Times,* May 15, 2015. There is also a New York State venture capital fund that is supposed to invest in “the commercialization efforts of start-up companies associated with New York’s universities.” See the governor’s office press release dated December 12, 2014, “Governor Cuomo Launches $50 Million Innovation Venture Capital Fund to Support and Attract New High-Growth Businesses.” https://www.governor.ny.gov/news/governor-cuomo-launches-50-million-innovation-venture-capital-fund-support-and-attract-new-high.
5. My quotes are taken from a manuscript of the speech that was kindly furnished me by Markell’s office.
6. Jack Markell, “Americans Need Jobs, Not Populism,” *Atlantic,* May 3, 2015.
7. These statistics are reported in the Boston Redevelopment Authority’s publication, “Retaining Recent College Graduates in Boston: Is There a Brain Drain?” (2014), available online at http://www.bostonredevelopmentauthority.org/getattachment/170db5fb-ad3b-4fbb-a143-82f7d7f4539e.

   The boast about Nobel laureates is a common one in Boston promotional materials. See Jonathan P. Marcus et al., *Our Boston* (MBI Publishing Co., 2003), p. 14. See also “The Prominence of Boston Area Colleges and Universities,” an article in the Bureau of Labor

Statistics' *Monthly Labor Review* for June 2009. The authors of the article are Denis M. McSweeney and Walter J. Marshall.

8. Massachusetts' achievements on these indices are reported in "Creative Intelligence," a newsletter produced in part by the Richard Florida Creativity Group and dated February, 2003. Boston itself does fairly well on Florida's "gay index," his "melting pot index," and his "bohemian index." See *The Rise of the Creative Class*, Table 14.3, p. 256; Table 14.2, p. 254; and Table 14.4, p. 261.
9. See Lily Geismer, *Don't Blame Us: Suburban Liberals and the Transformation of the Democratic Party* (Princeton, 2015).
10. Specifically, the report estimates, it would be "the eleventh-largest economy in the world." See Edward B. Roberts and Charles Eesley, "Entrepreneurial Impact: The Role of MIT," a Kauffman Foundation report dated February 2009. http://cdn.executive.mit.edu/17/a2/bdcaf61a49479de51861040707ac/mitimpactfullreport.pdf.
11. See Barry Bluestone and Alan Clayton-Matthews, "Life Sciences Innovation as a Catalyst for Economic Development: The Role of the Massachusetts Life Sciences Center," a May 2013 study published by the Kitty and Michael Dukakis Center at Northeastern University and downloadable here: https://repository.library.northeastern.edu/files/neu:330208.
12. Thanks to Harris Gruman for putting this unforgettable image in my head.
13. The Center on Budget and Policy Priorities' study, "Pulling Apart: A State-by-State Analysis of Income Trends," dated November 15, 2012, ranks Massachusetts number eight, seven, and two among the states, depending on the historical period in question. http://www.cbpp.org/research/poverty-and-inequality/pulling-apart-a-state-by-state-analysis-of-income-trends.

    According to 2013 Gini coefficients calculated by the Census Bureau, Massachusetts ranks fourth after New York, Connecticut, and Louisiana (it is tied with Georgia and Florida). See "Household Income: 2013," one of the Bureau's American Community Survey Briefs, dated September 2014. https://www.census.gov/content/dam/Census/library/publications/2014/acs/acsbr13-02.pdf.

    See also the Economic Policy Institute's report, "The Increasingly Unequal States of America," dated January 26, 2015. http://www.epi.org/publication/income-inequality-by-state-1917-to-2012.

14. See the U.S. Census Bureau's State and County QuickFacts. The unemployment percentage is drawn from an ABC News story by Samantha Lavien, "Fall River Unemployment Rate Is the Worst in MA," March 11, 2014.
15. See Jessica Geller, "Amazon Inks Deal on Fulfillment Center in Fall River," *Boston Globe*, November 24, 2015.
16. "Fall River's on the Bike Trail to Nowhere," Fall River *Herald-News*, October 11, 2015; "Stand Up, Wal-Mart!," creators.com, October 15, 2012; "Notes from a Liquor Store Before the Debate," creators .com, October 8, 2012.
17. Dion, "A Sicker Fall River Eases Its Pain By Getting High," Fall River *Herald-News*, October 4, 2015.
18. Mayor of Boston: These quotations are headlines from obituaries for Tom Menino from the *Boston Globe* and the WGBH radio station. Innovation Institute: See the introduction to their 2014 annual index, "Massachusetts Innovation Economy," available online at http://www.masstech.org/sites/mtc/files/documents/Innovation Institute/2014_index_web.pdf.
19. The fund is the XFund; it invests in ideas of former students from anywhere, but most of them so far have come from Harvard.
20. You can read it here for yourself: http://innovation.mit.edu/about. I learned about this from one of the only sarcastic stories about innovation that I have been able to find, Eric Levenson's "Deval Patrick Joins MIT to Innovate Their Innovation Initiative," a post on Boston.com dated January 13, 2015.
21. Obama even drew certain of his famous 2008 campaign themes from Patrick's 2006 run for the Massachusetts governorship. On the connection between the two men, see Gwen Ifill's book, *The Breakthrough: Politics and Race in the Age of Obama* (Doubleday, 2009).
22. Watch Harthorne's TED talk here: https://www.youtube.com /watch?v=hisa30dJfP4.
23. For a concise summary of the life and times of Ameriquest, see the *Financial Crisis Inquiry Report*, pp. 12–14: http://www.gpo .gov/fdsys/pkg/GPO-FCIC/pdf/GPO-FCIC.pdf. For a lengthier version, see Michael W. Hudson, *The Monster: How a Gang of Predatory Lenders and Wall Street Bankers Fleeced America—and Spawned a Global Crisis* (Holt, 2010).
24. Ameriquest was one of the only subprime companies that journalists investigated thoroughly before the financial crisis hit; in its

response to one of the landmark stories published in the *Los Angeles Times*, the company claimed, "Ameriquest pioneered innovative best practices in the mortgage industry" and insisted that they had "helped hundreds of thousands of homeowners purchase or refinance their homes, making it possible for them to achieve their financial goals and enhance their quality of life." See Mike Hudson and E. Scott Reckard, "Workers Say Lender Ran 'Boiler Rooms': Critics say Ameriquest, Touted as an Industry Model, Fabricated Data, Forged Documents and Hid Fees. The Company Denies Wrongdoing," *Los Angeles Times*, February 4, 2005.

25. "The Massachusetts economy": Patrick said this at a groundbreaking for a pharmaceutical office complex, December 8, 2010, according to a story on BusinessWire. http://www.businesswire.com/news/home/20100908007027/en/Cubist-Pharmaceuticals-Prepares-Continued-Growth. "Innovation is a centerpiece": Patrick said this while opening an IBM software development lab in 2010, according to Hiawatha Bray, "IBM Unveils Two New Campuses," *Boston Globe*, June 17, 2010.
26. On the latter, see the press release dated April 21, 2010: "Massachusetts Governor Signs Social Innovation Compact at Year Up Boston." http://www.prnewswire.com/news-releases/massachusetts-governor-signs-social-innovation-compact-at-year-up-boston-91702664.html.
27. "It's a pleasure to partner with the Churchill Club to host this evening's town hall," said the Hewlett Packard executive introducing the governor. Patrick replied, in his easy, self-assured way: "I'm a great, great admirer of this company of Hewlett Packard and of the many ways that you partner with us in Massachusetts." See http://www.google.com/url?q=http://www.youtube.com/watch%3Fv%3DaOG44e3nZLE&sa=U&ei=Z-BhVenCFISHsAWdkYGoCg&ved=0CBUQtwIwAA&sig2=ze2ch111WRR12fLfinIt7A&usg=AFQjCNF2LQQ9N2BAx9cNu33iGoMmgnNNWQ.
28. On Patrick's courting the CEO of a large company, see Brian Johnson, "Gov. Deval Patrick's life sciences legacy," MassDevice.com, January 12, 2015. "To provide assistance, mentoring," etc., is the language of the law itself: House Bill Number 4377, dated July 30, 2014.
29. Matt Stout, "Gov Candidates Digging Deep in Final Days," *Boston Herald*, November 2, 2014.

30. The Schmidt and Harthorne remarks are from Dennis Keohane, "MassChallenge Celebrates Innovation, Deval Patrick's Influence in Tech Community," *Boston Globe*, dated October 29, 2014.
31. Ryan Dezember, "Massachusetts Ex-Gov. Patrick to Run New Bain Unit," *Wall Street Journal*, April 13, 2015.

10: THE INNOVATION CLASS

1. https://www.whitehouse.gov/sites/default/files/uploads/InnovationStrategy.pdf.
2. On the allure of San Francisco and the tech industry for members of the Obama administration, see Edward-Isaac Dovere, "The City on the Hill(s) for Obama Alums," *Politico*, July 5, 2015. For a comprehensive list of all the Obama personnel who came from or departed to Silicon Valley, see Cecilia Kang and Juliet Eilperin, "Why Silicon Valley Is the New Revolving Door for Obama Staffers," *Washington Post*, February 28, 2015. "Obama's lean startup" is also known as "18F"; it's a unit of the General Services Administration. See Elaine Chen, "Building Obama's Lean Startup in America's Biggest Bureaucracy," *TechBeacon*, July 23, 2015; Jon Gertner, "Inside Obama's Stealth Startup," *Fast Company*, June 15, 2015.
3. The exchange can be watched on YouTube at https://www.youtube.com/watch?v=8URYPna1lhw.
4. This last is called The Groundwork; very little is known about it at present. See "Hillary Clinton Leans on Eric Schmidt's Startup for Campaign Technology," *Quartz*, October 16, 2015.
5. Eric Schmidt and Jonathan Rosenberg with Alan Eagle, *How Google Works* (Grand Central Publishing, 2014), pp. 5, 42.
6. Ibid., pp. 17, 18–19.
7. See "Only Connect," an "Annotation" on the subject by Whitney Terrell and Shannon Jackson, *Harper's Magazine,* April 2013. See also Scott Canon, "Within its Fiberhoods, Google Rules the Roost, Survey Says," *Kansas City Star*, May 6, 2014.
8. Jaron Lanier, *Who Owns the Future?* (Simon & Schuster, 2013), pp. 44, 52.
9. Eric Schmidt and Jared Cohen, *The New Digital Age: Reshaping the Future of People, Nations and Business* (Knopf, 2013), p. 36.
10. Interview with Maria Bartiromo, December 3, 2009.
11. Andreessen: Alessandra Stanley, "The Tech Gods Giveth," *New*

York Times, November 1, 2015. Lehane: Conor Dougherty and Mike Isaac, "Airbnb and Uber Mobilize Vast User Base to Sway Policy," *New York Times*, November 5, 2015.

12. "Uber and the American Worker," a speech Plouffe delivered at "the DC tech incubator 1776," dated November 3, 2015, and available on the Uber website. http://newsroom.uber.com/2015/11/1776.
13. Schmidt can be seen making these statements in a YouTube recording of his SXSW talk, which also featured his coauthor, Jared Cohen, and the interviewer Steven Levy: https://www.youtube.com/watch?v=bmzcCSF_zXQ.
14. *It Takes a Village: And Other Lessons Children Teach Us* (Simon & Schuster, 1996), p. 294.
15. The economist Dean Baker suggested to me this interpretation of inno-as-circumvention. See "The Opportunities and Risks of the Sharing Economy," his testimony before the House Subcommittee on Commerce, Manufacturing, and Trade, September 29, 2015.
16. Lanier, *Who Owns the Future?*, chapter 7. See also Astra Taylor's account in *The People's Platform*.
17. On Amazon, see Franklin Foer, "Amazon Must Be Stopped," *New Republic*, October 9, 2014. On the retailer's dispute with Hachette, see David Streitfeld, "Literary Lions Unite in Protest Over Amazon's E-Book Tactics," *New York Times*, September 29, 2014. On Google and the FTC, see Brody Mullins, "Inside the U.S. Antitrust Probe of Google," *Wall Street Journal*, March 19, 2015.
18. Pharma executives often use innovation to justify their pricing decisions. Consider the innovation remarks of Martin Shkreli, the former CEO of Turing Pharmaceuticals, a company that in 2015 dramatically raised the price of an old drug it had acquired. Asked Shkreli of Bernie Sanders, a Democratic presidential candidate who had criticized him, "Is he willing to sort of accept that there is a tradeoff, that to take risks for innovation, companies have to invest lots of money and they need some kind of return for that, and what does he think that should look like?" See David Nather, "Bernie Sanders Rejects Donation from Drug Company CEO," *Boston Globe*, October 15, 2015.

    Another good example of this sort of thinking can be found in a 2003 speech by Sidney Taurel, then the CEO of Eli Lilly, at the American Enterprise Institute in Washington, D.C. Taurel warned that "under a regime of weaker I[ntellectual] P[roperty] protection or harsher market controls, our R&D would no longer be able to deliver true innovation." Read the whole thing at: http://www.lilly.com/news/speeches/Pages/030318.aspx.

19. See Mark Ames, "The Techtopus," *Pando Daily*, January 23, 2014, and Mark Ames, "Newly Unsealed Documents Show Steve Jobs' Brutal Response after Getting a Google Employee Fired," *Pando Daily*, March 25, 2014.
20. White collar: "Inside Amazon," *New York Times*, August 16, 2015. Blue collar: See Dave Jamieson's excellent *Huffington Post* article, "The Life and Death of an Amazon Warehouse Temp," n.d. [2015], http://highline.huffingtonpost.com/articles/en/life-and-death-amazon-temp.

    See also "Amazon workers face 'increased risk of mental illness,'" an article on the BBC's website dated November 25, 2013, in which an English worker reports, "We are machines, we are robots, we plug our scanner in, we're holding it, but we might as well be plugging it into ourselves."
21. The CEO in question is named Lukas Biewald. He is quoted in a shocking article by Moshe Z. Marvit, "How Crowdworkers Became the Ghosts in the Digital Machine," *The Nation*, February 24, 2014.
22. Describing Harper Reed, the chief technology officer of Obama's 2012 campaign, Biewald writes as follows: "I remember meeting with him as he worked with me and other Silicon Valley tech CEOs asking for techniques to deal with the large databases of voter and donors the Obama campaign was dealing with." "Three Levels of Big Data," November 20, 2013; https://www.crowdflower.com/blog/2013/11/three-levels-of-big-data.
23. This is from the second sentence of an address by Belinda A. Barnett, senior counsel to the deputy assistant attorney general for criminal enforcement of the Antitrust Division called "Criminalization of Cartel Conduct—The Changing Landscape," given in Adelaide, Australia, April 3, 2009, and available on the DOJ website: http://www.justice.gov/atr/public/speeches/247824.htm.
24. See the DOJ's statement on the matter, http://www.justice.gov/opa/pr/justice-department-requires-six-high-tech-companies-stop-entering-anticompetitive-employee. On the class-action lawsuit and its result, see Jeff Elder, "Judge Approves Final Settlement

in Silicon Valley Wage Case," *Wall Street Journal*, September 3, 2015.

25. Cuomo as quoted in the *New York Post*, "Cuomo Drops Bombshell on de Blasio over Uber," July 22, 2015.
26. Robert Reich, "The 'Sharing Economy'? More Like the 'Share the Crumbs' Economy," *In These Times*, February 4, 2015.

11: LIBERAL GILT

1. John Mack interviewed by Neil Cavuto of Fox Business, June 8, 2015. Watch it here: http://video.foxbusiness.com/v/4283714937001/john-mack-standing-by-hillary-clinton/?#sp=show-clips.
2. William Cohan, "Why Wall Street Loves Hillary," *Politico*, November 11, 2014.
3. Rubin, *In an Uncertain World*, pp. 128, 353.
4. Deploring the revolving door: See "To Restore Trust in Government, Slow Wall Street's Revolving Door," an article HRC cowrote with Senator Tammy Baldwin for the *Huffington Post*, August 31, 2015. Her hires from Wall Street included Thomas Nides, described above, and Jack Lew. Trade: Her opinions on trade are summarized in a story by Domenico Montanaro on the website of NPR, "A Timeline of Hillary Clinton's Evolution on Trade," dated April 21, 2015. See http://www.npr.org/sections/itsallpolitics/2015/04/21/401123124/a-timeline-of-hillary-clintons-evolution-on-trade.
5. More prison: These are HRC's remarks to a Women in Policing Awards Ceremony in 1994. She continued:

   > We need more prisons to keep violent offenders for as long as it takes to keep them off the streets. . . . We will be able to say, loudly and clearly, that for repeat, violent, criminal offenders—three strikes and you're out. We are tired of putting you back in through the revolving door.

   HRC as quoted in Eli Hager, "A (More or Less) Definitive Guide to Hillary Clinton's Record on Law and Order," an article on the website of the Marshall Project dated May 7, 2015. A nearly identical transcription of this particular Clinton speech appears on p. 189 of *The Unique Voice of Hillary Rodham Clinton*, a compendium of HRC quotes assembled by Clair G. Osborne (Avon,

1997). "Dare to care": From HRC's Class Day speech at Yale University, 2001.

6. Hillary describes her role in the welfare-reform debate in her 2003 book, *Living History*. The old Aid to Families with Dependent Children system, she writes, "had helped to create generations of welfare-dependent Americans. . . . I strongly argued that we had to change the system, although my endorsement of welfare reform came at some personal cost." She then recounts how the Republicans in Congress passed two versions of welfare reform that she found too punitive, but that their third try was acceptable. Bill Clinton signed this third version. "Even with its flaws," Hillary continues, this bill "was a critical first step to reforming our nation's welfare system. I agreed that he should sign it and worked hard to round up votes for its passage—though he and the legislation were roundly criticized by some liberals, advocacy groups for immigrants and most people who worked with the welfare system."

   Hillary then goes into a meditation on her favorite subject—how "Principles and values in politics should not be compromised, but strategies and tactics must be flexible enough to make progress possible, especially under the difficult political conditions we faced." *Living History*, pp. 365, 368, 369.
7. Stephanie Hannon, "What I Heard from Hillary about the Sharing Economy," a post on *Medium* dated July 13, 2015.
8. From the *New York Times* transcript of the Democratic presidential debate: http://www.nytimes.com/2015/10/14/us/politics/democratic-debate-transcript.html.
9. How she made the hard choice between law schools: See her speech on Class Day 2001 at Yale. "Talent is universal": See her remarks at the Female Heads of State and Foreign Ministers Luncheon, September 24, 2009, http://www.state.gov/secretary/20092013clinton/rm/2009a/09/129598.htm. Clinton used this phrase on many occasions as secretary of state. For example, see her speech about Haiti dated April 14, 2009, or her speech in Vietnam dated July 10, 2012, also available on the State Department website.
10. Sheehy, *Hillary's Choice* (Random House, 1999), p. 38. Brock, *The Seduction of Hillary Rodham* (Free Press, 1996), p. 147. Ann Lewis, quoted in Dan Balz and Haynes Johnson, *The Battle for America: The Story of an Extraordinary Election* (Penguin, 2010), p. 140. NB: Lewis attributes this famous saying to John Wesley,

but Methodist scholars deny he ever said it. See Josh Tinley, "Checking our Facts," *Ministry Matters*, May 12, 2011.

11. Bernstein, *A Woman in Charge*, p. 62.
12. Ibid., p. 79.
13. These quotations and the ones that follow are all from my own transcription of the "No Ceilings" event at the Best Buy Theater, New York City, March 9, 2015.
14. Joby Warrick, "Hillary's War: How Conviction Replaced Skepticism in Libya Intervention," *Washington Post*, October 30, 2011.
15. The State Department press release is called "21st Century Statecraft"; it is unsigned and undated but the State Department informed my research assistant that it was issued in 2011 by the office of Alec Ross, Secretary Clinton's senior adviser for innovation. High-profile speech: "Remarks on Internet Freedom," a speech delivered by Secretary Clinton on January 21, 2010, at the Newseum in Washington, D.C., the text is available on the website of the State Department.
16. On this subject, see my 2000 book, *One Market Under God*. The "Twitter Revolution" in Iran, by the way, turned out to have little to do with Twitter at all. See Evgeny Morozov, *The Net Delusion: The Dark Side of Internet Freedom* (PublicAffairs, 2011), chapter 1.
17. More quotes from Clinton's speech of January 21, 2010.
18. "Conference on Internet Freedom," remarks by Hillary Rodham Clinton, secretary of state, Fokker Terminal, The Hague, Netherlands, December 8, 2011, available on the State Department's website as of August 31, 2015. Schmidt's introduction is described by Steven Lee Myers, "Hillary Clinton's Last Tour as a Rock-Star Diplomat," *New York Times Magazine*, June 27, 2012.
19. Read it yourself at http://www.state.gov/statecraft/overview/index.htm. The document on the State Department website is undated; in an email to my researcher, the State Department confirmed that it was initially posted in 2011.
20. Valerie Hudson and Patricia Leidl, *The Hillary Doctrine: Sex and American Foreign Policy* (Columbia, 2015).
21. TEDWomen, Washington, D.C., 2010: http://blog.ted.com/ted-blog-exclusive-hillary-rodham-clinton-at-tedwomen.
22. Ibid. See also Clinton's essay, "Leading Through Civilian Power: Redefining American Diplomacy and Development," *Foreign Affairs*, November/December 2010.

23. These quotations are drawn from "Remarks at Breakfast with Women Entrepreneurs Attending the Presidential Summit on Entrepreneurship," dated April 28, 2010, and available on the State Department website.
24. See the TV remarks of George W. Bush, "Bush: Stay in Afghanistan for Women's Sake," *Politico*, April 1, 2011. For an amusing example of how the Hillary Doctrine was implemented in Iraq, see Peter Van Buren, *We Meant Well: How I Helped Lose the Battle for the Hearts and Minds of the Iraqi People* (Metropolitan, 2011), especially the chapter "Widowed Tractors, Bees for Widows."
25. Here I am following the narratives of Milford Bateman, *Why Doesn't Microfinance Work?: The Destructive Rise of Local Neoliberalism* (Zed Books, 2010), and Philip Mader, *The Political Economy of Microfinance: Financializing Poverty* (Palgrave Macmillan, 2015).
26. "This is a big idea, an idea with vast potential," Hillary Clinton said. "Whether we are talking about a rural area in South Asia or an inner city in the United States, microcredit is an invaluable tool in alleviating poverty, promoting self-sufficiency and stimulating economic activity in some of the world's most destitute and disadvantaged communities."

    The president of the Citicorp Foundation at the time was Paul Ostergard. His remarks are found on p. 21 of "The Microcredit Summit Report," a booklet dated April 1997 and apparently published by the RESULTS Educational Fund. Hillary Clinton's remarks are found on p. 29. A pdf of the report may be downloaded here: http://www.microcreditsummit.org/resource/59/1997-microcredit-summit-report.html.
27. Verveer: "Launch of the State of the Microcredit Summit Campaign Report 2011," March 7, 2011. Otero: "Keynote Address to the Mobile Money Policy Forum," Nairobi, Kenya, November 30, 2010. Hillary herself: *Hard Choices*, p. 149.
28. On microcredit in Bosnia, see Bateman's blog post, "A New Balkan Tragedy? The Case of Microcredit in Bosnia," April 8, 2014. In "From Poverty to Power," an Oxfam blog post dated April 20, 2011, Bateman poses the following rhetorical question: "With so many countries having achieved microfinance 'saturation' this last decade or so (notably Bolivia, Bosnia, Mexico, Peru, Cambodia and others), why is it that in none of these countries can we see

obvious substantive poverty reduction and 'bottom-up' development gains?"

29. See Bateman, *Why Doesn't Microfinance Work? The Destructive Rise of Local Neoliberalism* (Zed Books), chapter 5. The headline-making development here was a Mexican microlender that decided to go public in 2007, revealing along the way that it charged its clients (nearly all of them poor women) the kinds of interest rates that would be unusual in the U.S. See also Hugh Sinclair, *Confessions of a Microfinance Heretic: How Microlending Lost Its Way and Betrayed the Poor* (Barrett-Koehler, 2012).
30. See "Public Private Partnerships & Social Entrepreneurship: Building Solutions for Good," remarks by Nancy Smith Nissley delivered on September 10, 2012, and available on the website of the State Department.
31. See the "Women's Entrepreneurship in the Americas" factsheet, dated April 13, 2012, and available on the website of the State Department. See also the Wal-Mart press release from the same day: "Walmart, U.S. Secretary of State Hillary Clinton and the Inter-American Development Bank Partner to Change the Lives of Women and Youth." http://corporate.walmart.com/_news_/news-archive/2012/04/13/walmart-us-secretary-of-state-hillary-clinton-the-inter-american-development-bank-partner-to-change-the-lives-of-women-youth.
32. Did you catch it, reader? I took this metaphor from F. Scott Fitzgerald, who used it in *This Side of Paradise* to describe not liberalism but youth: "Just as a cooling pot gives off heat, so all through youth and adolescence we give off calories of virtue. That's what's called ingenuousness. . . . That's why a 'good man going wrong' attracts people. They stand around and literally *warm themselves* at the calories of virtue he gives off." (Scribner's, 1921, p. 277)
33. Matthew Bishop and Michael Green, *Philanthrocapitalism: How Giving Can Save the World* (Bloomsbury, 2009), p. xii. Bill Clinton wrote the Foreword to the paperback edition of this book, which originally bore the subtitle, "How the Rich Can Save the World."

CONCLUSION

1. Tom Rowley, "On Martha's Vineyard, Casual Meets Political," *Washington Post*, August 15, 2015.

2. Remy Tumin, "A Peek Past the Gate of Key Beaches," *Vineyard Gazette*, August 2, 2012.
3. Reporter Carol Felsenthal gave a good description of Schulte's biography and political activities in *Chicago Magazine*: "What You Need to Know About the Guy Who Owns the Obamas' Vineyard Rental," August 2013.
4. Michelle Higgins, "Politics at Play," *New York Times*, August 17, 2007. There were other complications as well. The Boston tycoon who owns the Vineyard house in which the Clintons vacationed during their presidential days was, in 2007, helping the long-shot presidential campaign of Chris Dodd.
5. There is an interesting story behind the Clinton-Rothschild relationship. Once Obama had triumphed in 2008, Lady de Rothschild publicly denounced him as a kind of secret radical, determined to wreck the American Dream with his unspoken leftist policies. Then, in a 2010 email to Hillary Clinton that was released by the State Department, Lynn Forester de Rothschild could be found signing herself "Your loyal adoring pal." And in 2015, this same Lady de Rothschild was reportedly asking $1,000 a head to attend "A Conversation with Hillary" at a Martha's Vineyard estate. If you wanted to get your picture taken with the candidate, the price was higher.

   On Obama's nefarious designs on the American Dream, see Lynn Forester de Rothschild, "Barack Obama's America," *Huffington Post*, December 1, 2008. On the 2015 Hillary fund-raiser, see Tom Rowley, "On Martha's Vineyard, Casual Meets Political," *Washington Post*, August 15, 2015.
6. Wolfe, "Mauve Gloves and Madmen, Clutter & Vine," in the anthology of the same name (Farrar, Straus and Giroux, 1976).
7. On average, executives in Decatur, which Mills called "Central City," made $137 per week, while wage workers made $59. See "The Middle Classes in Middle-Sized Cities," *American Sociological Review*, vol. 11, number 5, October 1946, p. 521.
8. According to data compiled by the AFL-CIO's "Executive Paywatch" website. See http://www.aflcio.org/Corporate-Watch/Paywatch-2015.
9. Quality of life metrics: http://www.growdecatur.org/community-assessment-survey.html. Threatened photographer: http://www.illinoisinfocus.com/central-park.html.

AFTERWORD TO THE 2017 EDITION: THE YEAR THEY FOUND SOMEWHERE ELSE TO GO

1. Denial: See Nate Silver, "The Mythology of Trump's 'Working Class' Support," *FiveThirtyEight*, May 3, 2016. "To have a lifelong job," Thomas Friedman, "Web People vs. Wall People," *The New York Times*, July 27, 2016.
2. See Matt Karp, "Fairfax County, USA," *Jacobin*, November 28, 2016.
3. The national poll numbers come from exit polls collated by the *Washington Post* and are available online at "2016 Election Exit Polls," https://www.washingtonpost.com/graphics/politics/2016-election/exit-polls/?tid=a_inl. On black voters in Milwaukee, see Sabrina Tavernise, "Many in Milwaukee Neighborhood Didn't Vote—and Don't Regret It," *The New York Times*, November 20, 2016.
4. The detailed exit polls are posted, among other places, on the Fox News website: http://www.foxnews.com/politics/elections/2016/exit-polls

ACKNOWLEDGMENTS

This book owes a tremendous debt to my two researchers, Alex Kelly and Zachary Davis, who did so much capable work on so many different subjects. The first round of thanks also includes the people who helped me with the passages of this book that were first published elsewhere: Dave Daley at *Salon*, Chris Lehman at *Bookforum*, and James Marcus and the crew at *Harper's*.

John Summers of *The Baffler* drew my attention to the innovation theme, persuaded me to use Massachusetts as my model blue state, and then helped out enormously during my time there. For their help in understanding Massachusetts, I also wish to thank Noah McCormack, Chris Sturr, Chris Faraone, Elena Letona, John Redford, and Harris Gruman, who was not only a source of information but also of several excellent ideas. Debra Fastino acted as a tour guide to Fall River. Jonathan Soroff provided valuable insights on Martha's Vineyard. Art and Linda Dhermy spent a day showing me the corporate sights of Decatur, Illinois.

Eric Klinenberg, Kate Zaloom, Tom Geoghegan, and Dave Mulcahey all encouraged me in the early days of the project. Jim McNeill and George Scialabba came through with excellent preliminary edits. Dean Baker was a good sport through my many, many queries to him.

Jeff Schmidt helped me comprehend professionalism; Zillah Eisenstein had special understanding of the character of Hillary Clinton; Brendan Williams explained Obamacare to me; Milford Bateman walked me through the disasters of microfinance; Barry Lynn helped me understand antitrust; Bill Black knew about Dodd-Frank and the decline of professionalism; Peter Edelman gets welfare reform like nobody else; Heather Ann Thompson and Jessica Steinberg were enormously helpful on mass incarceration; Paul Maliszewski helped me track the creative class; and Bill Curry laid out the grand narrative of Democratic failure. Johann Hari had many brilliant suggestions for this book; Chris Shiflett had one big genius insight; Barbara Ehrenreich effortlessly saw through and diagnosed the nonsense latent in any subject I brought to her attention.

Joe Spieler handled my literary affairs with humor and proficiency. Prudence Crowther did a superlative copy edit. Sara Bershtel and Riva Hocherman deserve the biggest helping of gratitude there is, this time for transforming a sprawling manuscript into a proper book. It was one hell of a sprint this time, but thanks to them it got done.

INDEX